DARK SECRETS OF THE NEW AGE

DARK SECRETS
OF THE NEW AGE

Satan's Plan
For a One World Religion

TEXE MARRS

CROSSWAY BOOKS □ WESTCHESTER, ILLINOIS
A DIVISION OF GOOD NEWS PUBLISHERS

Cover design: Britt Taylor Collins

Seventh printing, 1988

Printed in the United States of America

Library of Congress Catalog Card Number 86-72066

ISBN 0-89107-421-X

TABLE OF

Contents

PREFACE

S atan has a Plan for a One World Religion and a One World Government. How do we know this? It is revealed in Bible prophecy.

If we examine God's Word closely and contrast its prophecies with the events transpiring around us, we come to a most astonishing conclusion: the last years of the twentieth century may well comprise one of the final chapters in the age-old battle between the powers of evil and God and His people.

The Bible envisions a period of increasing rebellion against God culminating in the Great Tribulation, a frightening time of worldwide brutality and religious apostasy. During this period, the nations of earth will be transformed into a one world political system and religion. This will be accomplished according to The Plan of the dark forces that oppose God.

In my book *Rush to Armageddon* I stated:

Powerful forces are swirling around mankind today—forces that are destined to bring about a profound change in both our physical and spiritual worlds. Man cannot avoid those forces, no more than he could avoid being brought forth into this world and having breath entered into his lungs.

In this present book, I closely examine these powerful forces and, with God's help, expose their evil objectives. The Bible warned us about these forces. For example, Daniel, one of the Lord's great prophets, foresaw that in the last days, Satan would install a world ruler. This ruler, Daniel said, would magnify himself above all while contemptuously disregarding the laws of God. In place of the true God, this evil ruler will honor "the God of forces" (Dan. 11:36-45).

Even now, a man is perhaps being groomed to be this world ruler. I do not know when he will come forth, though the time must surely be drawing near, based on current events. However, after years of research into the objectives of the New Age Movement, I am convinced of one thing: this man of Satan, called the Beast with the number 666 in Revelation, will find already in place a popularly acclaimed One World Religion perfectly suited for his style of leadership. The Antichrist will therefore find great satisfaction in assuming the reigns of the New Age World Religion.

If this statement shocks you, that is understandable. It is best for us to be very skeptical about claims that this or that group or church is the Satan-led, end-time religion prophesied in the Holy Bible. God wants us to be discerning. What's more, having a scientific orientation and with my background as a career Air Force officer, I am not prone to hasty, ill-considered judgments or snap decisions, especially about important spiritual matters. This is why I decided to investigate for myself by thoroughly researching the New Age Movement, its roots, and its activities and goals.

What I discovered staggers the imagination. The New Age Movement has undeniably taken on the definite form of a religion, complete with an agreed-upon body of doctrine, printed scripture, a pattern of worship and ritual, a functioning group of ministers and lay leaders, and an effective outreach program carried out by an active core of proselytizing believers. Furthermore, because of its astonishing success in attracting new followers, the New Age Church now has a large and growing membership worldwide. Its avowed aim, however, is to become the *only* world religion.

In the free marketplace of ideas, it is perfectly acceptable that a religion strive to convert others to its belief system. This is as true of the New Age World Religion as it is for Christianity. But the horrible truth about the New Age is that its leaders do not wish to freely compete with Christianity. They seek to destroy Christianity.

New Age leaders know that only if they are able to undermine credibility in the Bible, discredit Jesus Christ, and weaken the example of Christian churches can they succeed in their ultimate objective: the ascension to power of a New Age Messiah (the Antichrist) and the establishment of a one world order. At the pinnacle of this one world order will be the religious system described in Revelation 17: MYSTERY, BABYLON THE GREAT, THE MOTHER OF HARLOTS AND ABOMINATIONS OF THE EARTH.

To accomplish its insidious and perverse objectives, the leaders of this new religion have set forth a New Age Plan which they call The Divine Plan or simply The Plan, designed by none other than the master of deceit, Satan himself.

You should know, if you are a Christian—a Biblical Christian who believes in the inspired Word of God—*that you are a primary target of The Plan*. In fact, the only thing that stands between Satan and the successful implementation of this horrible, lawless Plan for humanity is you and millions of other determined Christians throughout the world. This is why the subversion and conquest of Christianity is the number one priority for those involved in carrying out The Plan.

Who Will Prevail?

As we look at the New Age with our Bibles open and plainly understand its darker side, our minds grow numb. But finally we recognize this movement for what it truly is. A sense of mounting horror grips us as we understand that this is almost certainly the end-time harlot church prophesied in the Bible. Our hearts sag because it is evident The Plan has made startling progress toward fulfillment. The New Age World Religion has already become the fastest-growing religious movement on earth.

In the parable of the wheat and the tares (Matt. 13:24–30), Jesus taught that evil would grow and grow, intermingling with the good until the time of the "harvest." Evil will not gradually disappear before good, but will ever develop and ripen until its highest manifestation in the last days. When we survey the damage to souls being caused by New Age doctrines and the incredible popularity of these doctrines, it is difficult not to view this development with alarm.

However, ". . . God hath not given us the spirit of fear; but of power, and of love, and of a sound mind" (2 Tim. 1:7). Basic to our "sound mind" is the knowledge that greater is He who is in us than he who is in the world (see 1 John 4:4). The rise to power of an evil Antichrist and the move toward a dominant One World Religion is no surprise to God's people. His prophets told us everything that was to come.

What is needed today is revival—a revival of the power of God on earth. Satan cannot withstand this, and his New Age World Religion shrinks before it. May each one of us be an instrument of this supernatural power. As one of God's great twentieth-century spiritual leaders, the late pastor Gresham Machen, wrote:

> God has brought His church through many perils, and the darkest hour has often preceded the dawn. So it may be in our day. The gospel may yet break forth, sooner than we expect, to bring light and liberty to mankind. But that will be done by the . . . instrumentality, not of theological pacifists who avoid controversy, but of earnest contenders for the faith. God give us men in our time who will stand with Luther and say, "Here I stand. I cannot do otherwise, God help me. Amen."

Texe Marrs
Austin, Texas

ONE

The Plan

We wrestle not against flesh and blood, but against
principalities, against powers, against the rulers of the
darkness of this world, against spiritual wickedness in
high places.   (Eph. 6:12)

A World Religion for the New Age . . . is needed to meet
the needs of thinking people . . . and to unify mankind.
(Lola Davis, *Toward a World Religion for the New Age*)

In a stunningly brief period of time, a new and powerful world religion has swept across America and the entire planet. Popularly called the New Age Movement by its own leaders, this new religion is rapidly and dramatically reshaping man's views of God and the universe.

Claiming to represent a radical new global culture, the New Age World Religion denies the existence of a personal God who loves His own, while it exalts human potential and scientific progress. Its leaders point out that they are forerunners of the New Age Messiah, a great superhuman world teacher and leader who is soon to come. He will, they have declared, establish a glorious Kingdom of man on earth in which all men will live in peace, harmony, and unity. Possessing unparalleled wisdom and knowledge, and wielding marvelous psychic abilities, all the powers of the universe will be at his command.

The Fantastic Drawing Power of the New Age

The New Age World Religion holds great appeal for modern man. New Age author and researcher Marilyn Ferguson, publisher of *Brain/Mind Bulletin,* says that New Age believers come from all levels of income and education. Among them she lists "schoolteachers and office workers, famous scientists, government officials and lawmakers, artists and millionaires, taxi drivers and celebrities, leaders in medicine, education, law, and psychology." She also says there are New Age advocates in corporations, universities, public schools, and even on the White House staff.[1]

As Ferguson states, the New Age World Religion is strongly supported by influential leaders from every realm of our culture. These include such personages as singer John Denver, former astronaut Edgar Mitchell, former University of Notre Dame head Theodore Hesburgh, former chancellor of the Federal Republic of Germany Willy Brandt, science fiction writer Isaac Asimov, physicist Fritjof Capra, *Megatrends* author John Naisbitt, and actress Shirley MacLaine.

Just as Hitler was able to inspire both the intellectual elite and the masses, the spirit of the New Age has taken in millions of men and women from all economic and social categories and from all walks of life, even supposed ministers of the Christian faith. Inclusive, it welcomes those of every political persuasion, liberal or conservative, and those from practically every ethnic group. What's more, it extends an invitation to those in all religions, holding itself up as the world's one great religious arbiter: a single beacon of light in which all religions can experience unity. The clarion call of the New Age to other religions is: "Come, let us be one."

The growth of the New Age World Religion is truly phenomenal and reveals how close we are to the last days. Only a decade ago, many viewed the New Age Movement as an assemblage of assorted nuts and weird, hippie-like personalities. In the years since, the New Age has matured into a monstrously enlarged religion and social movement that threatens to swallow up all other religions, philosophies, and social systems.

John Randolph Price, head of two major New Age groups—the Quartus Foundation for Spiritual Research and the Planetary Commission for Global Healing—claims that "more than half-a-billion (New Age) believers are on the planet at this time working in various religious groups." Boastfully he adds, "New thought [New Age] concepts are spreading more rapidly than any other spiritual teaching."[2]

From Witches to Humanists and Scientists

The reasons for such growth are obvious. Until now, most cults, Mystery Religions, and splinter churches attempted to be exclusive and open only to a select few. But the New Age World Religion is unlike any other apostate church or pagan cult the Christian world has confronted since the days of the early Church. The New Age is a universal, open-arms religion that excludes from its ranks only those who believe in Jesus Christ and a personal God. Buddhists, Shintoists, Satanists, Secular Humanists, witches, witch doctors, and shamans—all who reject Christianity are invited to become trusted members of the New Age family. Worshipers of separate faiths and denominations are to be unified in a common purpose: the glorification of man.

While pagans and occultists openly declare themselves to be New Agers, the religion is also broad-based enough to include those in the most respectable professions. As I mentioned in *Rush to Armageddon*, the New Age doctrine combines the worst of modern psychology, so-called "progressive education," medicine, science, and economics in a dangerous and new formulation perfectly compatible with the abominations of paganism and occultism. New Age professionals claim that this is a "High Religion" more attuned to the needs of "thinking" people than Christianity—which they deem outmoded and unsophisticated. They are drawn to the New Age belief that man is himself an evolving god and that the greatest love of all is self-love.

The essence of New Age religious doctrine is that man is neither sinful nor evil, and that Jesus' sacrifice on the cross was meaningless and futile. Man did not need a Savior to atone for sin, says the New Age, because man has for millennia been inevitably evolving toward perfection and godhood.

Predictably, a religious philosophy that deifies man and is totally void of absolute moral restraints is extremely attractive to those who do not know the Lord Jesus Christ as their personal Savior. In a world rampant with sin and unethical conduct, a world devoid of the *agape* love that is in Christ Jesus, the New Age sadly has become a narcissistic religion that readily finds converts.

Understanding the New Age Vocabulary

Being the earthly emissaries of another gospel and another Christ, leaders of the New Age are expert in the application of confusing and deceitful terminology. When Satan's representatives use such familiar Christian terms as God, Christ, Messiah, the Second Coming, born again, salvation, angel, heaven and hell, and the Kingdom of God, their meaning is radically different than that given in the Word of God.

In addition, the New Ager often uses terms, phrases, and euphemisms totally unfamiliar to all but persons who have studied esoteric doctrine. Again, the intent is to cloud and obscure the true meaning from the uninitiated.

Below are several Christian terms that the New Age has twisted and perverted, along with a few terms unique to the New Age lexicon. I have taken the liberty of revealing the hidden New Age meaning of each.

God: An impersonal energy force, immanent in all things. To the New Age, "God" can be referred to either as she or he, mother or father, god or goddess. Most New Age teachers hold that Mother Earth, the sun, the moon, and the stars—indeed all of nature—can be worshiped as "God."

Christ: A reincarnated avatar, Messiah, or messenger sent from the "hierarchy" (see *Angels* below) to give the living on earth spiritually advanced revelation. The New Age contends that Buddha, Mohammed, Confucius, Jesus, and many others were "Christs," but one greater than all of them will soon come to usher in the New Age. To the Christian, this coming New Age "Christ" is, in fact, the Antichrist.

Angels: More frequently called Ascended Masters, Masters of Wisdom, Ancient Masters, spirit guides, inner guides, spirit counselors, one's Higher Self, the Self, Superbeings, aeons, muses, or walk-ins." Collectively called the "hierarchy." Whichever term is used, the discerning Christian will recognize these shadowy entities not as "angels," but as demons.

Born Again (Rebirth): Personal or planetary transformation and healing. The point at which a New Age believer "lets go" and allows his Higher Self or Inner Guide (translated: demon) to guide and direct his life. Some New Agers describe this as *Kundalini,* a Hindu term meaning "serpent power," a moment of instant rebirth when the recipient is said to be transformed by a flash of light, receiving the benefit of higher consciousness as well as greater spiritual awareness and wisdom. Such a rebirth is said to convey "Christ consciousness" on the individual.

The Second Coming: The New Age assigns two definitions to this phrase, each of which subverts the true meaning of the Second Coming of Jesus prophesied in the Bible. First, it is claimed that at the Second Coming a New Age believer achieves "Christ consciousness," an exalted, higher state in which he is spiritually transformed into a divine being. This phrase also can mean the appearance on earth of the New Age Mesisah, or "Christ," and his hierarchy of demons from the spirit world.

Heaven/Kingdom of God: The terms heaven and Kingdom of God are often indistinguishable to the New Ager. Each refers to a spiritually cleansed and purified earth in which mankind has achieved "Christ consciousness" and has become akin to godkind. The New Age, or Aquarian Age, is expected to be the era when heaven and the Kingdom of God are realized on earth. The reincarnated "Christ" (the Antichrist) is to reign over the New Age, bringing in a One World Religion and consolidating all nations into one monolithic government.

Hell: New Agers deny the existence of a hell and a judgment. They also deny that sin and evil exist. God is alleged to be beyond good and evil, neither of which is a relevant term to the New Age.

Understanding the special definitions assigned Christian words and phrases by New Age leaders, we see the subtle deceit and confusion they employ. With this in mind, let's examine Satan's Plan for our world.

The Plan Exposed

When we analyze The Plan for the New Age—as publicly expressed by its own leadership—we cannot avoid the horrible conclusion that this apostate religion is demonic. The astonishing truth is that the New Age World Religion fits all the criteria of the Babylonian harlot church of the latter days. Revelation 17 reveals this as a Satanic religious system that just prior to the Second Coming of our Lord Jesus shall rule "peoples, and multitudes, and nations, and tongues" and shall be full of "abominations and filthiness." Led by the Beast who ascends "out of the bottomless pit," it will be, at its core, the mirror image of the Mystery Religion established by the founders of ancient Babylon.

To bring this prophesied anti-God religious system to reality in the last days, Satan has concocted a thirteen-point Master Plan, called simply The Plan by New Age leaders. Here is that chilling plan for world domination:

Point #1
The principal aim of The Plan is to establish a One World, New Age Religion and a one world political and social order.

Point #2
The New Age World Religion will be a revival of the idolatrous religion of ancient Babylon in which mystery cults, sorcery and occultism, and immorality flourished.

Point #3
The Plan is to come to fullness when the New Age Messiah, the Antichrist with the number 666, comes in the flesh to lead the unified New Age World Religion and oversee the new one world order.

Point #4
Spirit guides (demons) will help man inaugurate the New Age and will pave the way for the Antichrist, the New Age man-god, to be acclaimed by humanity as the Great World Teacher.

Point #5
"World Peace!," "Love!" and "Unity!" will be the rallying cries of the New Age World Religion.

Point #6
New Age teachings are to be taught and propagated in every sphere of society around the globe.

Point #7
New Age leaders and believers will spread the apostasy that Jesus is neither God nor the Christ.

Point #8
Christianity and all other religions are to become integral parts of the New Age World Religion.

Point #9
Christian principles must be discredited and abandoned.

Point #10
Children will be spiritually seduced and indoctrinated and the classroom used to promote New Age dogma.

Point #11
Flattery will be employed to entice the world into believing that man is a divine god.

Point #12
Science and the New Age World Religion will become one.

Point #13
Christians who resist The Plan will be dealt with. If necessary, they will be exterminated and the world "purified."

The Plan has such tremendous consequences for mankind and for Christianity that we cannot neglect to take stock of what is going on before our very eyes. Every Christian man and woman must face up to the harsh reality that there is, in fact, a New Age Plan for a One World Religion and a One World Government.

The Main Event

New Age leaders maintain that we are on the threshold of a New Order, that this is the Great Awakening—the dawning of the New Age. And all agree that The Plan will bring everything to pass. Vera Alder writes:

> There is actually a Plan and a Purpose behind all creation. . . .
> World Unity is the goal towards which evolution is moving.
> The World Plan includes: A World Organization . . . A World
> Economy . . . A World Religion.[3]

John Randolph Price has said that the Plan's centerpiece—
the Main Event as he calls it—will be the coming of the New
Age "Christ" and the building of the Kingdom on earth, to be
accomplished by a new race of god-men:

> The Gathering is taking place. (New Age believers) in all
> religions are uniting again—this time in a New Commission
> to reveal the Light of the World . . . and begin the Aquarian
> Age of Spirituality on Planet Earth. . . .[4]

> The revolution has begun . . . the pace is quickening.
> Throughout the world, men and women are joining in the
> uprising (and rising up) and are coming forward to be
> counted as part of a new race that will someday rule the
> universe.[5]

> Now we can co-create the future according to the Divine
> Plan.[6]

According to Price, the Plan includes "the elimination of
fear, the dissolving of false beliefs, and the erasing of karmic
debts in each individual soul." Price says that sin need not
disqualify you: "There is no such thing as a 'lost soul'—for every
soul is a page in the Master Plan."[7]

M. E. Haselhurst, writing for the Lucis Trust, emphasizes
that The Plan is positive and "concerned with rebuilding mankind." To those who doubt The Plan exists, he declares:

> Humanity needs to realize that there IS a Plan and to
> recognize its influence in unfolding world events, even when
> these appear as hindering factors, operating by means of
> destruction.[8]

What does Haselhurst mean when he speaks of "rebuilding
mankind" and hints of "hindering factors, operating by means of

destruction"? As we'll see in later chapters, New Age spokesmen teach that the earth must soon undergo chaos through a "purification process," and Christians are at the top of the New Age list of those to be "purified."

The concept of purification was perhaps first elaborated by Meishu Sama, a New Age pioneer from Japan. Sama reportedly meandered from atheism to Shintoism into the New Age philosophy. In 1931, at the age of forty-five, he was given a "revelation" that disclosed to him "God's divine plan for the New Age." He supposedly learned that humanity is to go through a great transitional period, turning from the old age of darkness to the New Age of light. During this transitional period, those with "negative vibrations" will be removed from the earth in an earthshaking *purification process.*[9]

This removal from the earth of those who rebel against the coming New Age World Order will evidently be supervised by a "Messiah" whom many in the New Age believe to be the Lord Maitreya:

> What is The Plan? It includes the installation of a new world government and new world religion under Maitreya.[10]

David Spangler claims he has communicated a number of times with this New Age Messiah. In his communications with Spangler, this spirit calls himself "John" or "Limitless Love and Truth." This demon spirit has indeed verified that a Plan is being rapidly implemented, declaring: "I . . . present to you, therefore, the revelation of man's destiny, for behold! I have placed my seal upon this planet."[11]

Spangler's demon guide also contends that The Plan is concerned with rebuilding mankind after a cleansing of the earth through the eradication of negative forces. This is necessary, claims the demonic spirit, to bring in a joyous new heaven and a new earth:

> This is the message of Revelation: we are now the builders of a New Age. We are called upon to embark on a creative project . . . in order to reveal the new heaven and build the New earth.[12]

One New Age organization that has publicly stated its endorsement of The Plan is the New Group of World Servers, a group intensely dedicated to a One World Government and a One World Religion. The New Group of World Servers says of its members: "They believe in an inner world government *and an emerging evolutionary plan.*" The group's official statement of purpose includes these four objectives:

1. Bring about world peace, guide world destiny and usher in the New Age.
2. Form the vanguard for the Reappearance of the Christ and his Great Disciples (the Masters of Wisdom).
3. Recognize and change those aspects of religion and government which delay the full manifestation of planetary unity and love.
4. Provide a center of light within humanity and hold the vision of the *Divine Plan* before mankind.[13]

Barry McWaters, founder and co-director of the Institute for the Study of Conscious Evolution, attributes the goal of *evolution* to the intelligence that created The Plan. McWaters, who terms this intelligence (actually Satan) the "Higher Will," provides this quote from the book *The Rainbow Bridge:*

Evolution is . . . the response to the call of Logos, of God. It is the purpose behind the Plan. It is God's drawing of creation back to himself.[14]

According to McWaters, man is evolving toward union with the universe, as planned by the "Higher Will," becoming a little god serving a greater god: the planet earth, or GAIA.[15]

New Age leaders have begun to publicize previously hidden aspects of The Plan. Alice Bailey has said that her "hidden Masters" told her that beginning in 1975 the time would be ripe for open propagation of The Plan. This same, demonic message may have been telepathically given to other New Age leaders as well, for a flood of information has poured forth about The Plan.

Still, there are apparently some elements of The Plan that are disclosed only to an inner circle.

George Christie, formerly a communications executive and now with the internationalist group The International Center for Integrative Studies (ICS), has intimated that some aspects of The Plan should be kept from the public. Asked about the work of the ICS at a meeting of the Lucis Trust, Christie defensively remarked: "Now, we don't publish it—it's not in our literature, you're not going to find it there—it's not right out there, you're not going to find it!"

When a participant inquired about The Plan, Christie grew even more guarded, offering only the cryptic comment: "Now when you speak of The Plan, capital P, I, of course, probably think the same thing as most of you do here."[16]

When Will the Plan Be Realized?

New Age leaders have said that The Plan is progressing extremely well. The final stage—the materialization of a heaven on earth presided over by their "Christ"—is said to be on the immediate horizon. Some project the year 2000 as the key date for the appearance of the "Christ" and his hierarchy. Others believe that this cardinal event is imminent and may occur at any time.

In the interim, they continue to work The Plan, educate believers, and bring into the fold thousands of new converts. They also work to spread insidious, often subtle propaganda throughout the media praising the New Age World Religion and its objectives. The way is being prepared for the Antichrist.

Lola Davis speaks of these preparations in her pivotal book *Toward a World Religion for the New Age:*

> The good news . . . is that there is already much activity toward required actions and conditions and that an increasing number of people are *either consciously or unconsciously* preparing mankind for a World Religion that's compatible with the New Age.[17]

Davis explains that The Plan cannot be fully realized until the New Age "Christ" or "Messiah" comes. "The leadership of the Messiah is the catalyst needed to materialize the New Age Kingdom." After his arrival the New Age Messiah will:

. . . help mankind learn to cooperate consciously with God's plan for the peace and well-being of the world . . . we will have, before the total program is in place, the guidance of the Avatar or Messiah.[18]

John Randolph Price echoes Davis, confidently proclaiming:

This New Age *will be*. A new Heaven on Earth *will be*. Preparations are being made now, and out of chaos will come the beginning of peace on earth, a New Order for Mankind.[19]

An effective leader, Price rallies his faithful around the call to preach the New Age gospel to the world so The Plan will more quickly be realized:

For you to be an effective member of the Planetary Commission, you should understand your role in the implementation of the Divine Plan. Yes, the salvation of the world does depend on you.[20]

Terry Cole-Whittaker, a flamboyant New Age minister from California whose television ministry and best-selling books brought her international fame and success, intimated recently in an interview with *Magical Blend* magazine that the world is very close to the day when the New Age will suddenly arrive in all its splendor: "I feel that we are right on the edge and we are going to 'pop' into a new dimension. Everybody senses it."[21]

The Real Plan

The God of the Bible also has a Plan for Mankind. I like to call it The Real Plan. John wonderfully summarized this Divine Plan with these momentous words:

For God so loved the world, that he gave his only begotten Son, that whosoever believeth in him should not perish, but have everlasting life. (John 3:16)

God's Plan was that His crucified Son, Jesus, would rise from the dead, ascend to heaven, and be our Mediator and our Savior:

> For there is one God, and one mediator between God and men, the man Christ Jesus; who gave himself a ransom for all, to be testified in due time. (1 Tim. 2:5, 6)

The Real Plan—designed by the only God there is—will be completed only when Jesus Christ returns to earth with a shout, descending in glory from out of the clouds. He will judge the living and the dead and reign as Lord of Lords and King of Kings forever and ever (see 1 Thess. 4:13; Rev. 19:11-21; 21; 22). Then and only then—after the Second Coming of Jesus Christ—will peace and harmony envelop the globe.

The best news about God's Real Plan is that salvation through Jesus Christ is intended for all. Unfortunately, the vast majority rebel against God and His Plan, falling victim to the Great Lie. That lie is incorporated in another Plan, drafted by the New Age Movement under direct command from Satan. The New Age Plan of Lucifer is in marked contrast to that of God's. It calls for another gospel and another "Christ." It falsely promises a reprobate humanity a quantum leap in consciousness that will result in man's becoming a god. Satan's Plan seductively offers prosperity and peace to a world hungry for material goods and fearful of nuclear destruction.

The deceptive Plan of Satan is finding great favor in the world today. New Age leaders tell us that it is destined to succeed. The Bible prophesied that this evil Plan would, for a time, win out (Dan. 11:24). But in the end Satan and all those who become embroiled in his dark Plan will end tragically, going down to resounding defeat.

Until the day when Christ returns and Satan's Plan is defeated, the world will experience a terrible period of untold misery and horror. Satan's Antichrist, the Beast with the number 666, will establish his malignant reign over all nations and peoples, and Christians will be severely persecuted for their beliefs. The prophesied One World Religion, the global church of Satan, will demand—and get—obedience from everyone on earth except the people who make up the Church of the living God.

Mystery Babylon: Satan's Church, Yesterday and Today

And upon her forehead was a name written, MYSTERY, BABYLON THE GREAT, THE MOTHER OF HARLOTS AND ABOMINATIONS OF THE EARTH. And I saw the woman drunken with the blood of the saints, and with the blood of the martyrs of Jesus. (Rev. 17:5, 6)

Christianity came face to face with the Babylonian paganism in its various forms that had been established in the Roman Empire. . . . Much persecution resulted. Many Christians were falsely accused, thrown to the lions, burned at the stake, and in other ways tortured and martyred. . . . Over the centuries God has called His people out of the bondage of Babylon. Still today His voice is saying, "Come out of her, my people, that ye be not partakers of her sins!"

(Ralph Woodrow, *Babylon Mystery Religion*)

The Scriptures reveal that from the time Satan rebelled and was banished to earth, *two churches* have existed on the planet. God's true Church is described as the chaste bride of Christ, a pure woman without blemish, redeemed by the sacrifice of God's Son, Jesus (Eph. 5:27; Rev. 19:7, 8).

The opposing world church is likened to a defiled woman, a drunken whore. She has on her forehead the revealing title, MYSTERY, BABYLON THE GREAT, THE MOTHER OF HARLOTS AND ABOMINATIONS OF THE EARTH. In her hand is a golden cup full of the filthiness of her fornications. This is the church of Satan.

God has determined that His Church be preserved until the Second Coming of His Son, Jesus, at which time Satan and his followers will be destroyed. But Satan, knowing he has only a short time until his fiery judgment, seeks all the temporal pleasures that counterfeit godhood can bestow on him. So he is determined that the evil Mystery Religion he first set up in Babylon now grow and expand.

More than seventy years ago, Anglican Bishop Alexander Hislop observed that Satan has worked hard over the centuries on behalf of the Babylonian Mystery Religion that serves as his church:

> Again and again has power been arrayed against it; but hitherto, every obstacle it has surmounted, every difficulty it has overcome. Cyrus, Xerxes and many of the Medo-Persian kings banished its priests from Babylon, and laboured to root it out of their empire; but then it found a secure retreat in Pergamos, and "Satan's seat" was erected there. The glory of Pergamos and the cities of Asia Minor departed; but the worship of the Queen of Heaven (Satan's false goddess) did not wane. It took a higher flight and seated itself on the throne of Imperial Rome.[1]

Hislop went on to explain how the Babylonian Mystery Religion continually rose above all attempts to put it down. The early Roman Catholic Church, for example, incorporated many of its elements into Catholic doctrine and worship. Mystery Babylon lived on!

As we survey the world around us today, we find that Mystery Babylon has again reared her ugly head. She has healed her wound and now invites all the world to partake of her drunkenness and her fornication. Shamelessly, she claims to be the one and only true Church. She calls herself the New Age World Religion, but this modern-day scarlet woman's real name is MYSTERY, BABYLON, THE MOTHER OF HARLOTS AND ABOMINATIONS OF THE EARTH.

Modern Babylon

The remarkable parallels between the Mystery Religion and cults of Babylon and the New Age World Religion provide definitive proof that these two anti-God religious systems are in fact *one and the same*. Here is just a partial list of the religious practices and rituals and the doctrinal beliefs mutually embraced by the Babylon of yesterday and today:

man-god doctrine	palmistry
karma	fire worship
self-love	occult visualization
reincarnation	sexual licentiousness
numerology	necromancy
psychic mind powers	astrology
levitation	evolution doctrine
astral travel	divination
hypnotism	drug abuse
shamanism	alcohol abuse
nature/earth worship	occult meditation
magic words (mantras)	occult symbolism
decrees	Mystery Teachings and initiation
goddess worship	altered states of consciousness

These perverse doctrines and practices, begun by the mighty Babylonian King Nimrod and his evil queen Semiramis, were in much evidence in the days of Abraham. The sensuously beautiful Semiramis grew to be worshiped as Mother Goddess, the central figure in a Satanic trinity composed of the father (Nimrod), the mother (Semiramis), and their son (also named Nimrod).[2]

In the Babylonian religion, Nimrod and Semiramis were thought to be the first of the man-gods, spiritually powerful reincarnated souls whose superwills catapulted them to exalted status as deities. Similarly, in today's New Age doctrine, man is depicted as evolving toward divinity through successive reincarnations and psychic willpower.

Semiramis was a supremely wicked woman. Declaring herself the Queen of Heaven, she demanded blood sacrifices and instituted temple prostitution. Following her death, word of her mystical exploits spread and her dark fame grew. The Babylonian Empire was able to dominate much of the world culturally, economically, and militarily. As a result, the Babylonian religious system also spread. Soon Semiramis was worshiped throughout the known world: as Ishtar and Astarte in Babylon, as Asherah and Ashteroth in Israel and Canaan, as Diana and Artemis in Ephesus and Asia Minor, as Cybele in Roman, Isis in Egypt, GAIA in Greece, and Kali in India. Her husband and son were also worshiped as gods, again under a variety of names. In Israel, Nimrod was venerated as Baal; in Egypt he was called Osiris and his son Horus.

The perverted Babylonian Mystery Religion, mocking the Holy Trinity, taught that the father-mother-son aspects of the godhead were separate deities but also were united as one. Therefore, in Egypt Ra the Sun God was worshiped as a combined, male and female, androgynous (unisex) god. This has significant implications for today's New Age World Religion. For example, there is now a modern-day revival of the worship of the Mother Goddess, especially by feminist New Agers.

This explains why, although the Bible clearly prophesies that the Antichrist will be a man, many in the New Age have actually begun to worship the Mother Goddess, whom they claim to have "reawakened" from her long sleep during the past two millennia of Christendom. Some New Age feminists go so far as to claim that their coming "Christ" will be the reincarnated goddess who physically reigned during the Babylonian era.

New Age proponents of witchcraft are especially active in the revival of the Babylonian Goddess Mystery Religion. Miriam Starhawk, a prominent witch, is president of the Covenant of the Goddess, a union of New Age, pagan, and goddess traditions officially recognized as a church in California. Starhawk and other witches of the official Church of WICCA (the "Wise Ones") have been invited by feminist organizations and even by Catholic priests and nuns to present their teachings.

Starhawk in a recent interview said of the growing belief by the New Age in the goddess:

Mother Goddess is reawakening and we can begin to recover our primal birthright, the sheer intoxicating joy of being alive. We can open our eyes and see that there is nothing to be saved from . . . no God outside the world to be feared and obeyed.[3]

Worship of the Mother Goddess is also prevalent in such churches as Unity and Unitarian. The Unity Church teaches, for example, that: "God is. Man is. We are now in the presence of that eternal Is-ness—Osiris and Isis are now our Father-Mother as fully as they were of old Egypt."[4]

A number of prominent feminist leaders today encourage women to abandon Christianity and Judaism in favor of the worship of Isis or another goddess from Babylonian origination. One of the tarot cards, "The High Priestess," depicts Isis. Feminist writer Kathleen Alexander-Berghorn illuminates us on the current campaign to revive the ancient goddess religion for modern-day women:

> Today women are rediscovering Isis. . . . The reawakening of Isis as a source of inspiration for contemporary women is exemplified by the healing ministry of Selena Fox, co-founder and High Priestess of Circle Sanctuary near Madison, Wisconsin. Every month at the New Moon, Selena holds a Spiritual Healing Circle centered around an Isis Healing Altar. . . . Each of us can personally experience the healing presence of the Goddess within us. All women are Isis and Isis is all women.[5]

Lucifer and the Babylonian/New Age Sun God

As a child, I marveled when I read that some primitive peoples actually worshiped the moon, the sun, the stars, and the earth as gods. Today I marvel that many in the New Age have revived this same primitive worship. Added is the concept that Lucifer was sent from the Sun God to bring man the truths of the New Age.

The symbol of Unity Village, a New Age community in Missouri with a worldwide ministry, is a Babylonian temple with the sun hovering above it. This is appropriate because in the Mystery cults the Babylonian deities were popularized as the Sun God. Today the New Age holds the sun to be a divine, living being, often called the Solar Father. Lucifer is claimed by the New Age to be the Solar Logos (Word), a god spirit appointed by the Solar Father to usher in the New Age through the Luciferic Initiation of humanity. We will examine this twisted, Luciferian doctrine of the New Age more thoroughly in a later chapter.

Satan's Final Act: The Revival of the Babylonian Mystery Religion

The Bible tells us there will be massive apostasy during the last church age. The vast majority of people will fall prey to the doctrines of demons. False prophets and false "Christs" will seduce people's minds and initiate them into the Mystery of Iniquity (2 Thess. 2:7). Babylon will be revived as a worldwide religious and political system headed by the Antichrist. Then the Great Tribulation period will occur, a time of universal bloodshed and persecution.

Are we at the threshold of this brutal period of bloodshed and turmoil? Are we soon to see a One World Religion and a One World Government headed by a Satanically inspired Antichrist? Literally thousands of hours of research and prayer convince me that the answer can only be in the affirmative.

I am not alone in this conclusion. Hal Lindsey recently told listeners of the Trinity Broadcasting Network (TBN), "We now have a movement that is unparalleled in history called the New Age. . . . This movement is preparing the way for the Antichrist—rapidly. . . . The religious deception is here."[6] Paul Crouch, president of TBN, remarked, "The octopus tentacles of the New Age movement go directly to the great deceiver himself, the Devil."[7]

Other Christian leaders have expressed much the same sentiments. Pat Robertson and his "700 Club" have discussed the New Age movement. Constance Cumbey stated in her best-selling *Hidden Dangers of the Rainbow* that the New Age fulfills all the prophetic requirements of the Babylonian Harlot Church of the last days. Dave Hunt wrote of this modern-day descendant of Babylon's Mystery Religion in his powerful *Peace, Prosperity and the Coming Holocaust*. Evangelists Jimmy Swaggart and David Wilkerson have expressed their intense concern.

The New Age could well be the last age. Babylon has sprung back to life in the form of the New Age Movement. Satan's day is at hand.

The Prince of Darkness is apparently ready to unveil his bloody Plan. In doing so, mankind will be hurled with magnum force into a boiling caldron as the final chapter ensues in the battle between the forces of evil and God and His people.

The Spiritual Warfare Raging Today

If you are a Christian, you are on the front line of battle. And there's no way out. You'll either have to see this war through—and come out on the other end victorious—or through your inaction you will become an accomplice in Satan's Plan. The fact is, once you surrendered your life to Jesus Christ, Satan declared war on you. Now you are counted by him as a sheep to slaughter (see Psa. 44:22).

The leaders of the New Age World Religion are Satan's generals and admirals. In concert with their demon advisors, these men and women have already drawn up their battle plan. They have also identified the enemy.

"The radical Christian Right is working hard to destroy the New Age movement," reports an alarmed Dick Sutphen, author of many best-selling New Age books and tapes. Sutphen says that Christian "forces of ignorance and intolerance" must be defeated. He states that Christians are now trying to censor books in schoolrooms and dictate what magazines convenience stores can sell. Sutphen singles out Christian authors Robert Morey and Constance Cumbey, as well as Christian ministers and evangelists Charles Stanley (former head of the Southern Baptist Convention), Jerry Falwell, James Robison, Tim LaHaye, Jimmy Swaggart, Pat Robertson, "and others of their ilk," branding these men as "zealots."[8]

To combat what he calls the "Fundamental Fascism" of these and other Christians, Sutphen and his associates have founded an adversary group named New Age Activists. He describes this group as follows:

> New Age Activists is a spiritual action group of
> Reincarnationists, Inc., a nonprofit (nontaxable) educational
> organization structured to promote peaceful planetary
> transformation by *sharing* awareness of metaphysical
> principles, *alerting* others of the (Christian) efforts to block
> our dreams, and *networking* New Agers for support
> programs.[9]

Sutphen and his New Age Activists evidently will use any and all means at their disposal in their war against Christianity. Sutphen himself has stated that "New Agers are best at infiltrating society," hinting that much of his organization's aggressive behavior may be concealed behind the scenes.[10]

Christians must therefore expect determined New Age opposition. William Irwin Thompson, founder of the New Age's Lindisfarne Association, which now operates out of the Cathedral of St. John the Divine in New York City, has emphatically stated, "There is no escaping it, religious warfare will continue."[11] The Quartus Foundation's John Randolph Price speaks of this conflict in stark military terms, calling it an "offensive" and announcing that the "true believers . . . are now stepping forth from every religion on earth and are now moving into the staging area."[12] The demon spirit Djwhal Khul, whom Alice Bailey calls "the Tibetan," is quoted as saying that every problem in society "is essentially a religious problem, and behind all strife . . . is to be found the religious element." But, says this demon spirit defiantly, "Nothing in heaven or hell, on earth or elsewhere, can prevent the progress of the (New Age) man who has awakened to . . . the clarion call of his own soul."[13]

We are experiencing outbreaks of spiritual hostilities in our schools, within the media and entertainment industries, and even within our churches. The business world is not immune from the New Age onslaught either. Incredible though it may seem, the *New York Times* reported on September 28, 1986 that the previous July, "Representatives of some of the nation's largest corporations, including IBM, AT&T, and General Motors, met in New Mexico to discuss how metaphysics, the occult, and Hindu mysticism might help executives compete in the world marketplace."[14] At Stanford University's renowned Graduate School of Business, a seminar called "Creativity in Business" includes such topics as chanting, meditation, the use of tarot cards, and the "New Age Capitalist." Meanwhile, a recent survey of five hundred corporate presidents and company owners revealed that half had sponsored some type of New Age "consciousness raising technique" for their employees.[15]

Our nation's military also seems to have become susceptible to New Age influence. In the early 1980s, officers at the Army War College, some of whom were graduates of EST and the radical Students for a Democratic Society, conducted a study aimed at creating a "New Age Army." The study recommended meditation for soldiers and training in psychic skills and in magic.[16]

Carl A. Raschke, professor of religious studies at the University of Denver, describes the New Age as "the most powerful social force in the country today." He adds:

> I think it is as much a political movement as a religious movement and it's spreading into business management theory and a lot of other areas. If you look at it carefully you see it represents a complete rejection of Judeo-Christian and bedrock American values.[17]

Onward New Age Soldiers?

As we'll discover in the chapters that follow, the early stages of spiritual warfare have been successfully won by the New Age. Now comes the decisive, more ominous stage: the determined effort by the New Age to subvert and take over the Christian churches and to seize complete social and political power.

The foundation is now being laid for the Antichrist's reign of terror. It is ironic that at this very moment, when so many liberal Christian churchmen seek to remove older songs of worship like "Onward Christian Soldiers" from our hymnals, claiming them to be militaristic, a slow but steady drumbeat of violence has begun within the New Age movement. This seething undercurrent of violence threatens to openly explode into savage acts once Satan unleashes against mankind all his powers through the Antichrist.

A shrewd dictator convinces his subjects that a certain group is a threat to their welfare. This is how Nero and Caligula were able to marshal public rage against the early Christians; this was the ruse Hitler used to inflame the German people against the Jews. Now there are early signs that this same tactic may be employed by the New Age masters.

In the influential publication *Life Times: Forum for a New Age,* publisher and editor-in-chief Jack Underhill recently called for "The Second American Revolution," which he likened to "The New Crusades." "There is a New American Revolution brewing today," Underhill writes, "and the outcome of it will decide the fate of the world in the next decade." This modern-day conflict can, he says, result in "a higher nobility, a more pure idealism."[18]

According to Underhill, the fate of the planet and the human race hinges on the outcome of this new revolution. He calls the struggle for New Age spiritual supremacy "the biggest war of all times" and announces that only full victory can bring "freedom to create our own reality." Underhill also advises New Age disciples on how they can achieve this total victory over "the enemy":

> We start the revolution within each of us and work out from there, getting groups of similar minded rebels together and drafting campaigns to make the enemy surrender.[19]

Like a general giving an inspirational pitch to his troops, Underhill continues with these combative and dramatic words:

> In this New Age we are our own commanders and infantry, truly special forces of a sort that has never been seen at war before. . . . Charge on to the only true victory there is, that of spiritual liberation. . . .
> Like the colonists of this country who began this struggle for liberation, we owe it to ourselves to complete it. The fate of the world depends on us.[20]

The New Age is dead serious about what it sees as a special mission for mankind: the conquest of the world for their "Christ," the Lord Maitreya. Satan has ignited in his New Age followers a desperate urge to become gods, and he and his demons accuse Christians and Jews of being impediments and stumbling blocks to man's godhood. Either the Christians and Jews will convert to the New Age faith . . . or they will have to go!

A Declaration of Spiritual War

Underhill flatly states this is *war.* John White has said that *survival* is at stake, and John Randolph Price talks about a *spiritual offensive* and about breaking up the *dark pockets* of resistance. Price tells New Agers who are worried that they may not get to be gods, "The salvation of the world *does* depend on you!"[21]

Other New Age leaders deceptively use Biblical imagery to provoke their followers to action. One group likens the New Age "Christ" to the first of the four horsemen of the Apocalypse from Revelation 6:2, a rider on a white horse who was given a crown and went forth to conquer.[22] (Christian Bible students know that this passage of Scripture as a whole refers to the coming of Jesus Christ. Any other interpretation amounts to blasphemy.)

The leaders of the New Age are fully aware that even though many Christian clergy and laymen can be tricked into believing in The Plan, a small core of Biblical Christians will never acquiesce to the New Age Kingdom. These stubborn believers in Jesus and a personal God are the "enemy" of whom Underhill wrote. These are the "dark pockets" of resistance that Price says must be smashed.

How can these enemies of the New Age best be dealt with? Let's see what Peter Lemesurier, premier New Age thinker, speaker, and best-selling author, proposes to do about these stubborn Christians as well as the Jews reluctant to support The Plan.

Referring to the New Age Plan to install Satan's man (the Antichrist) on the world throne, Lemesurier scathingly notes that "there are multitudes of Christians, long dazzled by a rabidly other-worldly messanic image, who will . . . be affronted at the suggestion that a mere man could ever fulfill that awesome role."[23] Lemesurier says that these troublesome Christians will undoubtedly believe the New Age "Christ," whom he calls the "New David," to be the Antichrist.

Christians who know their Bible will indeed recognize the New Age "Christ" as an impostor and they'll refuse to worship him as God. Lemesurier suggests that New Agers will battle the resisters under the banner of their impostor Messiah. "It is for the soul of man that the New David will have to fight," he writes. The supporters of this New David must be willing to die, if necessary, to insure the success of their New Age Kingdom. It is the New David who will prevail, Lemesurier confidently asserts. "The masked forces of the Old Age," he says, "will be unable to check (the) headlong rush" of the New Age.[24]

THREE

Toward a One World Religion and a Global Order

And the king shall do according to his will. . . . Neither
shall he regard the God of his fathers. . . . But in his
estate shall he honor the God of forces. . . . Thus shall
he do in the most strongholds with a strange god,
whom he shall acknowledge and increase with glory:
and he shall cause them to rule over many. . . .

(Dan. 11:36-39)

Religions should
    —Accelerate their ecumenism and create common
world religious institutions which would bring the
resources and inspirators of the religions to bear upon
the solution of world problems.
    —Display the UN (United Nations) flag in all their
houses of worship.
    —Pray and organize world prayers. . . .

(Robert Mueller, *The New Genesis*)

There can be no doubt whatsoever that one world religious and political leadership is the greedy, all-consuming goal of the New Age. Not a day goes by that New Age leaders somewhere in the world do not impress upon their followers the prediction that a new world order is coming—and soon.

Dozens of books have been written, hundreds of magazine articles published, and literally thousands of speeches presented detailing The Plan for this new world order. One of the most revealing and thorough books is *Toward a Human World Order,* by Gerald and Patricia Mische.[1] The Misches were one of five original co-sponsors of Planetary Initiative for the World We Choose, a group dedicated to world unity and a centralized government. Their book is a detailed account of how a New World Order can be instituted, complete with an economic system embodying a "whole earth personal identity system," as well as a plan for a New World Religion. The most amazing thing about this book is that it was published by an ostensibly Christian publisher, Paulist Press, a Catholic-operated press.

The Tara Center, a New Age group led by Benjamin Creme, on April 25, 1982, ran a full-page ad in twenty major newspapers around the globe, including dailies in New York City, Washington, D.C. London, and Paris. The ad boldly proclaimed that the New Age Messiah, identified as the Lord Maitreya, was now alive and ready to assume his rightful place on the throne of world power. The ad bluntly admitted that this goal was at the very essence of The Plan:

What is The Plan? It includes the installation of a new world government and new world religion under Maitreya.

Nearly five years later, on January 12, 1987, the Tara Center published a similar full-page ad in *USA Today*, trumpeting the lie that "THE CHRIST IS IN THE WORLD." The ad described the Lord Maitreya as "A great World Teacher for people of every religion and no religion."

Christians who have studied Scripture can easily identify Lord Maitreya, the New Age Messiah. He is none other than the Antichrist, the Beast with the number 666. However, the Bible tells us that in the end the Antichrist will not prevail. Instead, Jesus will return (the Second Coming) in full glory and power to destroy the Satanic world ruler and to establish His own One World Government and One World Religion:

And I heard a great voice out of heaven saying, Behold, the tabernacle of God is with men, and he will dwell with them, and they shall be his people, and God himself shall be with them, and be their God. (Rev. 21:3)

At the Second Coming, Will Men Become Gods?

Satan's intention is to discredit God's Holy Word by reinterpreting—that is, by perverting—the Scriptures that point to the certainty of Jesus' return. This is why many New Age leaders are spreading the false doctrine that the Second Coming does not mean the return of Jesus but instead refers to the realization by modern man that he, man himself, is "Christ," the one and only supreme deity. David Spangler, with the Lucis Trust ("Lucis" is the Greek word for Lucifer) and director of the occultic Findhorn Community in Scotland, has flatly stated that "The Second Coming has already occurred. . . . Now is the time to begin building the new earth."[2]

John Randolph Price echoes the words of Spangler. He says that the Second Coming refers not to the return of Jesus, but to the awareness by an individual that he is a god, a supermind. A superminded person, Price says, achieves the higher state of "Christ Consciousness" that results from the awareness of one's own divinity. This for him is the Second Coming.[3]

New Agers maintain that Jesus is *not* returning; therefore, it is up to man to transform the earth—to bring in the Kingdom. According to Price, "We can *can* let the kingdom come . . . which means that this world can be transformed into a heaven—right now—in the 1980s and 90s."[4]

Lola Davis says that the coming New Age World Religion will be made possible because, through education, spiritual man "will have developed god-like qualities and sufficient knowledge and wisdom to cooperate with God (the universal energy force) in materializing the Kingdom of God on earth."[5]

Organizing the New World Order

Davis believes, as do many other New Agers, that the United Nations is an excellent first step for the coming New Age World Government. "Perhaps one way to prepare the people of the world for a World Religion," she remarks, "would be to encourage their participation in this admirable organization that is leading the way toward One World."[6]

Religious practices in most United Nations member countries are either pagan or shamanistic, or else the peoples are of the Islamic, Buddhist, or Hindu faiths. Many of the member nations have Marxist/Socialist governments vigorously opposed to Christian belief. One United Nations organization, UNESCO (United Nations Educational and Social Organization), is so openly hostile to democracy and the West that the United States Congress has refused to fund it anymore.

It is understandable then that the United Nations would be instrumental in the New Age push toward a New World Order. In October 1975 a convocation of spiritual leaders read this statement to the United Nations Assembly:

> The crises of our time are challenging the world religions to release a new spiritual force transcending religious, cultural, and national boundaries into a new consciousness of the oneness of the human community and so putting into effect a spiritual dynamic toward the solutions of the world's problems. . . . We affirm a new spirituality divested of isolarity and directed toward planetary consciousness.[7]

"New consciousness," "oneness," "human community," "spiritual dynamic," "new spirituality," "planetary conscious- ness"—these are all buzzwords of the New Age. Noticeably absent from the statement are references to a personal God who loves us or to Jesus Christ, His Son. Nor did these world spiritu- al leaders make mention of such meaningful Biblical terms as sin, redemption, salvation, and prayer. Evidently these men preach "another gospel," a New Age gospel.

The anti-Christian nature of the United Nations is exempli- fied by the attitude of its assistant secretary general, Robert Mueller, to whom all thirty-two directorates of this international body report. Mueller has advocated a One World Religion using the UN as a model. He has also proposed that the UN flag be displayed in every church throughout the world and that a uni- versal Bible be written and published. Mueller is also a promoter of a one world economic and political order.[8]

The One World Government planned by the New Age will be completely merged with the One World Religion. There will be no separation of church and state. LaVedi Lafferty and Bud Hollowell, leaders of the Collegians International Church, which they describe as a "Church Universal of the New Age" dedicated to revealing the "ancient mysteries" (the anti-God Babylonian religious system) to initiates, make this point clear. They say that "The New Age, in its full meaning, will be attained as humanity individually and collectively moves past self-centered awareness to self-realization of human and universal oneness."[9]

Lafferty and Hollowell assert that present religious systems fail to promote universal harmony because they are negative and ignorant. The New Age World Religion, on the other hand, is positive and endowed with knowledge and wisdom. "The formation of New Age religion," they conclude, "is necessary to fill the void left by the inability of old religious forms to meet modern spiritual needs."

For example, they note that the New Age Religion allows believers to discard "ignorant" notions of an external God and to accept such "wise" Eastern doctrines as that of the Law of Rebirth (reincarnation) and that of "Christ" as a *State of Consciousness* residing in many spiritually advanced men and not simply Jesus alone.[10] It's plain to see that the "new" religion espoused by the Colleagians International Church is simply a warmed-over version of the old Babylonian religious system which demonically led to the occultic Hindu and Buddhist religions.

The new world order will exalt the lie that all paths lead to "the one," and that "one" is the New Age. Even agnostic science will supposedly find a place in the pantheon of the New Age. Jonathan Stone has made this fake claim of universality for the coming "World Order:"

> I feel that there is coming a World Order in which science will merge with monistic philosophy and all the world will be swept up in a new consciousness.
> The one distinguishing feature in the World Order will be the credo: "All is one."[11]

Clearly, The Plan is to create a world order in which not only churches and religions but all of society will be controlled by Lord Maitreya—the Antichrist—and his demonic spirit guides. Benjamin Creme and his group, Tara Center, have proclaimed that Maitreya will establish both a world religion and a world Socialist government that will bring peace to the planet and finally solve our economic and hunger problems.[12]

Jean Houston, past president of the New Age-oriented Association for Humanistic Psychology and a firm believer in evolutionary transformation, has said:

> I predict that in our lifetime we will see the rise of essentially a New World Religion. . . . I believe a new spiritual *system* will emerge. . . .[13]

According to The Plan, cosmetic changes to present government systems just won't do. A wholescale change is necessary to purify and spiritualize the political process. Marilyn Ferguson insists that "the political system needs to be *transformed,* not reformed. We need something else, not just something more."[14] Such a transformation will mean no national boundaries and borders, no division among governments, and the end of patriotism and nationalism.

The New Age sees the world as an interconnected global village, or as Lewis Mumford phrases it, "a World Culture." Mumford enthusiastically lauds this New World Culture:

> The destiny of mankind, after its long preparatory period . . . is at last to become one. . . . This unity is on the point of being expressed in a world government that will unite nations and regions.[15]

The New World Culture will be achieved, William Irwin Thompson says, through "planetization"—the implementation of a political regime brought about by a growing world consciousness of unity.[16] Mark Satin prophetically remarks: "Planetary events are, in a sense, *conspiring to inspire us* to recognize our oneness and interdependence."[17]

Satin finds this conspiracy a favorable development that should lead to a "planetary guidance system," a leadership structure that can levy a planetary tax on the rich so that the economic resources of the wealthy nations can be redistributed to the poorer ones.[18]

Similar to Satin's proposal for a planetary guidance system is

Donald Keys's call for a "planetary management system" which will, he theorizes, advance us toward "Omega," a sort of Kingdom on Earth in which all consciousness (man's thoughts) and culture will be unified.[19] Keys is founder of Planetary Citizens, a New Age group seeking to transform the world's political systems. A former United Nations worker, Keys has enlisted the likes of David Spangler, Edgar Mitchell, Norman Cousins, and Isaac Asimov in his group's quest for a centralized one world system.

Another New Age organization whose goal is the establishment of a one world system is World Goodwill. Headquartered on United Nations Plaza, this group pushes The Plan for a one world governmental and religious system espoused by Alice Bailey. In *The Externalization of the Hierarchy* and other works, Bailey has spread the teachings of her mentor-spirit—"the Tibetan," Djwhal Khul. "The Tibetan apparently has an open line to Satan because everything he has taught Bailey about The Plan is in perfect accord with the Satanic "revelations" received telepathically from demon spirits by many other New Agers.[20]

Lola Davis, in her book *Toward a World Religion for the New Age,* gives a glowing "appreciation" to Djwhal Khul and Alice Bailey for all "the thought and planning" they have done toward a world religion for the New Age.[21] Britisher Benjamin Creme of the occultic Tara Center in London is also a follower of the Tibetan and Alice Bailey.

The Coming New Age "Christ": Lord Maitreya

According to Bailey, "the Tibetan" predicts a New World Order to be brought about when the "Christ" (not Jesus, but Maitreya) appears on the world scene. This "Christ" or world leader is expected to establish a New World Religion to supplant the "false teachings" of traditional Christianity.[22]

World Goodwill offers for individual use The Great Invocation, a printed meditation which pleads for Maitreya to come swiftly so a new world can be built, man can recognize his divinity, and global peace and tranquillity can come to pass.

Evidently Maitreya is to lead us into a new astrological era: the Age of Aquarius. Reverend Matthew Fox, a Catholic Dominican priest whose endorsement of paganism and nature worship has shocked many of the Catholic faithful, says we are "on the verge of breaking into a new spiritual age." It is imperative, Fox warns, that we "beware of the Gods of the past"—apparently a reference to the Holy Trinity: Father, Son, and Holy Spirit. Fox says we must not look back at the fading age, but instead should embrace the New Age. "To look back piningly," he cautions, "is to commit idolatry."[23]

Like other New Agers, Fox insists that the "Kingdom/Queendom of God has begun," but that it is up to man to finish this Great Work. In his *Manifesto for a Global Civilization*, Fox avows that:

> Our era lures us to create the first global civilization on earth. We are that generation that begins the creative transformation out of the whole world into a single community out of the diverse peoples of the planet.[24]

For Fox, what Christianity should be all about involves everything from the perversion of homosexuality to witchcraft to the worship of both the planet earth and the reawakened ancient goddess. To those who might protest that these activities are clearly abominations before God, Fox snaps back that "the Holy Spirit will not be locked into any one form of religious faith.[25]

New Age advocate Robert Mueller, assistant secretary general of the United Nations, is also highly respected within the U.S. Catholic community as a Christian educator. Yet he has said, "I am not so fanatical as not to respect other faiths. I would never fight with another religion about the superiority of mine."[26]

Asked "What is the best religion?" Mueller replies, "You have about five thousand religions on the planet. You'd be dead before you studied them all to decide which is the best."[27]

Uniting the World's Religions

Mueller is pushing for "a convergence of the different religions" on earth, believing that mankind should and will discover the "cosmic and divine laws" that unite all religions. He even claims that this is what Christ would want us to do: "Worldwide spiritual ecumenism, expressed in new forms of religious cooperation and institutions would probably be closest to the heart of the resurrection of Christ."[28]

It is preposterous that Jesus would find heathen and pagan religions such as witchcraft, Buddhism, and Hinduism close to His heart. But observe that *Mueller never says that Jesus is the Christ to whom he is referring.* Most New Agers believe that the "Christ" is not a man but an *office* or a *spiritual state of higher consciousness.* The New Age claims that Buddha, Jesus, Lao Tse, and other enlightened teachers were all the same reincarnated person.

Mueller mentions the "resurrected Christ," but to Mueller resurrection is not exclusive to Jesus—it is simply a synonym for *reincarnation:*

> We will be resurrected materially in other life forms on this planet and ultimately into atoms of other stars, but most of all we will continue to live by the contributions we have made to humanity's improvement through our deeds, thoughts, love, and reverence for life during our own incarnations.[29]

Mueller believes that merging all religions into one and establishing a One World Government will fulfill all man's dreams and hopes. Furthermore, it will complete the *evolutionary plan* designed to lift man to divine status:

> It was now very clear to me: there was a pattern in all this; it was a response to a prodigious evolutionary march by the human species toward total consciousness, an attempt by man to become the all-understanding, all-enlightened master of his planet and his being. Something gigantic was going on. . . .[30]

In rapturous tones, Mueller describes this evolutionary march toward a One World Order as "glorious and beautiful like Aphrodite emerging from the sea."[31] What a revealing choice of words! Aphrodite is ancient Greece's version of Babylon's Mother Goddess, the very personality who polluted the world with Satanism and who is depicted in Revelation 17:1 as "the great whore that sitteth upon many waters," and in Revelation 13:1 as *a beast rising up out of the sea.*

This all makes sense when we note Mueller's belief in the evolving godhood of man and the unity of all religions. He has stated, for example, that "Unity in diversity is one of the basic laws of the universe, as it is the law for a garden."[32] Evidently his analogy refers to the result that sprang out of the Garden of Eden after Eve was seduced by Satan into disobeying God.

He writes that the story of the Tree of Knowledge vividly describes that all of us, "having decided to become like God . . . have become Masters in deciding between good and bad." Mueller says that "this gives Catholic, Christian and all Christian educators a marvelous opportunity to teach a new morality and ethics."[33]

Christians who know their Bible know that Adam and Eve did not "become like God" by their act of disobedence in the Garden of Eden, but became servants of the evil ruler of this temporal world, Satan. The Bible reveals that we are not "Masters in deciding between good and bad," but are to rely on the Holy Spirit in discerning the difference between right and wrong.

Mueller's New Age ideas do indeed represent a "new morality and ethics," but any Christian educator who irresponsibly teaches such warped, un-Biblical doctrine will have to answer to God.

Where did Robert Mueller acquire these un-Biblical ideas? He has admitted that the demon spirit, "the Tibetan," has advised him on a core curriculm for the New Age, to be used in public and private schools to teach children "Global Education." Furthermore, Mueller confesses that his "Master" was U Thant, the Burmese Buddhist and one world propagandist who was Mueller's superior as secretary general of the United Nations Assembly. Mueller explains his personal conversion to the New Age this way:

I have never been a deeply religious person. I was raised in a good Catholic family, but for long in my life, I had never met anyone who inspired me to become a really spiritual person. . . . At the age of 46, I became director of Secretary-General U. Thant's office. Here, for the first time in my life, I met a person who inspired me, a man who was deeply religious. . . . He was one of the most marvelous human beings I ever met in my life. . . . I studied Buddhism to know him better. We became great friends. . . . Here, in the middle of my life, was the Master, the one who inspired me, someone I could imitate like a father. . . . From the moment I became interested in the spiritual dimension of life, everything started to change. . . . I studied the mystics. . . . I was invited to participate in an East-West monastic encounter.[34]

Robert Mueller has become an unknowing captive of the Great Deception and now seeks to bring other lost souls into delusion and captivity. Sadly, Mueller concludes his testimony with these words: "I would like the whole world to benefit from my experience and to derive the same enlightenment, happiness, serenity and hope in the future as I derived from my contact with U. Thant."[35]

All Paths Lead to God (Except Those That Profess a Belief in God)

According to the New Age theology, any and all religious practices and beliefs are fully acceptable, no matter how bizarre or incredible. What the New Age does aggressively object to, however, is the suggestion that any one religion, faith, or set of moral and ethical rules is *the way.*

This seems at first glance tolerant; but in practice, it is diabolically clever and disingenuous. It portrays the Christian who professes belief in Jesus Christ as *the way* of salvation as intolerant and biased. The same is true for the Jew who refuses to accord witchcraft manuals equal standing with the books of the Old Testament.

An alleged doctrine of universality turns out to be a wicked strategy to extinguish the world's only major religions that believe in a loving, personal God: Christianity and Judaism—the same religions that historically have opposed the ancient Babylonian religious system now being revived for the New Age. After centuries of hatred for those who believe in a personal God, Satan hopes to get his revenge through New Age One World Religion.

With which of the great religions of the world does the New Age find itself most in accord? Hinduism and Buddhism. Robert Mueller, though Catholic, has kind words for Hinduism and Buddhism. Embracing the Hindu (and New Age) doctrine of successive reincarnations, as opposed to the Christian (and Catholic) doctrine of death and judgment, Mueller states:

> O God, I know that I come from you, that I am part of you, that I will return to you, and that there will be no end to my rebirth in the eternal stream of your splendid creation.[36]

In his book *The New Genesis,* Mueller eloquently calls for the New Age to be ushered in by the year 2000 and the formation of a New Order which he euphorically calls "A Bimillennium Celebration of Life, the advent of an Era of Peace, a Golden Age, and the First Millennium of World Harmony and Human Happiness."

"Yes," he writes, "we must join our Hindu brethren and call henceforth our planet 'Brahma' or the Planet of God."[37]

With its many idolatrous temples, thousands of gods, belief that man is himself a deity, practices of a caste system, belief in karma and reincarnation, and almost every other abominable act and doctrine, the Hindu religion is in most respects a mirror image of the Babylonian religious system. The sensual Mother Kali, the Hindu creator of the universe as well as its destroyer, is counterpart to the Goddess of Babylon, Semiramis, who with her mate-god Nimrod, the "mighty warrior," built the Tower of Babel that so angered God.

Gurus from India, where Hinduism flourishes, have been coming to America for several decades now. The tumultuous sixties saw a heightened interest among drug freaks, hippies, and rebellious youth in the ungodly religious philosophies of the gurus. Now in their forties, many still possess the Satanic desires and lies they embraced in their youth. To these millions of confused Americans, the planned New Age World Order is synonymous with the Kingdom of Heaven on earth.

Many who in the sixties sought to integrate Hindu religion with Western culture founded hundreds of New Age organizations. They have become Western-style gurus. They wear tailored suits and drive expensive foreign automobiles, but the religious philosophies they teach are no different than those of Maharaj Ji, Maharishi Mahesh Yogi, and Baghwan Rajneesh.

This weird blend of Eastern and Western philosophies is what gives the New Age World Religion its seductive appeal. New Agers now tell those they seek to recruit that they can incorporate the "best" of Eastern mysticism with traditional Western values and even Judeo-Christian tradition.

The Preaching of Another Gospel

Paul warned the Church against those who preach "another gospel." There is no way the Hindu and Christian faiths can be reconciled. Whereas the former preaches a gospel of occultic, idolatrous practices, man-gods and worship of devils, the latter—Christianity—points to the exclusive Lordship of the King of Kings, Jesus Christ, and instructs us to keep our eyes fixed *only* on Him.

One sees in twentieth-century India the damage Hinduism can wreak on a nation. The poverty-stricken and diseased Indian masses disprove the New Age lie that this religion can bring prosperity and health. The horrendous caste system of India shows the harm that can befall people who trust in the false doctrines of karma and reincarnation. Yet, millions of New Age believers in America and the West insist that Hinduism is a scientific religion able to meet all of man's spiritual and material needs.

The Maharishi Mahesh Yogi, who brought Transcendental Meditation (TM) to America, teaches his followers here and in Europe that the New Age began in 1975 when he inaugurated an "Age of Enlightenment." He also has organized a New World Government with himself as overseer. Assisting Maharishi when his World Government assumes full power sometime in the future will be "Governors of the Age of Enlightenment."[38]

To the solid Christian, it seems ludicrous that anyone would support a graying guru with long unkempt hair and flowing robes who sits in a lotuslike stance preaching that he is head of a new world political and religious system. Yet, hundreds of thousands have already been initiated into his TM program, which is titled, "Enlightenment and the Siddhis, a New Breakthrough in Human Potential."

Maharishi promises his initiates unparalleled, godlike powers such as the ability to communicate with the dead, to levitate and even fly through the air, to walk through walls, to discern the future, and to visit the past in spirit. Maharishi has said that through advanced meditation, man enters a new state of consciousness. In this enlightened state, superhuman powers—the "Siddis"—become possible:

> Enlightenment and its expression in the Siddhis will produce an ideal man. . . . A few enlightened individuals in all areas of society will surely lead to an ideal society . . . and an ideal world.[39]

Maharishi Mahesh Yogi is only one of a long string of latter-day, New Age Messiahs who have appeared recently on the world scene offering enlightenment and godhood to gullible New Age seekers. Jesus Himself prophesied that many would come claiming to be Christ: "For there shall arise false Christs, and false prophets, and shall show great signs and wonders; insomuch that, if it were possible, they shall deceive the very elect" (Matt. 24:24).

Yogi and many other New Age Messiahs are forerunners of a more powerful, more malignant leader—the Antichrist—possibly now waiting in the wings. The Antichrist sees the adoration and veneration that millions around the world now give to the many so-called New Age Messiahs and teachers who are his pale imitations. How much more will these legions of believers worship and venerate *him,* for he will be filled with the power of Satan and will come as a miracle worker and an angel of light. We see in the work of men like Yogi only a foretaste of what lies ahead for mankind.

Conspiracy and Propaganda: Spreading the New Age Gospel

Associate yourselves, O ye people, and ye shall be broken in pieces. . . . Take counsel together, and it shall come to nought; speak the word, and it shall not stand: for God is with us. . . . (Isa. 8:9, 10)

Say ye not, a confederacy. . . . (Isa. 8:12)

The open conspiracy must begin as a movement of explanation and propaganda. (H. G. Wells)

The New Age World Religion has experienced stupendous success in getting its message before the public. Its success is fostered by extraordinarily cunning *propaganda* and the astounding power that lies in the phenomenon called *networking*.

Seeding Lies: The Usefulness of Propaganda

New Age theorists believe that their Plan can succeed only if they reach the public with enough propaganda. H. G. Wells, whose book *The Open Conspiracy* is much admired by today's New Age elite, stated, "The open conspiracy must begin as a movement of explanation and propaganda."[1] Alice Bailey, head of the Lucis Trust, has told her followers, "It must be remembered that the forerunner of all movements which appear upon the physical plane is an educational propaganda."[2]

The New Age has taken this advice to heart and has made

49

important inroads in Western culture because of its masterful use of propaganda.

Every would-be world dictator, from Napoleon to Hitler to Stalin, has sought to use the written word to promote lies. Today, with television, movies, computer networks, and an array of high-tech media possibilities, the ability of a determined minority or a world dictator to delude a gullible public is simply phenomenal.

The New Age has in its fold many articulate public relations-oriented spokesmen who flood the airwaves with broadcasts that subtly reflect New Age doctrine. Even many kids' television programs are impacted. Saturday morning cartoon shows are almost predominantly New Age-oriented with definite overtones of sorcery, witchcraft, and Satanism. The printed media is flooded with New Age propaganda as New Age authors find it easy to have their views printed in the most elite magazines and their books published by the top publishers in the United States and Europe. Movies with occult and other New Age themes are being heavily promoted.

New Age propaganda pictures Christian fundamentalists as bigots unsympathetic to world problems such as hunger and militarism. Meanwhile, New Age spokesmen are permitted to showcase their groups and leaders as broad-minded, humanitarian, and caring. New Age groups such as the Hunger Project, which has taken in millions and millions of dollars in donations, are commended; yet many of these groups have never spent even one cent on food for the needy! The Hunger Project, for example, admits that *all* of its money goes for a massive public relations campaign designed to promote "consciousness," a New Age doctrine.[3]

Many persons are drawn to the New Age movement because of its extremely effective public relations campaign about correcting social injustices and ending world hunger. New Age leaders would have the West redistribute its income to the Third World and set up a one world, Socialistic government to oversee this redistribution. While Western governments and many compassionate Christian organizations are actively working to help hundreds of thousands in desperately starving countries, New Age leaders do little but criticize the United States and other Western governments and call for a "World Consciousness" of love for the hungry and needy.

Toward One-Worldism

Many New Age groups promoting one-worldism are active in propagandizing The Plan. Most define themselves as "educational" and therefore receive tax-exempt status and obtain government grants to prepare humanity for a One World Order.

Planetary Citizens, a networking group founded in 1974 by United Nations executive Robert Mueller, well-known author/editor Norman Cousins, and New Age peace activist Donald Keys, is one such organization. Planetary Citizens' intention is to encourage all the citizens of the globe to force their nations into a One World Government and Planetary Consciousness by the year 2000. As Keys explains:

> The first objective of Planetary Citizens is to help people around the world cross the threshold of consciousness from a limited, local perspective to the inclusive and global view required in a planetary era.[4]

Such organizations as the Club of Rome, the Lucis Trust, and World Goodwill are also busy proselytizing throughout the world to drum up support for the New age blueprint. Officials of the liberal-oriented Club of Rome, expressing support for a one world system, have stated:

> Mankind cannot afford to wait for change to occur spontaneously and fortuitously. . . . Man must initiate . . . changes. . . . (The) crises confronting mankind now and in the immediate future can be successfully met provided there is *genuine international cooperation* in the creation of a *Master Plan* for world "organic growth."[5]

These same Club of Rome officials stress that "there is no other viable alternative to the future survival of civilization than a new global community under a common leadership."[6]

Networking the New Age

The New Age is composed of a wide assortment of loosely interlinked groups. The strength of the movement comes from its masterful ability to network to achieve common goals and objectives.

Marilyn Ferguson, author of what many New Agers consider their manual for action, describes this networking activity as an "open conspiracy." Borrowing an astrological term, she calls the movement the "Aquarian Conspiracy." She proudly trumpets that the Aquarian conspiracy "has triggered the most rapid cultural realignment in history," and tells us that the movement is nothing less than a "new mind—the ascendance of a startling world view."[7]

Ferguson's New Age manifesto was published in 1980 under the title, *The Aquarian Conspiracy: Personal and Social Transformation in the 1980s.* In the intervening years, the New Age religious movement has continued its phenomenal growth spiral. Literally thousands of organizations are now integral parts of the New Age Movement. Many of these groups are openly proselytizing for new members and are even advertising their meetings and other activities in the media. Other New Age groups remain secretive, conducting their operations behind closed doors and strictly limiting access or knowledge of their activities to only those who have been properly initiated and found trustworthy enough to become active participants.

Ardent New Agers recognize that their plans to subvert and destroy Biblical Christianity and replace it with a world church based on supposed scientific laws and Eastern mysticism can best be achieved by a large number of separate organizations. Many of these can best be described as cults. Some but not all New Age organizations call themselves "churches."

New Age groups, sensing a rising tide of Christian opposition, now prefer such euphemisms as the Human Potential Movement, New Thought, Consciousness Movement, Holistic Movement, Whole Earth, East/West, Unity, and so forth.

Whatever their label and whether they are formal or informal, a group or a church, a cult or a denomination, the New Age believers have much in common. Some derive great satisfaction in identifying their movement as a conspiracy. But is the New Age a conspiracy?

Certainly the New Age leaders know and collude with one another, and they parrot almost identical doctrines. Moreover, they possess a common hostility toward Christian belief that Jesus Christ died on the cross for our sins.

The Unity Behind the Multiheaded New Age Monster

A multiheaded, invincible, conspiratorial network is the goal of the New Age. It is amazing how supposedly independent New Age groups can quickly coalesce. As John G. Bennet explains the New Age strategy:

> The part of wisdom is to establish, here and there, centers in which right relationship can exist by the power of a common understanding of what is ultimately important. From such centers there can spread throughout the world—perhaps more quickly than you can imagine possible—the seeds of a new world.[8]

LaVedi Lafferty and Bud Hollowell suggest that New Age networking is made possible by the hidden work of invisible spirit "Masters." In other words, Satan's demons are operating like a mental television network, planting messages in the minds of New Agers. The disembodied Masters are said to be able to communicate much more freely with the living today because our "psychic receptivity" and "collective consciousness" is much higher. Lafferty and Hollowell say that New Age groups around the globe function as central psychic receiving stations:

> Light centers have developed into a worldwide network that purposely link-up telepathically in meditation to serve as "superconscious" receiving, anchoring and sending stations. Many such groups exist. We have even "seen" their "lights" twinkling across Russia. Some are known this way, intuitively, but many are now consciously aware of each other and are in direct contact.[9]

An important focus for this link-up has been the Unity-in-Diversity Council in Los Angeles, which publishes an annual directory of member and supporting organizations and sponsors an annual conference where group representatives from around the world gather to meet, conduct workshops, and exchange information. Also, the *Spiritual Community Guide* is published by a Berkeley, California New Age organization. In Scotland the Findhorn

Communications Center keeps a computerized referral list of New Age-oriented individuals, groups, and communities. Also, the United Nations, under the guidance of its resident New Age leader Robert Mueller, has sponsored the publication of an international guide called simply *Networks.*

In Menlo Park, California, the Spiritual Emergency Network (SEN) was started by Stan and Christina Grof "in response to a great international demand for a new understanding of 'unusual' states of consciousness." Now SEN's network, located at the California Institute of Transpersonal Psychology, reportedly encompasses ten thousand individuals and organizations, and its resource file includes fifteen hundred active New Age leaders.[10]

Clearly, when the call comes from their Master (Satan), the entire panoply of New Age organizations can spring into action. *There is definitely a conspiracy.* However, these groups and their masters retain separate identities for now, to ward off attack from outsiders (Christians) by offering dispersed targets.

The strategy was explained by Donald Keys, consultant to the United Nations and cofounder of Planetary Citizens. In his book *Earth at Omega,* which he dedicates to Max Heindel, the famous Rosicrucian, to "The Tibetan," and to Ascended Master El Morya, Keys reveals:

> We mentioned earlier how the dominant straight "society" has apparently not recognized the strength and pervasiveness of the new consciouness culture. Perhaps this is just as well, as so far a polarization between the old culture and the new one has been avoided. If the New Age movement does become a target of alarmed forces and defenders of the *status quo ante,* however, it will offer a widely dispersed and decentralized target, very hard to identify and impossible to dissuade or subvert from its life-serving values.[11]

Christians opposed to New Age philosophies should not concern themselves with whether a conspiracy exists. More profitable would be firm opposition to all New Age beliefs and activities, recognizing Satan is behind them all.

It may be true that there is no one organizational chart that places all New Age groups under a particular hierarchy or any document that unites them all. However, considering the characteristics common to New Agers, it is difficult to deny that most of the groups alleged to be autonomous are, in fact, integral components of the entire apparatus. Furthermore, all who are active in promoting the New Age World Religion are, in fact, answering the call of Satan. "By their fruits ye shall know them."

FIVE

The New Age Antichrist and His Will to Power

And in the latter time . . . when the transgressors are come to the full, a king of fierce countenance, and understanding dark sentences, shall stand up. And his power shall be mighty, but not by his own power: and he shall destroy wonderfully, and shall prosper, and practice, and shall destroy the mighty and the holy people. And through his policy also he shall cause craft to prosper in his hand; and he shall magnify himself in his heart, and by peace shall destroy many: he shall also stand up against the Prince of princes; but he shall be broken. . . . (Dan. 8:23-25)

The new Messiah should himself believe in his identity and mission sufficiently to inspire others with that same belief—just as Jesus and John the Baptist before him . . . the leader must have the courage to step forward and play out his role to the full if the greater prophetic plan is to go forward.
(Peter Lemesurier, *The Armageddon Script*)

The most significant tenet of the New Age World Religion is its teaching that the planet earth is on the threshold of a cardinal event in its history: the arrival of a "Messiah" or "Christ." The New Age believes that its "Messiah," also called the Great World Teacher, will lead a One World Government and a One World Religion. Light-years ahead of anyone else on earth, he will teach marvelous new revelations and bring peace and prosperity. He will come as a savior, arriving just as the world is sliding into chaos and destruction to lead man into a bright, shining, glorious New Age.

If this description of the New Age "Christ" sounds to you suspiciously like that of the real Messiah, Jesus Christ, found in the Holy Bible, your suspicion is confirmed. The New Age "Christ" is a blasphemous imitation of the true Christ of the Bible. But Satan's use of a fake Messiah does not surprise those of us who know God's Word. Isaiah revealed the evil one's traitorous goal: "I will be like the Most High."

The Plan of Satan, now being meticulously executed by his New Age followers, is to mimic the prophesied return of Jesus Christ. This will be Satan's boldest trick ever. His fake "Messiah" will imitate the real Christ by performing miracles. His charismatic charm and perceived spiritual wisdom will so enchant world leaders and the masses that they will hail this "Christ" as the greatest and most advanced man to have ever lived. Eventually almost every man, woman, and child in the world will worship him as God.

New Age literature abounds with predictions about the imminent appearance of this false "Christ." *The Aquarian Gospel of Jesus Christ,* a fake Biblical text given in a Satanic vision to an Ohio man, Levi Dowling, and now frequently quoted as truth by New Agers, prophesies:

> But in the ages to come, man will attain to greater heights.
> And then, at last, a mighty Master Soul will come to earth to light the way up to the throne of perfect man.[1]

Lola Davis identifies the New Age "Christ" as "the One for whom all religions wait, called Lord Maitreya by some in the East, Krishna, Messiah, Bodhisattva, Christ, Immam Mahdi." She promises, he "will bring new revelations and further guidance for establishing the World Religion."[2]

Currently, Davis explains, the New Age "Christ" resides on a different plane of consciousness from that which we experience. There he directs the Masters, "a group of advanced souls, most of them discarnate . . . known variously as the White Brotherhood, The Great White Lodge, the Masters of Wisdom, the Hierarchy, and the Angels around the Throne."[3]

Davis says that the Mystery Schools and the Ageless Wisdom teach that:

The Hierarchy is composed of souls of several levels of advancement, degrees of initiations. This group is directed by the One called Lord Maitreya in the East and Christ in the West. All of its members have lived many lives on earth, and just like us, have learned from them.[4]

According to Davis, until this great avatar or leader returns to earth, it is man's responsibility to "create a new global society that will welcome a World Religion for the New Age." Furthermore, she suggests

. . . that we assist his earthly and heavenly helpers prepare humanity to recognize and receive him joyously and appropriately whether he be called Lord Maitreya, Buddha, Messiah, Christ or Imam Mahdi.[5]

Alice Bailey, head of both the Arcane School and the Lucis Trust, has written a number of books which detail The Plan. She leaves little doubt that the New One World Order will be realized only with "the reappearance of the Christ." Bailey's *The Externalization of the Hierarchy* predicts that the New Age will be in full bloom soon after a global crisis occurs and in desperation the world turns to the "Christ" for leadership. This New Age "Christ" will affirm the essential divine nature of humanity, says Bailey, and a New World Religion will come about, led by the "Christ" and his spiritual hierarchy manifest on earth. Christianity will be eclipsed by the new religion.[6]

The New Age Christ: A Reincarnated Hindu Avatar?

The New Age holds that the term *Christ* can be applied to any person who reaches an elevated state of consciousness and thereby achieves divine status. It is said that we are all simply Christs-in-the-making. Nevertheless, historically only a few souls have found enough favor with the spiritual hierarchy of reincarnated ancient Masters to be chosen to return to earth as an *avatar.*

The concept of the avatar is derived from the Hindu religion, which teaches that avatars are reincarnations-in-the-flesh of the god Vishnu, messengers sent to the living from the "gods." (There are at least thirty-three hundred Hindu gods—some authorities on Eastern religions say there are over a million!) This corresponds to the New Age belief in the hierarchy of reincarnated ancient Masters.

New Agers claim that Gandhi, Mohammed, Buddha, and Jesus were avatars and that each was therefore a "Christ." Some avatars are more enlightened than others. In the New Age scheme of things Jesus is not the Son of God, but just another enlightened, reincarnated spirit.

New Age disciples claim that in the near future we can expect an avatar to come who is far greater than either Jesus, Buddha, Krishna, Mohammed, or Gandhi. Rather than just *another* "Christ," this is to be *the* "Christ." He will be god realized, god incarnate.

Lord Maitreya, avatar and world teacher, is now claimed to be living in London, preparing himself for his eventual reign at the world's helm. According to the Tara Center, Lord Maitreya is the one Christians call Christ and whom the Jews term Messiah, the Buddhists the Fifth Buddha, and the Hindus Krishna. "These are all names for one individual. His presence in the world guarantees there will be no third world war."[7]

"Lord Maitreya" is identified by most New Age groups as their coming "Christ." However, to deflect criticism, many refrain from naming him. Instead, such general titles as "the enlightened one to come," the "Cosmic Christ," the "Universal One," or the "New Age World Teacher" are used.

The Unity-in-Diversity Council is one large New Age organization that is proud to identify Lord Maitreya as the spiritual leader on whom the world awaits. Unity-in-Diversity has described its major goal as follows:

To establish a church based upon universal premises . . . for those who wish to follow a universal path (often called the "Maitreyan path," the Maitreya being the enlightened one yet to come).[8]

There is a long list of New Age groups and leaders who have endorsed Maitreya as their Messiah. Elizabeth Clare Prophet, head of the Church Universal and Triumphant, is one. Another group is the Collegians International Church. This thoroughly New Age church claims that Jesus and Maitreya were one and the same:

> At Collegians we acknowledge the World Teacher who appeared as Jesus the Christ, also known variously as the Lord Maitreya and the Bodhisattva, as well as other appearances of the Christ through such personalities as Melchizedek, Khrishna, and Mithra.[9]

The Lord Maitreya has also become "The 21st century Jesus" for many New Agers who futilely try to remain Christians, calling themselves "Cosmic Christians" or "Aquarian Christians" and claiming that hidden in the Bible are the Mystery Teachings of the New Age. A pathetic example is given by Elissa Lindsey McClain, a woman who for twenty-nine years was intimately involved in the New Age. After becoming a Christian in 1978, she wanted to represent her new Master with a picture or a figurine. So she went to her local cosmic (translated, "New Age") bookstore and asked for a picture of Christ.

> I was handed an artistic rendition of a man with long hair but the caption read "Lord Maitreya."
> "Excuse me, but this isn't Jesus Christ," I complained to the owner. "This is Maitreya."
> "Yes, but you see, Maitreya is the Christ of the Aquarian Age. Jesus was the Christ for the Piscean Age," the shopowner answered, smiling sweetly.[10]

Though a new Christian, McClain knew the difference between Maitreya and the *real Christ,* and so refused the picture of Maitreya. Thousands of others, however, vainly worship Maitreya, believing that he is merely the most recent—and most advanced—reincarnation of the Christ.

Any Christian with even a rudimentary knowledge of the Bible will recognize this Lord Maitreya for who and what he really is: a deceiver and a servant of the Devil. The Bible warns us of the false "Christs" to come and gives us tests for judging the truth. One test is that anyone who comes as other than Jesus cannot be the Christ, but is instead of Antichrist.

First Corinthians 8:6 tells us "there is but one God, the Father . . . and one Lord Jesus Christ." The disciple John labeled as a liar he "that denieth that Jesus is the Christ. He is antichrist, that denieth the Father and the Son" (1 John 2:22). And in Philippians 2:5-11 we see that Jesus is given a name which is above every other name. Accordingly, "at the name of Jesus every knee should bow, of things in heaven . . . and things under the earth."

The Christian is advised to stay away from and oppose corrupting doctrines of false Christs: "Believe not every spirit, but try the spirits whether they are of God" (1 John 4:1).

Is the New Age "Christ" the Antichrist?

Whether he comes as the Lord Maitreya, as the reincarnated Buddha, Immam Mahdi of Islam, or as another "divine being," the question Christians surely must ask about the coming New Age "Christ" is, Is he the Antichrist prophesied in Revelation 13, in the Book of Daniel, and elsewhere in the Bible? My own answer is, Yes, the man for whom the New Age waits will almost certainly be the Antichrist.

Do not, however, expect a devoted New Ager to admit that his "Christ" is the Antichrist. That would be considered negative thinking, even impossible, for many in the New Age Religion deny that *any* one man will come as the Antichrist. They do not foresee the coming of evil into the world, but only of good. New Age prophets consistently paint a bright, shining picture of the glorious future that shortly awaits mankind.

Elissa Lindsey McClain reports that as a New Ager she was taught, "There is no such thing as the devil or a fallen angel leading the forces of evil. Man alone is responsible for the present discord in the world."[11] Evidently the New Age teachers who propound this "new gospel" are either unfamiliar with or purposely reject Scripture, because the reality of Satan is a frequently stated Biblical truth.

New Age teachers are quick to twist God's Word when

doing so serves their purpose. For a prime example, read what John Randolph Price had to say when he was asked, "How do you define the Antichrist?"

> Answer: "Any individual or group who denies the divinity of man as exemplified by Jesus Christ; i.e., to be in opposition to 'Christ in you'—the indwelling Christ or Higher Self of each individual."[12]

Price's warped view that *the Antichrist is any person or group who denies that man is a god* is a diabolical twist of Biblical truth. Jesus did not come to exemplify man as a divine being. He came as the one and only living Christ, the Son of God, to offer salvation and the redemption of sins. *The Bible unequivocally states that the Antichrist is he who denies that Jesus came in the flesh as Christ.*

> Hereby know ye the Spirit of God: Every spirit that confesseth that Jesus Christ is come in the flesh is of God: and every spirit that confesseth not that Jesus Christ is come in the flesh is not of God: and this is that spirit of antichrist, whereof ye have heard that it should come. (1 John 4:2, 3)

The horrendous conclusion of Price's Satan-inspired teaching is to label all Bible-believing Christians as being of Antichrist, because no true Christian would ever confess that man is a deity. This is a clever but despicable ruse by Satan to undermine the Scriptures and threaten Christian believers by labeling them as the Antichrist.

Another popular New Age misconception is that the Antichrist is all those persons and groups who represent the *material* world, whereas all those who adopt the New Age consciousness and lifestyle are of the *spiritual* realm.

LaVedi Lafferty and Bud Hollowell appear to accept this concept of the Antichrist as being those who are of lesser, material essence.

> The Battle of Armageddon is not a war fought with weapons, it is a battle of Consciousness—Christ (Cosmic) Consciousness

against the Antichrist (earth/material illusions). These two polarities will produce the third, the "Kingdom."[13]

The teaching of Lafferty and Hollowell suggests that once the New Age Religion and One World Order come into existence, Christians may face very hard times. Lafferty and Hollowell give one indication of that dangerous and precarious future era of persecution and trial when they remark that a "new world" is coming and ominously proclaim:

This is a time of opportunity for those who will take it. *For others, if earth is unsuitable for them, they will go on to other worlds. The Yogic Kingdom will be coming to pass for this planet.*[14]

Christian fundamentalists—those who insist on believing in Jesus Christ—are certainly "unsuitable" for the "Yogic Kingdom." Therefore it is undoubtedly Christian fundamentalists who "will go on to other worlds." If we recall that the New Age preaches that *at death* we are reincarnated into other worlds—that is, other planes of existence—we begin to understand just what is being suggested by the New Age as the eventual fate of Christians and other "materialist" unbelievers.

The Antichrist Is a Man and His Number Is 666

The Bible convincingly foretells the coming rise to world power of the Antichrist. Scripture reveals that this false Messiah will come just before the return of Jesus. He is identified in the Book of Revelation as a man with the number 666 and is horrifyingly described as "the beast." Revelation also informs us that he was given power "to make war . . . to overcome . . . power was given him over all kindreds, and tongues, and nations. All that dwell upon the earth shall worship him" (13:5-8).

The Beast, the man with the number 666, will be so consumed by the spirit of Satan and his demons that he will become Satan personified on earth. The Antichrist "spirit" has been on earth for aeons. It was Satan's link with possessed men who actively opposed the teachings of the early Christian Church (see

1 John 2:18-23; 4:1-4). Now, in the last days, this spirit of Antichrist will totally possess the soul of the living man of evil and darkness whom Satan has chosen.

The Antichrist, or Beast, is to be given tremendous powers by Satan, "the dragon" (Rev. 12:9), and is to be admired by the masses for his supernatural power and his apparently unconquerable spirit:

> And they worshipped the dragon which gave power unto the beast: and they worshipped the beast, saying, Who is like unto the beast? who is able to make war with him? (Rev. 13:4)

The Blasphemy of the Antichrist

This man, the Antichrist, will have temporal power over Christians who dwell on earth until Jesus returns, when he and his followers will be destroyed. Until that momentous event, however, the Antichrist will wax stronger and stronger. The Bible tells us that he will dare to speak blasphemies, or lies and falsehoods about God. He will also blaspheme the heavenly host (Christians who have died) who reside in heaven with God (Rev. 13:5, 6).

Already we see this blasphemy. New Age teachers have been inspired by the spirit of Antichrist to declare that there is no personal God in heaven who loves and cares for man, no God whom man should fear and obey. They have blasphemed God's Son by spreading lies that Jesus was not who He and His disciples claimed, and that He will not return to earth again as the Messiah.

The spirit of Antichrist also is busy attacking the heavenly host—those saints who have died in Christ. This vile attack is clearly seen in the growing practice of "channeling," or communication with demon spirits. With regularity, New Agers report that the spirit of "Jesus," "Jonah," "Isaiah," "Paul," "John," "Abraham," or another Biblical saint has come to them while they were meditating. Christians know that these spirits masquerading as Christ or as dead saints are demons. The Bible condemns communication with the dead as sorcery (see Deut. 18:9-12 and Isa. 8:19); and Jesus, in the story of Lazarus, told us that the dead cannot contact the living.

Satan is deceiving millions by having his demons pretend they are long-dead saints or wise men who wish to help those now living to know "the truth." The truth these demons impart in invariably the same: namely, that an external God does not exist and that man is himself a god. The New Age believes these lies and perverts the gospel by attributing them to Jesus and the saints who have been channeled, or contacted, by New Age mediums. This is the spirit of Antichrist working in the world today (see 1 John 4:1-3). It is blasphemy.

How Will We Know the Antichrist?

And then shall that Wicked be revealed, whom the Lord shall consume with the spirit of his mouth, and shall destroy with the brightness of his coming: even him, whose coming is after the working of Satan with all power and signs and lying wonders. (2 Thess. 2:8, 9)

Drugs . . . A.I.D.S. . . . poverty . . . rampant crime . . . mass starvation . . . nuclear threat . . . terrorism . . . Is there a solution? In answer to our urgent need . . . THE CHRIST IS IN THE WORLD. A great World Teacher for people of every religion and no religion. A practical man with solutions to our problems. He loves ALL humanity . . . Christ is here, my friends. Your Brother walks among you. (Tara Center, full-page ad in USA *Today,* January 12, 1987)

When we turn to God's own Scriptures, the Bible, for insight, we find seven signs or marks to help us recognize the Antichrist:

1) He will come disguised as an angel of light.

2) He will exalt himself and magnify himself above every god.

3) He will come as a man of peace.

4) He will corrupt men and gain their allegiance through deceit and flatteries.

5) He will be given supernatural strength to show signs and perform wonders.

6) His rise to power will result from his exercise of will.

7) He will be a destroyer, a slayer.

It comes as no surprise that New Age leaders paint a vivid picture of their coming "Christ" or "Messiah" that exactly corresponds to these seven identifying marks of the Antichrist. Let's investigate this astonishing correspondence.

He Will Come Disguised As an Angel of Light

Those who expect to easily recognize the Antichrist because of his wicked countenance and thus avoid his snares will be sorely disappointed. Satan comes to us in human form, not as a devil but as an angel of light (2 Cor. 11:14).

New Agers report many experiences of communicating during deep meditation or trance with a spirit being shrouded in light, a being who brought them inner peace and a sense of rebirth and transformation. But this same being is said to encourage them to reject the religion of their fathers; he tells them the Bible is tainted throughout with error. The "angel of light" denies that Jesus is the Christ and guides the individual toward such practices as astrology, spiritism, black magic, witchcraft, homosexuality, and free sex.

He Will Exalt Himself and Magnify Himself Above Every God

The New Age Religion holds that man is an evolving god and that Jesus Christ is not man's master. Man is encouraged to worship other gods and to follow whatever path he chooses. He may worship the many Hindu deities, Buddha, pagan gods, the Mother Goddess, or incredibly, even Lucifer. But, in fact, these many gods are considered nothing more than forerunners of man's own inevitable ascension to godhood.

This unholy doctrine is tailor-made for the Antichrist, who is described in the Bible as a man who will exalt himself above every other man and will portray himself as more worthy of worship than any other god. The Antichrist will say, "Worship me because I come to initiate you into the Mysteries of the Ages, after which you will be your own god." Only after their initiation will men learn the awful truth: they will not be gods but slaves to Satan.

He Will Come As a Man of Peace

Daniel prophesied that "by peace" the Antichrist will "destroy many." The Antichrist will imitate Christ Jesus, whom the prophet Isaiah heralded as the "Prince of Peace" (Isa. 9:6).

The New Age boasts that its "Christ" will ensure there will be no third world war. In an age when man stands at the very precipice of widespread nuclear destruction, with missiles, atomic weapons, and other tools of death proliferating, this idle promise will surely be welcomed by all peoples.

If we wish to catch a revealing glimpse of how the Antichrist might use man's fear of nuclear destruction to seize world power, we need only turn to an astonishing book, *The Armageddon Script* by New Age authority Peter Lemesurier. Lemesurier proposes that the New Age use the Jewish and Christian belief in Biblical prophecy to catapult their chosen man-god to prominence. "Basically, it could be said that the prophecies . . . make up a kit of parts for constructing humanity's house of the future."[1]

Lemesurier's scheme is that as soon as world chaos strikes sometime in the future, the New Age "Christ" immediately will proceed to Jerusalem so he can fulfill the prophetic scenario. This is Phase One of The Plan, which runs as follows:

(a) The restored Messiah must reappear on Jerusalem's Mount of Olives at the time of a great earthquake.

(b) He must enter Jerusalem from the east, escorted by a procession of rejoicing followers dressed in shining white.

(c) Visiting the tomb of his spiritual ancestor, King David, he must emerge in suitably-perfumed royal robes as the great monarch returned.

(d) Supported by a popular rising, he must proceed with his followers to the Temple Mount, there to be enthroned, anointed and crowned King of the New Israel.

(e) In token of his power, the Cloud of the Divine Presence must descend upon him amid thunders and lightnings (created by man-made special effects such as in the movies).[2]

Lemesurier supposes that the world, seeing these things come to pass exactly as prophesied, will hail the New Age "Christ" as the Savior or Messiah of whom the Bible spoke.

As events go from bad to worse, it is more than likely that anxious, weary groupings and nations, only too glad to place all their burdens and responsibilities on other people's shoulders, will increasingly tend to offer the New David temporal power and even military command. The temptation for him to accept and play the dictator will be considerable. He may even be turned into a god, much as subsequently happened to Jesus himself.[3]

Until the time is ripe for this plot to unfold, Lemesurier suggests that the New Age "Christ"-to-be ready himself for the momentous task ahead:

In the meantime the new world-leader must prepare himself for his role. He must study the scriptures and the Dead Sea Scrolls, immerse himself in current Jewish messianic expectations, thoroughly survey the general locality and familiarize himself with all the major prophecies and the best in New Age religious thought. In short, he must create in his own mind a crystal-clear idea of the vision which he has to fulfill. For only in this way can that vision be guaranteed to come into manifestation.[4]

Jesus warned us that if it were possible, the very elect would be deceived. Lemesurier's proposed conspiracy to propel the Antichrist to power fulfills this prediction.

He Shall Corrupt Man and Gain His Allegiance Through Deceit and Flatteries

The Biblical prophecies tell us that the latter-days ruler of mankind will oppose those who have given their lives to God. At the same time, he will win over the unbelieving masses through deception and flattery.

And such as do wickedly against the covenant shall he corrupt by flatteries. . . . (Dan. 11:32)

And for this cause God shall send them strong delusion, that they should believe the lie. (2 Thess. 2:11)

There is no greater flattery than to convince a person he is an evolving god. This will be the smooth, seductive lie of the New Age "Christ." A second lie will be that man is neither bad nor sinful, but is instead naturally full of goodness and perfection. He will tell mankind that all they need to do is to believe in themselves, to awaken their "Christ consciousness," and to build their own self-esteem. You must love yourself, the New Age "Christ" will teach, if you hope to become God.

He Will Be Given Supernatural Strength to Show Signs and Perform Wonders

The Antichrist will perform supernatural feats, counterfeiting the gifts of the Spirit of the Lord (Dan. 11:28; Matt. 24:24). By these, the Antichrist will deceive the people of earth.

> And he doeth great wonders . . . and deceiveth them that dwell on the earth by the means of those miracles. . . . (Rev. 13:13, 14)

The New Age Messiah is reputed to possess miraculous spiritual gifts of a magical nature. For example, Benjamin Creme has said that the Lord Maitreya, the "Christ" of the New Age, will proclaim his arrival by suddenly appearing on all television sets around the globe and speaking telepathically to a world audience.[5] Other New Age leaders have described their "Christ" as one who will end world hunger, perform fantastic acts of healing, and display other marvelous powers of the mind.

His Rise to Power Will Result from the Exercise by the Antichrist of Superhuman Will

In the New Age scheme of things, human will is all-important. The Masters of Wisdom—the discarnate spirits in the other dimensions—are said to focus all their attention on serving the One Will.[6] George Bernard Shaw, who professed a vile hatred for God and Christianity, wrote of a "will" incarnated in man that shall "finally mould chaos itself into a race of gods."[7]

According to New Age teachers, the more a person evolves

and becomes the god he is intended to be, the greater *will* he has to freely exercise. The New Age Messiah shall therefore be endowed with unparalleled will, as evidenced by his superhuman mind powers.

The Bible alludes to the superior will of Antichrist. Daniel forewarned that he "shall do according to his will" (11:36), suggesting that he will freely exercise control over other men.

New Age doctrine associates higher consciousness, will, and power. Supreme power results when a man of higher consciousness is able to command whatever he desires and it is done. The New Age "Christ" is expected to be such a man. His will and that of the universe are to be one, giving him unequaled ability to actually create material reality with thought power.

In his sinister book *The Meaning of Christ for Our Age,* New Ager F. Aster Barnwell writes that the baser human has will, but gods have a more powerful will, which Barnwell terms Free Will. He recalls that in the Garden of Eden, Eve allowed the serpent to tempt her into eating of the Tree of Knowledge of Good and Evil. She and Adam were then banished from the Garden because God feared they would next eat of the Tree of Life and thus live forever as gods.[8]

But according to Barnwell, the mistake Eve made was in not eating of the Tree of Life *first.* Had she done so, he remarks, she would have become a goddess, or a "Christ," with Free Will. The goddess Eve could then have eaten of the Tree of Knowledge of Good and Evil without fear of God's wrath.

Barnwell equates Free Will with god-consciousness, explaining that god-consciousness is achieved when an individual releases pent-up psychic energy forces inside, so he can affect the world for good. He refers to this psychic energy force by the Hindu term "Kundalini," or "Serpent Power." Such a person does not need an external god, for he has himself become a god.[9]

Thus, we are being set up for the teaching that the New Age "Christ" possesses a superior morality and will: Serpent Power. Whatever he wills, is good.

A desire to impose his will on others motivated Adolf Hitler to power. Like today's New Age Messiah, the Nazi monster envisioned an empire founded on will. Hitler himself said of his messianic goal: "National Socialism is more than a religion; it is the will to create supermen."[10]

The supreme exercise of will is also the goal of all Satanists.

The late Aleister Crowley, the British Satanist and Black Magician so admired by many of today's New Agers, wrote that "Magick is the science or art of causing change to occur in conformity with will."[11]

"Thy will be done" is the only proper prayer for the Christian. But those outside God's grace seek to fulfill their own wills. The New Age "Christ," Satan in the flesh, will be a man whose mind is consumed with the desire to render all other men subject to his own evil will.

He Will Be a Destroyer, a Slayer

The Antichrist will take captive and destroy men's souls. But he will also prove to be a bloody world ruler who without hesitation stamps out opposition. Christians who refuse to join the New Age World Religion and to take the mark of the Beast will fall under the wrath of the Antichrist and will experience his brute power.

This, then, will be one more way the people of God will be able to identify the Antichrist. His destroyer mentality will be apparent *even though his mouth speaks of peace, love, and nonviolence*. If he preaches another gospel and claims himself to be another "Christ," Christians will know that he is not sent by God.

Eventually, to their amazement, the New Age masses will discover that they too are subject to the vicious caprice of the man whom they first heralded as savior and lord. They will learn the bitter truth that their "Christ" is not the Christ at all, but Satan. Their worst nightmares will be realized as they look upon the countenance of Lucifer.

SEVEN

Come, Lucifer

I saw Lucifer fall like lightning from heaven.
(Luke 10:18, NIV)

Lucifer was a created being, just as the angels. His big
mistake was in his conceit to exalt himself above God.
Satan . . . is the organizer of Babylon, a term used for
blasphemous religions.
(Elissa Lindsey McClain, Rest from the Quest)

Lucifer comes to give us the final . . . Luciferic initiation
. . . it is an invitation into the New Age.
(David Spangler, Reflections of the Christ)

I n exalting himself above all gods, including the God of Gods, Antichrist will reveal himself as Lucifer, or Satan, himself. In Isaiah 14:14 Lucifer boastfully pronounces, "I will ascend above the heights of the clouds; I will be like the Most High."

The most frightening aspect of the New Age World Religion is the adulation given to Lucifer, who has even been described as "God of Light and God of Good."[1] David Spangler, one of the most admired New Age teachers, has said that Lucifer is "in a sense the angel of man's inner evolution."

Spangler not only has taught that Lucifer is "an agent of God's love,"[2] but in a shockingly blatant perversion of truth he has declared:

Christ is the same force as Lucifer. . . . Lucifer prepares man for the experience of Christhood. . . . Lucifer works within each of us to bring us to wholeness as we move into the New Age."[3]

The Luciferian Initiation

When Spangler talks of Lucifer bringing us to "wholeness," he evidently refers to new converts being *initiated* into the Mysteries of the New Age World Religion. Spangler explains:

> The light that reveals to us the path to Christ comes from Lucifer . . . the great initiator. . . .
>
> Lucifer comes to give us the final . . . Luciferic initiation . . . that many people in the days ahead will be facing, for it is an invitation into the New Age.[4]

Spangler is not alone in teaching that Lucifer is the Christ-spirit who will initiate man into the New Age. Eklal Kueshana, a leader in a mystical organization called The Stelle Group, caused stir and excitement in New Age circles almost twenty-five years ago when he published his best-selling *The Ultimate Frontier*. In this revealing book Kueshana says that Lucifer is the head of a secret Brotherhood of Spirits, the highest order to which man can elevate himself. According to Kueshana, the Brotherhood is named after Lucifer "because the great Angel Lucifer had been responsible for the abolishment of Eden in order that men could begin on the road to spiritual advancement."[5]

In his book Kueshana makes the claim that through the ages only the spiritually advanced have been invited into the Luciferian Brotherhood. Benjamin Franklin and George Washington were, but Jesus, Moses, and John the Baptist didn't make the grade.

Apparently, by his own account, Kueshana is more spiritual than Jesus since, in his book, he reveals that he (under the pseudonym "Richard") has been initiated into this elite Brotherhood. Kueshana says that as part of his initiation, he was given a permanent mark on the lower part of his body.

Revelation 13:16 prophesies that the Beast (Antichrist) will cause all "to receive a mark in their right hand, or in their foreheads." For now, those initiated into the Luciferian Brotherhood may be receiving this mark elsewhere on the body to prevent widespread alarm by Christians. But once the New Age is fully ushered in and the Antichrist ascends to power, this same mark will be required on one's right hand or forehead.

Facts bear out that what Kueshana says in his book is substantially what other New Age leaders are teaching. Elissa McClain, for instance, has said that Kueshana's writings were taught by a study group at her Unity Church.[6] Furthermore, Kueshana's *The Ultimate Frontier* also identifies the Luciferian Brotherhood as the Great White Brotherhood. Lola Davis explains that the Great White Brotherhood is known variously as "the Great White Lodge, the Masters of Wisdom, the Hierarchy, and the Angels around the throne."[7] Its spirit head, Davis says, is Lord Maitreya. Elizabeth Clare Prophet, head of the Church Universal and Triumphant, also refers to her spiritual hierarchy as the Great White Brotherhood.

What we discover, then, is a consistent account among New Age authorities that Lucifer (Satan) is God and that Lord Maitreya is "Christ." Though the names for these two entities are often changed—Lucifer variously called Sat Nam, Sant Mat, Tanat, SatGuru, and Sanat—they remain the same beings. Discerning Christians can easily identify these two supremely evil entities as none other than Satan and his Antichrist.

The astonishing, revolting truth is that thousands of New Age believers are being duped into believing that these two occult creatures are "God" and "Christ." Accordingly, they are submitting themselves to the most unspeakable horror: soul initiation into the ranks of the Beast.

Lucifer, the Bright and Morning Star

The Lucis Trust is apparently named in Lucifer's honor, *lucis* being a Latin word for Lucifer. Headed by Alice Bailey, the publishing arm of the Lucis Trust was at first called the Lucifer Publishing Company, a continuation from the magazine *Lucifer,* published by Theosophy leader H. P. Blavatsky. The Lucis Trust explains that Lucis is the genitive case of the Latin word *lux,* which they choose to translate as "of light." The earlier term Lucifer, they contend, means "bringer of light" or the "morning star."[8]

While the Lucis Trust attempts to sidestep its use of the term Lucifer, other New Age groups openly admit that Lucifer is to be emulated. The Association for Research and Enlightenment (ARE), a Virginia Beach, Virginia, group that is the repository for the papers of late psychic Edgar Cayce, publishes religious education material for children and adults that praises Lucifer. In this material, ARE scoffs at Christians who believe in an evil power. Like the Lucis Trust, ARE claims that the word "Lucifer" means "light-bringer" in Latin and "morning star" in Hebrew. But ARE goes on to make the blasphemous statement that "Lucifer is that spiritual portion of ourselves that is perfect."[9] If we have Lucifer in our souls, says the ARE material, we have God within.

That ARE and other New Age groups actually praise Lucifer, exalting him as the "bright and the morning star," is shocking. These are descriptive terms that are reserved exclusively for Jesus Christ.

ARE also maintains that the term *Lucifer*, in English, stands for the planet Venus.[10] A common doctrine of the New Age is that Lucifer was wrongly banished to earth from Venus after his heavenly struggle with an unfair, jealous God. It is significant that the Satanic sign for Venus is a Satanic circle superimposed on top of a cross. This is also the symbol of the ankh, prominently displayed in ancient Egyptian temples.

In Austin, Texas, a woman at a Quaker fellowship related a vision she had in which she saw a star fall from Venus to earth like lightning. The star, she was told in the vision, represents a goddess whom she and the other Quakers must worship. As a result, a number of the Quakers believed her, and they have now formed a special group within their fellowship that meets frequently to meditate and worship this star goddess. In their ignorance, these people have become worshipers of Lucifer, whom both Jesus and Isaiah described as lightning fallen from heaven (see Luke 10:18 and Isa. 14:12-14). The Babylonian parallel is clear, too, for the goddess Venus was a Roman version of the great whore and harlot, the Mother Goddess of Babylon.[11] The Mother Goddess represents the end-time Satanic religious system discussed in Revelation 17. Also observe that in Babylon, the Goddess was also known as Astarte or Ishtar ("Star").[12]

Is Lucifer Man's Savior?

Many New Agers commend Lucifer because by tempting Eve he enabled man to evolve toward enlightened knowledge and godhood. Lucifer is thus credited as man's savior, a clear blasphemy of the truth as revealed in God's Word.

These heretical New Age teachers refer to the writings of fourteenth-century Gnostic groups, called Luciferians, who worshiped Lucifer and believed him to be the brother of God. The Gnostics taught that Lucifer was wrongly cast down from heaven and would someday be vindicated.

Meister Eckhart von Hochheim, a Catholic priest of the fourteenth century, was a leader in this heresy and was roundly condemned by a papal bull. Eckhart proposed that "Lucifer, the angel . . . had perfectly pure intellect and to this day knows much."[13]

It is no coincidence that Matthew Fox, the present-day heretic priest deeply involved in nature and goddess worship and other New Age atrocities, says that Eckhart's writings have deeply influenced him. Fox has remarked that Meister Eckhart is one of the two "greatest mystics the West has produced."[14]

Fox has even maintained that he regularly receives spiritual insight direct from the dead, fourteenth-century priest:

> I get more support from Eckhart than I do from most living Dominicans. I don't believe in the communion of saints. I know it.
>
> When I first fell in love with Eckhart, I was reading a book by the Hindu, Coomaraswami, on art and spirituality. I started his chapter on Eckhart and found whole sentences in Eckhart that I had written without having read him. It just blew my mind. . . .
>
> I think being receptive to these people is the key. . . .

Evidently, as Fox reveals, "being receptive" to these dead heretics—or, rather, to the demon spirits who emulate them—is "the key" for many of today's New Age leaders. Because of their rejection of Jesus Christ, Fox and others are easily deluded, just as was prophesied in the Bible:

> And for this cause God shall send them strong delusion, that they should believe a lie. (2 Thess. 2:11)

Millions are now under the delusion that Jesus is not coming again because He was not *the* Christ. They are therefore being made susceptible to the false teaching that Maitreya, or Lucifer himself, is the Christ. God is giving these people over to a reprobate mind.

Elissa Lindsey McClain, in her book *Rest from the Quest,* provides an ilustration of how the New Age is attempting to improve Lucifer's image. She tells of a friend—whom she thought of at the time as very advanced spiritually—who explained to her the "truth" about Lucifer.

> Sunny . . . had an explanation of Lucifer, the fallen angel. He had merely turned from the "light" and instead of hating him, we should reach out to him with love and compassion.
> Lucifer was just a mirror image of God's angels and mankind needed to restore him to wholeness. . . . Why couldn't (Christian) fundamentalists see that?

In *Hidden Dangers of the Rainbow* Constance Cumbey relates the story of a well-educated New Age woman who became angry when Cumbey brought up the subject of Lucifer and the Antichrist. After the woman related her belief that Jesus and the Christ are two distinct entities, Cumbey referred her to 1 John 2:22, which declares that particular teaching to be a mark of the spirit of Antichrist. Angered, the New Age believer asserted that the Bible "should not be allowed . . . the Antichrist is *not* the negative thing the Bible makes him out to be!"[16]

Hal Lindsey says that Satan is alive and well on planet earth.[17] The New Age says "Amen" and goes on to pronounce that the Satan who lives is destined to be man's savior.

Can Satan Be Restored to Wholeness?

Elissa McClain's friend, Sunny, told her that mankind needs to restore Lucifer to "wholeness." Richard Spangler has said that Lucifer comes to restore mankind to "wholeness." So we see a fiery circle of logic in which Satan and his followers are to love one another and restore one another to wholeness.

This is a mind-jarring doctrine because any rational person who reads his daily newspaper can see that Lucifer is still hard at work tumultuously despoiling God's creation and inciting evil of every kind. Rapes, murders, child abuse, robbery, adulterous affairs, and other incalculable horrors are commonplace. Is this the "wholeness" preached by the New Age? Is this evidence of Lucifer's rehabilitation?

It is preposterous to equate Lucifer with light. This is a sick doctrine straight from Hades. Satan began to spread this apostasy some one thousand years before Jesus' birth. In Babylonia and Persia, from about 1400 to 400 B.C., the religious cult of Mithraism thrived, teaching that in the last days the Devil and God would be reconciled. Mithraism taught reincarnation and the progression of the soul through stages, just as the New Age does today. The god Mithras later was worshiped as Sol Invictus, the Roman Sun God, because he was said to be the "light giver." This cult was brought to Rome by the Roman legions and was touted as a Mystery Religion. Mithraism was a strong rival to Christianity in the second and third centuries A.D.[18]

The idea of Lucifer and God being reconciled was also found in the Gnostic heresies of the second century. Various Gnostic-oriented Mystery Religions and Satanic worship cults perpetuated this lie throughout the centuries that followed. Recently in Canada, the United States, Germany, and England, the Process Church, a Satanic cult, gained some measure of support by promoting this un-Biblical doctrine. The Processeans, as they are called, believe in three gods: Jehovah, Lucifer, and Satan. Lucifer is known as the peace-loving god of joyful living and is a role model for man, whereas Jehovah is a strict, self-righteous god who seeks vengeance and demands obedience.[19]

The Processeans point to Jesus' commandment, "Love thine enemies" as proof that Jesus will eventually forgive Satan. Though it does not claim to be a formal part of the New Age Movement, the doctrine of the Process Church is decidedly New Age. In its worship services two silver chalices are used— one for Christ and one for Satan. A Satanic bible is used which combines authentic verses from the Bible with un-Scriptural statements and sayings. Its members claim that the end of this age is at hand and that the year 2000 will see the final reconciliation of Satan and Jehovah. This prediction closely parallels similar predictions by New Age prophets.

Satan as Sanat

For those who can't quite stomach Lucifer as the "Christ," the New Age offers a being called Sanat Kumara. "Sanat" is obviously a thinly veiled reference to Satan; nevertheless, New Age teachers evidently believe that the new spelling will alleviate the concerns of those not yet ready to confess Satan as their Lord and Messiah. The Church Universal and Triumphant teaches that The Great White Brotherhood of ascended Master spirits wants us to know that it was Sanat Kumura who came to earth to lead man into divinity:

> Long ago the Ancient of Days came to Earth from Venus . . . that you and I might . . . one day know the self as God. His name was Sanat Kumura. . . .[20]

According to some New Age "scriptures," Sanat Kumura was banished from Venus to earth many millennia ago after a war in the heavens. This is the same tale offered about Lucifer's fall to earth from Venus by many New Age groups.

Other New Age groups hold that Sanat will be a Messiah who will totally transform the earth into a heavenly dimension through a "purification process" in which all negative influences—for example, Christians—are removed. One group, head-quartered at the foot of Mt. Shasta in California, calls itself the Association of Sananda and Sanat Kumara. This group contends that Sanat, not the God of the Bible, will make all things new:

> For them which shall remain . . . shall be made whole, and they shall be as new. The Earth shall be purified and it shall give forth a *new life* from the place which is appointed her within the firmaments.[21]

The implication is that those who do not live the New Age religious philosophy will not be included in the coming kingdom of Sanat. What we find, then, is that the New Age seeks to distort the Biblical teaching that Jesus will return to establish on earth the true Kingdom of God. According to New Age deception, Sanat (Satan) is to be ruler of a counterfeit Kingdom where Christians shall be decidedly unwelcome.

Whether he comes as Sanat Kumara or Maitreya or bears another name, the New Age Antichrist will come proclaiming himself to be Lord of Lords and God of all Gods, the same titles held by Jesus Christ. He will also come heralded as the Word (Logos) who became flesh and dwelt among men.

Is Sanat the Word (Logos)?

John described Jesus as the Word, the eternal Creator:

> In the beginning was the Word (Logos), and the Word was with God, and the Word was God. The same was in the beginning with God. All things were made by him; and without him was not anything made that was made. In him was life; and the life was the light of men. And the light shineth in darkness; and the darkness comprehended it not. (John 1:1-5)

> And the Word was made flesh, and dwelt among us (and we beheld his glory, the glory as of the only begotten of the Father), full of grace and truth. (John 1:14)

John is telling us that Jesus *is the Word,* or Logos, *and the Word was with God from the beginning, and was God.* Jesus Himself stated, "I and the Father are one" (John 10:30). But since the early days of Babylon, the human custodians of Satan's Plan have attempted to deify their "Word," which is Satan. Contemporary New Agers seek to strip Jesus of His divinity, asserting that He is inferior to Sanat Kumara.

Benjamin Creme writes that Sanat is the Logos of our planet and therefore is our Savior and our God:

> That aspect of God to which we immediately aspire, can aspire to, is the Logos of our own planet, who is embodied for us as Sanat Kumara, on Shamballa. He is our "Father." God is both within us and can be known—you can see God. In this coming age many, many people will see God, as Sanat Kumara. They will come before Sanat Kumara and take the third Initiation. (Even more will come before the Christ and take the first and second Initiations.) When you take the third Initiation you see God, as Sanat Kumara, the Lord of the World, who is a real physical being in etheric matter on Shamballa.[22]

What Creme is saying is that Lord Maitreya, who Creme has on many occasions identified as the "Christ," is the underling of a greater master, Sanat. Once a person has been initiated by Christ Maitreya (the first and second Initiation) he becomes eligible for the later (third) Initiation by God: Sanat (Satan). In effect, people who first worship and obey the Antichrist will fall under the greater control of his master, the Devil.

Creme is right in at least two respects. Those who take what is called "the third Initiation" will indeed see god. Through this Luciferic Initiation, they will see *their* god: Satan, Sanat Kumara. But this won't be the God of the Bible, the mighty Spirit who created heaven and earth. What's more, just as Creme wrote, Sanat Kumara *is* the "Lord of the World," until Jesus' triumphant return in all power and glory to set up His millennial reign on earth.

Until Jesus' return, Satan, also called Sanat, will be lord of the world and the false logos, or word, of planet earth. Thus Alice Bailey refers to Sanat Kumara as the "Planetary Logos":

> The first or will energy is, as you know, focused in Sanat Kumara, the Ancient of Days (as He is called in the Christian Bible), the Lord of Shamballa, who is the embodiment of the Personality of the Planetary Logos.[23]

Bailey ascribes to Sanat the aspect of eternal being (the "Ancient of Days"). This is unquestionably blasphemy because this expression was used exclusively by the Old Testament prophets to describe Jehovah as a being of sovereignty, eternal nature, and unparalleled majesty. This powerful phrase of veneration should not be usurped by Satan and his minions.

Did Satan Create the Mind of Man Through Evolution?

The New Age also willingly commits blasphemy by claiming that Satan, through the process of evolution, created the mind of man. Creme spreads this apostasy:

> Eighteen-and-a-half million years ago, in Middle Lemurian times, early animal-man had reached a relatively high stage of

development: he had developed a strong physical body; a coordinated astral or emotional feeling body; and the germ of mind, incipient mind, which could form the nucleus of a mental body.

At that point the Logos of our planet took physical manifestation as Sanat Kumara, the Lord of the World, on Shamballa. The center we call Shamballa was formed.

With Sanat Kumara, from Venus, came the Lords of the Flame, who brought that energy we call mind. This energy stimulated the . . . Individualization of Man.[24]

Sanat, then, is alleged to be instrumental in moving man from being a brute of a caveman to a conscious soul on the verge of godhood. Still, man is declared not ready to be the captain of his own destiny, the master of his fate. This is where Sanat, the lord of man and his world, comes in. His is the *Master Mind,* and man must remain subservient to him.

Their lowliness as compared to their Satanic master, Sanat, is made clear to New Age quest-seekers in a number of ways. The Unity Church of Dallas holds seminars entitled, "The Master Mind Principle." Participants are told they must take "seven steps into the Master Mind Consciousness." The most momentous is this step:

I make a decision to place myself completely under the influence and direction of the Master Mind. I ask the Master Mind to take complete charge of my life. . . .[25]

It is frightening to realize that across America and our planet at this very moment men, women, and children—precious souls for whom Jesus shed His blood—are taking oaths totally committing themselves to Satan, the Master Mind of Shamballa (hell). It is even more chilling to learn that a number of deluded New Agers are now invoking this Master Mind to come soon to earth in the flesh to set up his Kingdom. Some actually meditate with their minds centered on the cryptic phrases, "Come, Lucifer" or "Come, 666." Surely, not since the days of Noah and of Lot has man become so reprobate and so insanely susceptible to Satanic confusion.

Where Does Satan Live?

Benjamin Creme, Alice Bailey, and other New Age spokespersons say that their Sanat, their Lord Maitreya, and the hierarchy of spirits reside in a place called Shamballa. We know it from the Bible as hell. The New Age sees fit to rename this unholy center of darkness in order to deceive the unsuspecting.

One fast-growing New Age church, Urantia, refers to a place named "Satania." Urantia has chapters forming all over the United States. This Satanic New Age organization has its own bible, *The Urantia Book*,[26] a 2,097-page behemoth supposedly given by divine inspiration. In this book, disciples learn that they can invite "Thought Adjusters" (demons) to dwell within. These Thought Adjusters allow the individual's Higher Self to experience "the presence of God."[27] Men should be thankful, says *The Urantia Book*, "that the Thought Adjusters *condescend* to offer themselves for actual existence in the minds of material creatures." Lowly humans are indeed blessed that the higher spirit beings are ready "to consummate a probationary union with the animal-origin beings of earth."[28]

Urantia teaches that the indwelling of these spirits should cast out fear and uncertainty. When such negative thoughts enter a person's mind, they should immediately look to "Satania" for relief:

> When the clouds gather overhead, your faith should accept
> the fact of the presence of the indwelling Adjusters. . . .
> Look beyond the mists of mortal uncertainty into the clear
> shining of the sun of eternal righteousness on the beckoning
> heights of the mansion worlds of Satania.[29]

Urantia students obviously believe Satania to be heaven and the Thought Adjusters to be angelic presences. I have no doubt that many who study the *Urantia Book* truly believe they are doing right. Tragically, the power of Satan has so engulfed the minds of these men and women that they can no longer discern the truth.

Satan's power is so strong an influence on the minds of New Agers that even when Satania is described for them in some detail, they still cannot avoid being deceived. A good example of this was a recent article in a prominent New Age magazine which was attributed to a channeled (demon) spirit named Kwan Yin.

Speaking through his human counterpart, a woman named Pam Davis, this demon spirit "told" readers that there are multitudes of spirit beings such as himself who wish to communicate with living human beings. "These (spirit) beings reach out to you. . . . They come to be in service . . . they place upon your brain mechanism beautiful thoughts."[30]

From where do these beings communicate to those on earth? Yin answers:

> Do you not know that the center of your Earth, it is not that
> which has been spoken by your scientists, the bubbling of
> the molten rocks. . . . It is beauteous. It is home for
> thousands upon thousands of Beings that have lived there in
> totality of harmony and understanding of love.[31]

Who controls these beings? Yin tells us that there is a greater being, a Master of all spirits, who has "come from such a great distance in space to be now upon the Earth."[32] He further states that this great "One" is now in a physical body, even though he has never lived one lifetime upon earth. Yin relates that this god-being is able to absorb all that happens on earth and to communicate by thought directly with humans.

Neither Yin nor his human channeler, Pam Davis, provide the name of this great "One" who is said to have a "beneficial effect upon Earth, now when there is such need." Regardless, Christians will quite easily recognize both this entity and the spirits from the inner realms of the earth whom he directs. He is, indeed, the master of the place known as Satania.

Lucifer, the Hindu God

The New Age view of Lucifer's true identity becomes more clear when we investigate the story of the Hindu god Shiva, and the Hindu goddess Mother Kali. Anton LaVey, the internationally know Satanist priest and author of *The Satanic Bible*, mentions the name "Shiva" as a synonym for Satan or Lucifer.[33]

Mother Kali, a goddess with a cruel side, is known as both the creator, or life-giver, and the destroyer. She is depicted as smeared with blood, wearing a garland of human heads, and chewing raw flesh.[34] Dressed in red or scarlet (note the parallel with the mother of harlots described in Revelation 17), she demands blood sacrifice, just as does Satan or Lucifer. Kali is also known as the goddess of becoming, of evolution, bringing to mind David Spangler's description of Lucifer as the "angel of man's inner evolution."[35]

Shiva, Kali's "soul-twin" and husband, was similarly blood-thirsty. Through sexual intercourse with Kali (Tantric Yoga), Shiva and Kali became *one* through sexual union; therefore, in calling on Shiva, Hindus also call on Kali. Shiva is known as the Lord of Dance, the guardian of the process of reincarnation. Those New Agers and Hindus who today practice Tantric Yoga maintain that through sexual union, they link up with the energy of the universe. In their ecstasy, some enjoy sex while exclaiming, "Shivaham": "I am Shiva."

Shiva is also believed to be the force that controls the rhythm of the universe. Fritjof Capra, a New Age physicist who lectures at the University of California, writes that while sitting on the beach contemplating the similarities between the new physics and Eastern mysticism, a "beautiful" vision came to him in which:

> I saw cascades of energy coming down from outer space, in which particles were created and destroyed in rhythmic pulses. I saw the atoms of the elements and those of my body participating in this cosmic dance of energy. I felt its rhythm and I heard its sound, and at that moment I *knew* that this was the dance of Shiva, the Lord of Dancers worshipped by the Hindus.[36]

Interestingly, Capra admits that his book *The Tao of Physics*, in which he relates this vision of the Dance of Shiva, was possibly written with some type of other-worldly spirit assistance:

> Sometimes while writing *The Tao of Physics*, I even felt that it was being written through me, rather than by me. The subsequent events have confirmed these feelings.[37]

As Christians, we see that these false gods are a bizarre blend of evil and good. But to the Hindu and to the New Ager, Shiva and Kali are *good only.* Evil is said not to exist—it is *maya* (illusion). The Law of Karma and the process of reincarnation portray eternity as a wheel, or a succession of cycles. Life-giving and creation reside on one side of the wheel, death and destruction on the other. Neither is intrinsically "bad."

Swami Vivekananda, a Hindu guru widely thought of in America, taught that because the Mother Goddess Kali is all, all is one, and all is cyclical, God is both good *and* evil:

> Who can say that God does not manifest Himself as Evil as well as Good? But only the Hindu dares to worship him in the evil. . . . How few have dared to worship death, or Kali! Let us worship death![38]

Likewise, Lucifer is said to be neither evil nor good. He simply *is.* Formerly a destroyer, Lucifer now becomes a god— perhaps *the* God—chosen to shepherd mankind into the brighteness of a New Age. He is the Shiva and Kali of the New Age.

The Word of God certainly does not agree with the New Age glorification of Lucifer. Far from it. Isaiah, inspired by God, spoke of Lucifer's traitorous thoughts and his unnatural craving for power. Isaiah also pronounced God's judgment on Lucifer's wrongful rebellion and his eventual end:[39]

> How art thou fallen from heaven, O Lucifer, son of the morning! how art thou cut down to the ground, which didst weaken the nations.
>
> For thou hast said in thine heart, I will ascend into heaven, I will exalt my throne above the stars of God: I will sit also upon the mount of the congregation, in the sides of the north: I will ascend above the heights of the clouds; I will be like the Most High. Yet thou shalt be brought down to hell, to the sides of the pit. (Isa. 14:12-15)

Call Not Evil Good

The Bible warns: "Woe unto them that call evil good, and good evil" (Isa. 5:20). God has no relationship with evil or with darkness. "Let no man say when he is tempted, I am tempted of God: for God cannot be tempted with evil, neither tempteth he any man" (Jas. 1:13).

Attributing both good and evil to God is an occultic and Satanist tactic to mock God. For example, below is a common prayer repeated at Satanic rituals during the Middle Ages and still in use today. (Observe that it is the Lord "Adonay" who is being implored by the Satan worshipers.)[40]

Prayer

Lord God, Adonay, who has formed man out of nothing to Thine own image and likeness . . . deign, I pray Thee, to bless and sanctify this water, that it may be healthful to my body and soul. . . . O Lord God, Almighty and Ineffable, who didst lead Thy people from the land of Egypt, and didst cause them to pass dry-shod over the Red Sea. Grant that I may be cleansed by this water from all my sins. . . .[41]

In this dark Satanic prayer Lucifer, in the form of "Adonay," is actually credited for having rescued the Israeli people from the clutches of Pharaoh. The Satan worshiper reciting this prayer is also addressing Lucifer as "Lord God," requesting Lucifer to cleanse his sins. This awful, blasphemous prayer attributes to Lucifer divine power to forgive sins, which is solely the prerogative of the God of the Bible.

In other prayers of contemporary Satanists, witches, and pagans, Lucifer is referred to by such divine names as God, Messiah, Immanuel, Lord of Hosts, and the Lord. Predictably, dedicated occultists report that Satan answers to God's names, even assuming a divine appearance when he wishes.

The religions of the ancient Babylonians and Persians taught that God and Satan were twin brothers, an idea later adopted by Gnostic traditions, but easily recognized by the early Christian Church as inspired by Satan and so rejected outright.

Today New Agers seek to revive this age-old lie by transforming Lucifer into Christ, perversely twisting logic and Scripture. The New Age truly calls black white, darkness light, and evil good. It is no wonder that our Bible brands Satan as the father of lies and that it cautions us against false apostles who transform themselves into the apostles of Christ (2 Cor. 11:13).

The Great Invocation: Calling on Satan

Satanists who wish to call on Lucifer summon him through *invocation* (prayer meditation or incantation). New Age scientific lingo presents this as linking up with the "collective unconscious" of the universe. The term "collective unconscious" was invented by occult German psychologist Carl Jung. It is in reality the Satanic realm which can be contacted by human effort.

Many in the New Age propose that man not passively wait on the New Age "Christ" (Lucifer) but, instead, fervently invoke him to come *now*. It is believed that if a *critical mass* of people throughout the world join in invoking the "Christ," the massive energy force thus created will somehow inspire him to action.

Alice Bailey's spirit guide, the Tibetan Master Djwhal Khul, has conveniently provided a vehicle for summoning the Christ: *The Great Invocation*.[42] It is now being used by hundreds of thousands in their meditation. Unfortunately, even a number of Christians are unknowingly reciting it under the false impression that they are hastening the arrival of peace and joy to our planet.

To illustrate the Satanic nature of The Great Invocation, here are a few brief stanzas, followed by a Christian interpretation of their hidden meaning:

> Let the Lords of Liberation issue forth
> Let the Rider from the Secret Place come forth
> And coming, save.
> Come forth, O Mighty One.
>
> Let Light and Love and Power and Death
> Fulfill the purpose of the Coming One.
>
> From the centre where the Will of God is known
> Let purpose guide the little wills of men
> The purpose which the Masters know and serve.
>
> Let the Plan of Love and light work out
> And may it seal the door where evil dwells.
>
> Let Light and Love and Power restore the Plan on Earth.

When we understand New Age doctrines and analyze those doctrines in light of the Bible, we can readily explain this invocation:

"*Let the Lords of Liberation issue forth*": Let the gates of hell be opened and the demons issue forth (see Rev. 6:8; 9:1-11).

"*Let the Rider from the Secret Place come forth*": Let Satan be loosed from the pit to take peace from the earth, to kill and slaughter, and to gather unsaved souls[43] (see Rev. 6:3-17; 9:11).

"*Let Light and Love and Power and Death fulfill the purpose of the Coming One*": Let Satan's ploys of "light" and "love" deceive so he can go forth with power to destroy souls.

"*From the centre where the Will of God is known*": From Shamballa, the mystical, invisible kingdom where the New Age "Christ" and demons reside (i.e., hell), where the will of Satan is known.

"*The purpose which the Masters know and serve*": The Plan of Satan to ascend unto the heavens and become God, which his demons know and serve.

"*Let the Plan of Love and Light work out*": Let Satan's Plan to rule the universe and have man worship him as God prevail.

"*And may it (The Plan) seal the door where evil dwells*": And may Satan's Plan succeed in extinguishing all traces of God and eliminating those who know His Word.

The Many Disguises of Satan

As the shadowy wording of The Great Invocation illustrates, Satan's Plan is to win victory over God by treachery, dishonesty, and deception. Satan excels in masks and disguises. He is a pretender to the throne, the world's most skilled actor. In taking on the part of God, Satan will play his greatest role. It is, moreover, a part that he has already carefully rehearsed.

One such rehearsal is documented in *Revelation: The Birth of a New Age*. There David Spangler prints word for word a spirit transmission received direct from the pit of hell. Yet Spangler insists that this is the voice of "Christ, the Savior." In his message, Satan first announces that he is to be addressed by the name "Limitless Love and Truth," then goes on to pronounce that he is in fact both God and Christ, *and yet more!*

> Am I God? Am I a Christ? Am I a Being come to you from
> the dwelling places of the infinite? I am all these things, yet
> more. I am revelation. I am the Presence which has been
> before the foundations of the Earth. . . .[44]

Just as Isaiah prophesied, Satan continues today to boastfully and arrogantly proclaim to his followers—who in these times
are called the "New Age"—that "I will ascend into heaven, I will
exalt my throne above the stars of God."

The Marvelous Doctrines of the Antichrist

Spangler suggests to readers that they should not be startled that
"Limitless Love and Truth" says he is God, Christ, *and yet more.*
Spangler explains that this "exalted" spirit is saying, in essence:

> I am all these recognizable thought forms which you have
> formed of God and of Christ and of great Beings, but I am
> also more. *I am aspects of Divinity of God which you have
> not yet learned to recognize but which will be revealed to you
> in this New Age.*[45]

In other words, Satan is readying his followers for the time
when he will reveal *marvelous things* beyond those which they
have previously been taught. This can only mean that following
the dawning of the New Age, after the Antichrist assumes world
power, he will teach the people of earth unholy doctrines defil-
ing God which they had not been taught by Biblical Christian
churches. This will bring to frightening fulfillment the prophecy
of Daniel:

> And the king (the Antichrist) shall do according to his will;
> and he shall exalt himself, and magnify himself above every
> god and shall speak marvelous things against the God of
> gods. . . . Neither shall he regard the God of his fathers. . . .
> But in his estate shall he honor the God of forces: and a god
> whom his fathers knew not shall he honor. . . . (Dan. 11:36-
> 38)

Lola Davis has said that the One World Religion will need new revelations and that "the most important source will come in the future in the person of the Avatar (Messiah) promised to all religions."[46] Evidently these revelations of the New Age Messiah will be to the effect that God is within everything, that the impersonal God is made up solely of energy patterns (a universal force), that reincarnated spirit Masters—forces from beyond—exist in an invisible realm accessible to the human mind, and that man's soul is an energy force system of seven centers or chakras. All of these concepts are of Hindu origin and are promoted in all Mystery Teachings.

Thus we can see that Davis is presaging a soon-coming era in which the Antichrist will initiate the world into the New Age by indoctrinating humanity with strange and "marvelous" new doctrines. Such doctrines will include the beliefs that God is nothing more than an impersonal energy *force* and that the real guardians of mankind are those forces that exist in the spirit world. This doctrine could well be the worship of the "God of forces" prophesied by Daniel.

In Service of Satan

David Spangler's many books, in which he willingly glorifies Lucifer while distorting the Word of God, provide convincing proof that he is serving a different master than the Great "I Am" of the Bible. Spangler apparently recognizes that the New Age "Christ" operates from the very depths of hell, from the *inner realms* of the earth:

> The New Age is here now and the Christ is functioning within the inner realms of the earth, both in his ascended state from the depths of his past ministry and in his greater state of Aquarian Revelation.[47]

Spangler furnishes us another insight by confiding that the spirit named "Limitless Love and Truth" can be best described as the "Deva of the New Age."[48] In the Hindu religion Deva is the great virgin Mother Goddess, "the way leading to the Gods," who reveals to initiates the teachings of Krishna and Shiva, two of the three gods of the Hindu trinity. Deva is simply another name for the Hindu Goddess Mother Kali and for Diana, goddess of the Ephesians, whom Paul talked about.

In identifying his false "Christ" as the Deva of the New Age, Spangler is revealing that this evil entity is the one destined to lead mankind to the false gods of the Hindu religion: gods that sprang from the occult Mystery Teachings, the sorcery and perversion of ancient Babylon. It is exactly this Babylonian religious system that the Book of Revelation condemns and identifies as that to be led by Antichrist in the last days—a world religion full of abominations and drunk with the blood of the saints (Rev. 17).

Spangler is not alone in his portrayal of the coming "Christ" as a deity of the Hindu religion. Note, for example, the writings of the Theosophists, a Mystery Religion group with links to Hinduism that has for decades provided the doctrinal core of New Age teaching. H. P. Blavatsky, the founder of Theosophy, identified the Maitreya "Christ"—the New Age Messiah—to be the same figure as Hermes (also known as Cush, the father of the idolatrous Babylonian ruler-god Nimrod). Blavatsky went on to trace the lifeline of this Satanic "Christ," showing that the coming New Age world ruler is none other than the "serpent" himself, the dragon:

> He is called the "Dragon of Wisdom" . . . as all the Logoi of all the ancient religious systems are connected with, and symbolized by serpents. In Old Egypt, the god Nahbkoon . . . was represented as a serpent on human legs . . . the serpent being an emblem of Christ with the Templars also (see the Templar degree in Masonry). This symbol is identical with one which . . . was called "the first of the celestial gods," the god Hermes, or Mercury with the Greeks, to which God Hermes Trismegistos attributes the invention of and the first initiation of men into magic. . . .[49]

The description of the New Age "Christ" by Blavatsky accurately portrays him as a *dragon serpent,* recognized as the prevailing god-spirit and *logos* in all ancient and ungodly religious systems. He is further traced as the "god" who invented and then initiated man into "magic" (witchcraft and sorcery).

Serpent, dragon, inventor of sorcery: this most definitely is

Satan. Revelation 12:9 informs us: "And the great dragon was cast out, that old serpent, called the Devil, and Satan, which deceiveth the whole world: he was cast out into the earth, and his angels were cast out with him."

New Agers readily admit their "Christ" is the serpent or dragon. He is Maitreya or Sanat, the reincarnation of Lucifer and the inventor of sorcery and witchcraft. But, they quickly add, he most certainly is *not* Satan, who is alleged to exist only in the warped minds of fundamentalist Christians.

Bible-believing Christians are far too wise to believe the Great Lie. The Holy Spirit directs them to this all-important determining factor: anyone or any doctrine that denies that *Jesus is the Christ* is of the Antichrist. This Bible truth is simple, clear, conclusive.

EIGHT

Messages From Demons: Communicating Satan's Blueprint for Chaos

Put on the whole armor of God, that ye may be able to stand against the wiles of the devil. For we wrestle not against flesh and blood, but against principalities, against powers, against the rulers of the darkness of this world, against spiritual wickedness in high places. **(Eph. 6:11, 12)**

People were crying. A few of them were at my feet. Some were saying Ramtha was the "one" people had been waiting for . . . the great Master of the Age and herald of truth. . . . (J. Z. Knight, channeler of Ramtha)

The seven hundred people packed into the Seattle auditorium have paid $400 each to hear Ramtha. They sit in excited expectation, their pulses pounding, their eyes rapturously cast upon the stage. Then Ramtha comes forth. He speaks marvelous words, exhorting the audience to know that each one of them is God and that nothing they do is· evil, because there is no good and evil in human nature. He scorns the teachings of Jesus, cynically proclaiming that because each person is God, they do not need anyone else to teach them. Ramtha also reveals that "in the seed of Lucifer lies God and divineness."[1]

Hearing Ramtha's resonant magical voice with all its "wisdom and knowledge" creates a sensation among the crowd. Some shout or begin to jerk their bodies. Others break out in uncontrollable laughter and tears of joy. "Surely," one woman exuberantly exclaims, "Ramtha is the Voice of Truth speaking to this last-days generation. The New Age is here and we are now God!" Hearing this, a man nearby says simply, "I love Ramtha, I love myself, I love everyone."

Who is Ramtha, and why do people react so wondrously to his message? Ramtha is a demon—more generously described by his growing legion of followers as a "spirit entity." Invisible, he speaks in a husky male voice through J. Z. Knight, a Seattle, Washington housewife who claims that Ramtha last lived on earth thirty-five thousand years ago. She further says that he was the great Ram, "the God" of the ancient Hindus.

"I did not die; I ascended," Ramtha tells J. Z. Knight, "for I learned to harness the power of my mind and to take my body with me into an unseen dimension of life." Ramtha says that before his "ascension," he was the world's first conqueror, a fierce lord who triumphantly led a sweeping horde of barbarians over a vast realm of territory, from the fabled Atlantis through Asia Minor to what is now India.

A thirty-five-thousand-year-old discarnate spirit speaking through a modern-day housewife, spouting blasphemies and lies, seems totally weird to many Christians. Yet, to most New Age believers, Ramtha and many other such spirits are not at all bizarre. They are "proof" of the existence of an invisible world inhabited by millions of spirits either awaiting reincarnation into a human body or existing in spirit indefinitely as part of a hierarchy led by the "Christ." It is this "Christ" and his hierarchical cohorts in spirit who plan soon to materialize on earth and usher in the New Age Kingdom of peace, unity and prosperity.

Are These Spirits Real?

I have carefully studied and researched this occult phenomenon of spirits spreading the New Age gospel. I am totally convinced that such spirits exist and increasingly are speaking to those they perceive to be "ready" for their Satanic message. Yes, there are human fakers running around who claim to be the mouthpiece of the spirits. But there is also little doubt that throughout the world today, literally millions of New Age believers are regularly communicating with demons.

Many are doing so independently of one another, and often unknown to each other; yet the messages they receive are the same. This defies the mathematical laws of probability and confirms that the same source is communicating with them. There are only two sources of power that can intelligently operate in thousands of sites around the globe, simultaneously communicating directly with hundreds or even thousands of people: God and Satan. And since the messages consistently deny the very existence of God and His Son and denigrate His Holy Word, we know with certainty that it is the Devil with whom these people commune.

The Reality of Satan and His Demons

It is astonishing that a number of Christian ministers today disclaim the reality of evil spirits or even that there is a Satan who leads his own force of dark angels. This is to deny the very Word of God.

The Bible says that Jesus Christ's mission to earth was for the express purpose of destroying the works of the Devil (1 John 3:8), and that at God's appointed time the Devil, his demons, and his human followers will indeed be condemned (Rev. 20:10-15). However, until that time Satan will exercise much authority on earth, and only the power available to believers in Jesus shall be sufficient to withstand him (Eph. 6:11, 12). A full one-fourth of Jesus' ministry as recorded in the Gospels has to do with His casting out demons and evil spirits. He was able to discern between mere physical illness and a person possessed by demonic spirits. In Matthew 4:24, 8:16, 10:1, 8, Luke 9:1, 2 and Mark 1:32 we find clear examples. For instance, in Matthew 8:16, it is recorded:

> When the even was come, they brought unto him many that were possessed with devils: and he cast out the spirits with his word, and healed all that were sick.

Also, note in Matthew 10:1 that Jesus gave His disciples power to cast out evil spirits.

Incredibly, the New Age teaches that these spirits are benign—"wise ones" sent to *guide and rule mankind*. On one hand, Satan has ingeniously convinced millions of people that they must trust, communicate with, and obey his many lying demon spirits. On the other hand, he has shrewdly whispered in the ear of unsuspecting Christians that they must not believe that spirits from beyond really exist!

As Kurt Koch, a German evangelist who has spent forty-five years studying the occult, has said:

> We . . . know from the prophetic parts of the Bible that in the last days Satan will try to obscure men's powers of judgment. He will try to confuse the mind, destroy people's sense of truth, and create uncontrollable intellectual chaos. This is the great strategy of the world below, which forms and controls the spirit of the age.[2]

Satan's strategy is working brilliantly. Some Christian ministers and congregations laughingly deny the reality of a Devil and his demons; meanwhile, across the world large numbers of New Age ministers and their followers talk to and obey the very same Devil and his demons.

Mission: To War Against the Word of God

Demonic spirits who appear as invited guests of human contacts wage war against the Word of God. The Bible instructs Christians to test the spirits to determine whether they are of God or Satan (1 John 4:1-3). We are also told that light and darkness cannot coexist (2 Cor. 6:14).

Using these Biblical guidelines, we can know that the clever spirits who are now deceiving New Age believers are of Satan, because they continually spread false doctrines that go against the Scripture.

In examining the utterances of these demons of the New Age, we find that among their many lies they consistently teach *eight spiritual falsehoods.*

1) A personal God does not exist.
2) Jesus is not the only begotten Son of God and is not the only Christ.
3) Jesus did not die for our sins.
4) There are no such things as sin and evil.

5) There is no Trinity of Father-Son-Holy Spirit.

6) The Bible is filled with errors.

7) There is no heaven and no hell.

8) Every man is God, and one's godhood can be realized through the attainment of a higher consciousness.

Satan is using demons to promote the New Age gospel, to defame Jesus Christ, and to discredit the Bible. He intends to soften up humanity for the arrival of the Antichrist, whom millions will believe is Christ because of the propaganda now being spread by these lying spirits. Elements of The Plan of Satan to bring in a New Age One World Religion and a one world political and social order are carefully woven into virtually every utterance of these demons.

The Conspiratorial Link: Satan's Impulse

I am often asked: Is the New Age Movement a conspiracy? My answer is that while the New Age may not be a secretive *human* conspiracy in the classic sense of that term, it *is* nevertheless a conspiracy, one of global dimensions. The most frightening feature of this end-time religious network is that though many of its leaders seemingly work and act independently, *all* are seized by the very same *Satanic impulse.* This is why they promote strikingly identical doctrines and philosophies so hostile to Christianity. Every New Age believer is a victim of a *demonic conspiracy* to promote Satan's Plan to rule humanity and overcome God.

The conspiratorial *impulse* is the throbbing vibration, or heartbeat, that universally grips the minds and souls of the New Age believer. It is the spirit of the Antichrist, the philosphy of seducing demons who work every minute of the day to drive The Plan to ultimate success. Vera Alder wrote that the "blueprint" or "ideal world plan" for the coming new world government has long been in existence. It has been lying in wait "until such time as the human intelligence (was) capable of contacting it."[3]

Evidently, that time has arrived. Alder noted that throughout the world people are awakening and arising. "This phenomenon," she said, "takes on somewhat the same form and quality in all parts of the globe."

Thus it would seem to show that there is a powerful inner influence at work, *a mighty impulse* pulsing throughout humanity. . . .[4]

In *The Eternal Dance,* a book project of The Collegians International Church, the authors also speak of "the impulse" to which humanity is responding. It is this impulse, they claim, that is the root cause for the "worldwide mushrooming of interest in spiritual growth, Eastern religions in the West, and an incredible number of New Age communities of all types."[5] They define this impulse as man's desire to return to the primal energy source that created him.

David Spangler calls this the "Christ impulse," adding:

Throughout the world a great sifting is taking place, not between those who are "saved" and those who are "lost," for these are meaningless terms . . . but (as to) allowing consciousness to . . . be reached by the Christ *impulse* that seeks to lift all mankind into the New Age. . . .[6]

A number of New Age leaders use the term *intuition* to describe a person's tuning his mind in to this universal (Satanic) impulse. This is much the same way a person tunes his radio into the broadcast of a particular station. Thus, an unidentified "advanced soul" tells John Randolph Price that:

Through the silent, hidden work of the Masters, men and women throughout the world are beginning to *intuitively* understand the Truth . . . and it is only a matter of time before the Dawning (of the New Age).[7]

As Price explains it, the Masters (i.e., demon spirits) "are releasing powerful waves of thought energy into the universal consciousness for the benefit and upliftment of each individual. To those who are receptive, their message is: 'Rise up out of the tomb of mortality and take your place among the enlightened of this world. Look up and see the unreality of sickness and poverty. Step out into the kingdom of wholeness and abundance, peace and joy. The time is near for the New Age to begin.' "[8]

Price would have us believe that the Masters are helping to seed the world with "Superbeings"—the first of a new species of mankind. "They are the Leaders, the Teachers, and their work is being accomplished through the great medium of mind."[9]

To become a Superbeing ourselves, we are supposed to develop our intuition. In fact, Lola Davis flatly states that we must "accept as truth for ourselves *only* that which is consistent with our intuition."[10]

Intuition is defined by Davis as the practice of receiving "impressions from our own souls and guidance and knowledge from the Divine and His helpers in the Hierarchy of advanced souls."[11] She adds that "A powerful tool for developing spiritual intuition is meditation." Through meditation, Davis says, man can seek guidance from "the One called Lord Maitreya."[12]

The Demonic Search for Suitable Human Subjects

Elena, one of the Superbeings Price says he has communicated with, has told him that the Masters are working to save mankind from self-destruction. They do so by selecting "suitable subjects" for New Age conversion so those selected can help establish the New Age order. Elena speaks favorably of these demons from hell, praising them for spreading the New Age gospel that man is God.

> I prefer to think of them as angels of light—whether from earth or other worlds. They search, select and guide those men and women who may be suitable subjects. . . . A Master may then instruct, or plant the seed of a new concept . . . and the Word is spread, taking hold and growing in the mind of others, until there is a wave of collective thinking sufficiently powerful to change events and shape the future.[13]

Why, if we are gods, can't we just develop *our own truth?* Elena conveniently explains that "the search for the Inner Kingdom may be stimulated from thoughts communicated by the Master Consciousness of another Soul. . . . All Truth must come from the Spirit of Truth within, but many souls are active in assisting mankind. . . ."[14] In other words, we need these demon spirits to assist us in our quest for perfection as gods because they are today wiser than we. Man needs their spiritual guidance to "awaken" to his full divine potential.

It would appear that a prime tactic of the demons now contacting so many "suitable subjects" is to convince them that The Plan comes from their own consciousness. The world's collective consciousness (called "mind-at-large") and the individual's consciousness are allegedly one and the same. *The New Age victim is led to believe that The Plan is his own creation.*

Willis W. Harman, a professor at Stanford University and one of the founders of the New Age-oriented Association for Humanistic Psychology, explains this concept as follows:

> Mind exists in co-extensive unity with the world. . . . There seems no reason to doubt that my creative/intuitive mind might "have in mind" a "plan." . . . This idea of a "plan" coming from beyond consciousness seems implausible. . . . Yet there is impressive testimony . . . in a vast literature on mysticism and religious experience.[15]

Harmon's idea is that by following this "plan," man will eventually be elevated to become a new species, *Homo Noeticus*, replacing *Homo Sapiens*. So convinced is Harman that The Plan will succeed in making man God that he has founded and is now president of a group called the Institute of Noetic Sciences.

Satan's deceitful scheme is working beautifully. His evil demon "John" revealed his intent when he implored the world through David Spangler to:

> Live my life. Be what I am. Let us co-create together the world that comes from our beingness. . . .
> Let these words go forth. I am with all men. Their destiny is mine. Their life is mine. Their yearnings are for me.[16]

Satan's Conspiracy Unmasked

The New Age person who opens his mind to Satan's impulse truly invites darkness to enter his heart. He becomes one, not with God, but with Satan's worldwide spiritual conspiracy. God invites man into the majesty of His light, and the Bible promises us that He is always faithful and will open Himself to us when we call on Him with righteous motives. The only mediator between man and God is His Son, Jesus Christ. Satan is deceiving man when he claims that to acquire wisdom in solving life's problems we must seek out the disembodied spirit of a *dead person* and put our own souls under his other-worldly direction.

This is the same lie that Satan told pagan man in Babylon and throughout the ancient world. The man-god Nimrod (and his namesakes Mithra, Janus, Osiris, etc.) was held up as man's mediator with the gods while the Queen of Heaven, Semiramis (and her many Mother Goddess representatives) was purported to be the mediatrix. Now, millennia later, man is once again told he cannot go direct to the Almighty. He must use intermediaries because, the lie goes, God is an impersonal God—some type of cosmic energy force. And how, the demons of Satan scornfully ask, can man talk to an energy force?

Satan's soul-destroying doctrine is exemplified by such New Age organizations as Eckankar, Quartus, and Transcendental Meditation. Each teaches their initiates to communicate with the spirit world because it is impossible to reach the ears of God.

For example, the Satanic foundations of Eckankar are apparent in that organization's doctrine that man can only reach an advanced spiritual state by communicating with "spiritual travelers" and "other highly developed persons in the other worlds."[17] Here's how Eckankar, an organization that believes in astral (out-of-body) experiences as the key to man's achieving Christ Consciousness, describes these spiritual travelers:

> . . . these travelers . . . are what we know as the supermen of the universes . . . a traveler . . . is equivalent to a saint, an agent of God, or what we might call a *Sat Guru;* and he is exactly what the term implies here. *Sat* means true and *guru* is light-giver. . . . Furthermore . . . his teachings . . . lead to the most complete religious experience, and the most happy.[18]

That Eckankar is secretly and subversively promoting Satan and his Antichrist spirit becomes clear when this group teaches that there is a shadowy etheric world lying beyond man's consciousness and headed by a being called Mahanta. Mahanta, says Eckankar, "means spiritual leader, or *Godman*."[19]

Initiates are taught that this god-man can be reached through meditation by chanting his name. He or a spiritual traveler will then escort you in soul travel, instructing you in the Mysteries and the sacred writings. Eckankar further tells the initiate that we can only reach the divine by going through Mahanta and the spirits who assist him.

Satan intends to build his world empire and bring his Plan to reality by winning over the hearts and minds of men one by one. The conspiracy of which he is chief operates worldwide. Its international agents—demon servants of the Devil—move about looking for lost souls vulnerable to manipulation. In the following chapter we will study further how these hellish agents accomplish their mission, and we will see the human tragedy that is occurring as New Age men and women willingly invite Satan and his demons into their very souls.

"It Said It Was Jesus"— The Leadership of the New Age Revealed

Then saith Jesus unto him, Get thee hence, Satan: for it is written, Thou shalt worship the Lord thy God, and him only shalt thou serve. (Matt. 4:10)

We want to talk to you of love. We want to blend with you—we want to blend our energy with yours so we can touch each other—so we can work together.

(Lazaris, a demon spirit)

New Age believers who communicate with Satan's demons see these spirit entities as their helpers—as "good." Therefore, these demonic beings are variously called *light bearers, spirits of light, spirit guides, inner guides, psychic guides, imaginary guides, spirit counselors, psychic advisors, inner teachers*. Some New Agers call these entities their *Self*, their *Higher Self*, or their *Inner Child*. In reference to the dominant New Age belief that the spirits are spiritually advanced souls from the invisible world, they are also called *Masters, Ancient Masters*, or *Ascended Masters*. In recognition of their supposedly superior spiritual wisdom, they often are referred to as the *Masters of Wisdom* or as the *Wise Ones*.

Frequently the demons are assigned the names of deceased humans. Most popular are Biblical and historical personages. Jane Roberts has published a number of books which purport to reveal messages from "Seth," a person mentioned in the Old Testament. The spirit that spoke through a human medium to actress Shirley Maclaine claimed to be "John," as did the demon whose message David Spangler published. Elizabeth Clare Prophet says she is able to speak with such curious characters as Confucius and a medieval mystic, Saint Germain. She also confesses to being visited by her late husband, now known in spirit as "Lanello," and a spirit that identifies himself as "Jesus."[1] As we'll soon discuss, the demons who claim to be "Jesus" are many, and they are doing incalculable harm.

"Michael the Archangel" also seems today to be speaking to many New Agers. "Moses," "Jeremiah," "Peter," "Paul," and other long-dead prophets and saints are frequently heard from, as are an assemblage of Babylonian kings and queens and Egyptian pharaohs and priestesses.

Jose Silva, founder of the Silva Mind Control System, a worldwide seminar training program reportedly completed by over six million persons, teaches students to link up with spirit guides that will teach them to live life more abundantly. Graduates report they are able to communicate with spirits who identify themselves as "George Washington," "Abraham Lincoln," "Shakespeare," or another famous wise man from the past. Some of the spirits claim to be religious teachers such as "Buddha," "Mohammed," and "Lao Tse."[2]

A most cruel device used by Satan is to have a demon come forth to identify himself as a dead husband, wife, father, mother, or other loved one. To a hurting relative who wants so desperately to believe, such a visitation can exert a profound influence.

Methods of Demon Contact

New Age believers are making contact with demons through a variety of methods, all of which put the person's mind in an *altered state of consciousness*. Visualization, meditation, music and color therapy, incense, gemology, sexual ritual, drug ingestion, Yoga, automatic writing, and the channeling of spirits by mediums or channelers are used to promote The Plan and wage war on God's Word and His Church.

The Demon's Pen

Automatic writing occurs when a Satanic spirit totally controls and guides an individual in writing a message. Entire books have been communicated in this way, and some have become the bibles of the New Age.

The late Helen Schucman, an atheistic psychologist, was responsible for the abomination *A Course in Miracles*.[3] The course, consisting of a text, a workbook for students, and a manual for teachers, comes to about twelve hundred pages— every word of which Schucman said was transmitted to her through automatic writing.

In *Science of Mind* magazine, Judith Skutch, president of the Foundation for Inner Peace, which publishes *A Course in Miracles*, discussed with New Age writer John White how this course came into being and why it has become so popular.[4] Skutch said that *A Course in Miracles* "tells us that . . . God did not make this world—we did." It also teaches that people do not need to atone for anything they've done wrong that is sinful or evil. Also included, according to Skutch, are the following doctrines:

> "Forgiveness is not something we ask from God but rather something we extend to others, to the world . . . we extend forgiveness to others and to the world as if we *are* God."
>
> "The Son of God . . . is not Jesus but our combined Christ consciousness. . . ."
>
> "The name Jesus refers to one who was a man but who saw the face of Christ in all his brothers. . . . So he became identified with Christ, a man no longer at one with God."
>
> "Jesus was an historical person, but the Christ is an eternal transpersonal condition."
>
> "Miracles are natural. When they do not occur, something has gone wrong."
>
> "Seek not to change the world but change instead the way you see it."[5]

How did Helen Schucman, then an associate professor of psychology at Columbia University, come by *A Course in Miracles?* Judith Skutch tells the story:

Helen believed it was Jesus speaking to her as an inner voice. . . . I asked her if there was a specific entity dictating to her, and if so, who. Imagine me, a little Jewish girl from Brooklyn asking a Jewish psychologist from Manhattan just who is the source of *A Course in Miracles,* and her muttering under her breath, "It said it was Jesus."

Now, do I believe it's Jesus? The answer is yes, although I think it's irrelevant . . . the Course itself says it's not necessary to believe in Jesus to use the Course. . . .

In October, 1965 . . . she heard a (channeled spirit) voice say "This is a course in miracles. Please take notes." . . . So Helen proceeded to transcribe this inner dictation.[6]

A Course in Miracles was transmitted to Helen Schucman over a period of seven years; then the demon spirit worked with her and an associate for two additional years polishing the text. It was published in 1975 by Skutch, then a professor of parapsychology at New York University, and her husband, who jointly founded the Foundation for Inner Peace to promote the course. Reportedly, over five hundred thousand people have taken this demon-written course of study. Sadly, some Christian churches have offered seminars and training classes using the materials. More frequently, Unity, Unitarian, and other "science of mind" churches use it.

A number of prominent success and positive-thinking seminar leaders and entertainment personalities have endorsed *A Course in Miracles.* Melanie Chartoff, who gained a measure of fame in ABC TV's "Fridays," told an interviewer, "The *Course in Miracles* has been a real mainstay for me, a true source of encouragement."[7]

In the same interview, Chartoff stated she was also high on the teachings of Emmanuel, a disembodied spirit channeled by Pat Rodegast. Proudly she hailed her fellow actors and performers, commenting, "I'm thankful I'm part of an industry that's at the vanguard of putting New Age platitudes into practice."[8]

Conjuring Up Spirits

Channeling is the process by which a person calls up a demon spirit to communicate with him. This can be accomplished either individually or in a group setting. The spirit usually speaks through the human channeler's mouth, sometimes taking possession of his entire body. Sometimes he speaks or appears after being contacted at a seance conducted by a medium. The conjuring up of demon spirits is often called *spiritism,* or spiritualism, and hundreds of spiritualist churches in America, Britain, South America, and elsewhere have engaged in it over the years. The United States' churches are members of the National Spiritualist Association.

The New Age has greatly refined the ancient and once discredited practice of spiritualism, also making communication with the dead (necromancy) an international pastime. Previously a means to communicate with one's departed loved ones, the New Age has tailored this un-Biblical practice into an occult happening by which millions of people trust their very lives to the wisdom of demons whom they obey as their personal spirit guides.

New Age believers who channel spirits say that the spirits are all-knowing, possessing the knowledge of the Mystery of the Ages. They are also said to be miracle workers. Reportedly, these demons have helped New Agers make better grades in school and find romantic lovers and mates. They sometimes diagnose illnesses and provide guidance on how the individual can "heal himself." Quite often a demon spirit is able to disclose confidential information regarding the stock market or financial centers which other human subjects have revealed to it. Also, a number of New Agers are put into touch with other New Agers of like mind, perhaps in a distant city, who can help them succeed.

Many New Agers say they are afraid to make any important life decisions without first asking their spirit guide. Reverend Laura Cameron Fraser, the first woman Episcopal priest in the Pacific Northwest, quit her job in 1986 when the bishop of her diocese demanded she repudiate her belief in "Jonah," a spirit who spoke to her through channeling. The courageous bishop also warned Fraser that failure to cease her spiritism might result in an investigation of her loyalty to the Scriptures.[9]

Fraser evidently intends to continue consorting with the Devil. She plans to found an institute of healing in Seattle to investigate faith and psychic healing.

The demon Seth, through psychic Jane Roberts, transmitted a series of doctrinal books, published by such major publishers as Prentice-Hall and Bantam, which have become best-sellers. Naturally, Seth's doctrines are totally opposite those of Christianity. This channeled demon entity writes: "it is natural to be bisexual," "evil and destruction do not exist," "we create our own reality," and "there is no authority superior to the guidance of a person's inner self."[10] Thousands of New Agers around the world believe in Seth's teachings, and annually an International Seth Seminar is held in Austin, Texas.

Obviously a diabolical and clever spirit, Seth advises us that we must follow our "impulses" so we can discover the purpose of our lives: "Our difficulties arise from our mistrust and repression of these vital directives sent out by our inner selves."[11]

Some New Agers have become wealthy by charging exorbitant fees to people willing to pay to hear from these "super-wise" disembodied spirits. In New Age bookstores, books, audio cassettes, and videotapes which feature these spirits are brisk sellers.

In addition to Ramtha, a current rage is the demon Lazaris (note the similarity to the Lazarus of the New Testament). Excited New Agers flock to hear Lazaris speak on the "mysteries, magick, and the muses of love" during his nationwide lecture tour. A recent advance flyer in Atlanta, Georgia, exuberantly told participants that Lazaris's love had already "touched the whole planet." The flyer went on to say:

> Once we have met Lazaris, he is like an old friend who somehow we have always known. His joy, his insight, his love makes us realize he has always known us, too. . . .[12]

The cost to hear the marvelous Lazaris was advertised to be $375 per person. Participants were promised "extraordinary experiences," and were told: ". . . Lazaris will again guide us through a meditation to retune, restore, and recharge us mentally, emotionally, psychically, and physically."[13]

Participants were also told that this will be a time of healing and that they were to bring with them a "power object" for meditation, such as "a small crystal, a special stone, a piece of jewelry."[14] Though the flyer of course made no mention of it, sorcerers, shamans, witches, Satanists, and voodoo practitioners have for centuries understood the occultic use of "magical" amulets and charms.

Meditation: Unleashing the Darkness Within

The most common method used in the New Age to make contact with Satan and his demons is the practice of *meditation*.

New Age meditation is not to be confused with that described in the Holy Bible. God wants us to seek guidance from His Holy Spirit through active meditation on His Word and through prayer. In contrast, New Age meditation involves an emptying of one's mind and an inviting in of spirits who are not from God.

The world has been sold a bill of goods regarding meditation. Some eight million people in America alone have gone through the initiation process required by the Transcendental Meditation group; another six million have graduated from Silva Mind Control System's meditation program, and millions more regularly practice some form of Yoga meditation. Possibly 25 percent of all American adults have practiced some form of supernatural meditation. Yet, New Age meditation is based on Hindu principles of linking the human mind with the Universal Mind and thus making contact with demons.

The New Age believes that through meditation man can become a god. A desire to be a god and to wield supernatural, superhuman powers thus compels the individual to meditate. As Roy Eugene Davis of the Center for Spiritual Awareness in Lakemont, Georgia, wrote recently:

> The practice of meditation is the way to God-realization and the fulfillment of destiny. Yogic processes have proven helpful to many thousands of truth seekers over the centuries.[15]

Satan glories each time a human asks him to come to them through meditation. Every New Age newcomer is taught that beyond the veil of our own visible dimension are large numbers of all-knowing spirit entities *hungry* to connect with and help humans through meditation:

> As we begin to connect with our personal power, we can connect with an even deeper source. There is within each of us a "wise one." . . . That's why meditation is so helpful. Through meditation the "wise one" is right there to say, "Oh, goody, goody, I've got a chance now." The "wise one" is waiting, as it were, for an invitation. When I introduce people to their "wise one," they're always astounded at how much they know. Because their "wise one" knows everything. It's all right there. It's truly amazing.[16]

In his *Quartus Report,* John Randolph Price told readers that meditation was the key to their becoming one with deity. Through meditation they could connect with the "Christ" within—"The Teacher":

> Following a Love Meditation with Spirit each morning, address the Presence in a manner such as this: "Beloved Christ within—the Living God of my Being—I humbly invite you to think through me now. . . ."[17]

Most New Age teachers instruct initiates to vacate or empty their minds and let a Presence come in. That Presence—whether it be a famous one such as "Jesus" or "Buddha," or some unknown disembodied soul—will be their personal guru, their inner guide.

German evangelist Kurt Koch writes of one woman, a master of the second stage of Yoga, who chose "Jesus" as her personal guru. Not her Lord and Savior, mind you. Her guru. During her Yoga exercises, Koch reported, the woman developed occult powers, apparently a gift from the demon who pretended to be Jesus. Frightened, she sought to free herself, only to find that the demonic force refused to yield. After turning to the real Jesus and after Christian friends prayed for her, she was finally able to escape. She has since written a book, *From Yoga to Christ.*[18]

Koch also wrote that sometimes when demons claiming to be Jesus are commanded *in the name of Jesus Christ* to reveal themselves, they are forced to utter, "I am the unholy Jesus" or "I am the Jesus of Satan."[19] Christians are well advised that to attempt to contact the real Jesus in any way that is un-Biblical—such as through New Age meditation, visualization, or spirit channeling—can possibly lead to catastrophe, giving lying demons a grand opportunity to pose as our Lord.

We can be quite positive that a spiritual method is wrong if in any way it does not glorify Jesus and conform to the Word of God. For example, Dave Hunt told of one woman who visualized a "Jesus" who had encouraged her, "Go ahead and cuss me out."

Another example is that of Jose Silva, founder of the Silva Mind Control System, who has said that Jesus taught His disciples the same (Silva) method of meditation. However, Silva revealed on TV's "John Ankerberg Show" that to succeed in the meditation taught by the Silva System, we need not believe that Jesus is the one and only Messiah. It is only necessary, Silva claims, "to believe in the *technique* that Jesus taught."[20]

There is, of course, not one shred of evidence that Jesus taught such a perverse method—the evidence is all to the contrary. For example, the Lord's Prayer which Jesus taught His disciples requires active participation rather than a meditative and silent emptying of thought from our minds.

Johanna Michaelson, in her chilling book *The Beautiful Side of Evil,* told of her frenzied and horrifying life after taking the Silva Mind Control System course. Through meditation her visualized guru was "Jesus," just as she requested. At first this Jesus appeared to be kind and loving. His physical countenance was perceived to be much like the artist's depictions in the paintings we have all seen of Jesus. But as the meditation sessions continued, "Jesus" showed himself as a beastly character and made it clear to Johanna that she would suffer immensely if she failed to carry out his instructions.[21]

Only after many harrowing experiences—and God's intervention—did Johanna manage to free herself from the demon's spiritual chains. Today a relaxed and confident Johanna Michaelson is a Christian, strong in her beliefs and dedicated to informing the world of the dangers of the occult.

Visualizing the Darkness

Johanna's nightmarish struggle with demons began in earnest after she visualized "Jesus" and invited him to be her New Age guru. In *visualization,* the individual conjures up an image of a spirit he wishes to contact. Visualization may be enhanced by focusing one's eyes on a centering device such as a candle flame, a crystal, or a mandala. A mandala is most often a circular pattern (the circle represents Satan and the karmic wheel of reincarnation and birth) comprised internally of a scene or symbols reflecting New Age themes.

In one recent New Age magazine, readers were rewarded with a mandala that was a full-page insert they could remove and use. Inside the circle were the names of various Mother Goddess figures such as Diana, Artemis, and Kali.[22] The user is to visualize and concentrate on these names and thereby summon his or her spirit guide, which most likely will be a demon purporting to be one of these goddesses from the past.

Keep in mind the difference between New Age occult visualization and the *visions* recorded in the Bible. Visions are from God *if* they glorify Him and His Word. In such cases, the vision is generated by God and *not* by man. In contrast, in visualization the *individual* initiates the image. He, not God, is the one who induces a spirit to enter into his mind.

Unholy Words

During meditation the New Age believer often uses a *mantra,* a mystical holy word of power, to invoke the demon spirit guide to come. A mantra also serves to relax the mind into a trance state. Elizabeth Clare Prophet's Church Universal and Triumphant teaches that the repeated chanting of a mantra "magnetizes" the "Presence" whom the meditator desires to communicate with. The magic word recommended is either *aum* in Sanskrit (Hindu) or *I am* in English. Prophet also says that this is the word originally used to command the universe into existence.[23]

Transcendental Meditation's (TM) founder, Maharishi Mahesh Yogi, claims that each individual in the universe has his own holy word (mantra) and that it should never be shared with anyone else. However, it has been revealed by other sources that the mantra which TM assigns is invariably the name of a Hindu god. Furthermore, there are only sixteen mantras in use, one for each of sixteen age groups. For example, all persons aged twenty to twenty-one chant the holy word *aem* to invoke their personal deity while persons forty to forty-four recite the word *hirim*.[24]

The concept of the mantra originated in the Hindu religion. The Mother Goddess Kali is said to have used her mantra word *om* (same as the Church Universal and Triumphant's mantra word *aum*) to create the world.[25]

In Babylon, Greece, and Rome, the mantra was used to command pagan deities to appear, and in Satan worship today such magical words are verbalized to summon Satan or one of his demon princes.

Thus, what the New Ager is doing by chanting these unholy words is putting himself into a vulnerable trance state at the same time that demons are invited to appear and do their horrible work.

Only the Power of Jesus Can Surmount the Demonic Powers

The demonic power of these channeled spirits is far greater than the New Age believer can ever hope to bring under control. As long as the individual does what the demon tells him, everything is fine. But once the person balks, and especially if he turns to the Bible or to prayer for deliverance, Satanic hostility breaks out as the angry spirit furiously attempts to whip the subject back into line. Yet, in the end these demons are no match for the sincere person who repents and calls on the name of Jesus (see Jas. 4:7).

Without Jesus, Lord of Lords and King of Kings, as his shield, any man is helpless when he encounters demon hordes. Once Satan is invited in, the individual finds himself defenseless. The great occult strength of these evil presences was recorded in Acts 19:13-16, in which we read of ungodly exorcists vainly attempting to cast out an angry demon from a possessed man by their own strength. The demon rebuked them, and they were brutally beaten.

Alone, man cannot reason with Satan's demons. The clever ability of these evil spirits to bend and warp the minds of men and women not attuned to God's Holy Spirit was manifested in the case of J. Z. Knight, the channeler of Ramtha.

Knight says that Ramtha monitors her thoughts and knows everything she is thinking. At first, she explains, she tried to challenge Ramtha by telling him of the doctrines she had learned as a child in the Baptist and Pentecostal churches (both of which she left). Undeterred, Ramtha pressed her and pressed her until she finally succumbed and began to think like him. Asked during an interview if a stronger-willed Ramtha had torn her basic belief system down, Knight replied, "He *allowed* me. I did it myself. He acted as the catalyst. . . ."[26]

To demonstrate how completely a demon can master the human will, I have included below a verbatim exchange between J. Z. Knight and Ramtha, as Knight told it to *Psychic Guide* magazine. Note how shrewdly and easily this Satanic being was able to inculcate his evil value system into the mind of an unprepared human subject who was unfamiliar with spiritual warfare, not clothed with the armor of God's Word, and not led by the Holy Spirit:

> He (Ramtha) asked me, "What think you God is?"
>
> I replied, "Well, He created us in His own image. He created the world and the heavens and the ocean." I went back and quoted some verses from Genesis and felt very arrogant that I could do that.
>
> He said, "So to you, God created everything. Who created God?"
>
> "No one did!" I said, "God always was!"
>
> He smiled and said, "But He has created all things?"
>
> I said, "Yes!"
>
> Ramtha continued, "Who think you to know who the Devil is?"
>
> I said, "I don't know." I was really getting ticked off at him because I thought he was trying to manipulate me. He was. I explained, "The Devil is a fallen angel. God created heaven, the earth and man. Grand angels were created and Lucifer acclaimed himself to be the most beautiful angel of all and even arrogantly proclaimed himself to be more beautiful than God. As a result he fell from grace and took with him the lot who sided with him. From then on a polarity was created consisting of good and evil."
>
> Ramtha said, "But who created this angel?"
>
> I said, "God did."
>
> He asked, "What did He create him out of?"
>
> "God stuff." It seemed logical, I thought.
>
> "So whatever God creates," he said, "is made up of God, correct?"
>
> I nodded, "Yes, God creates it out of Himself."
>
> "And so therefore it's divine and good?"
>
> I agreed.
>
> "Then Lucifer was divine and good, correct?"
>
> "Well, no he wasn't. He was a very evil entity," I said.
>
> "But then who created the evil?" He was getting right down to basics.
>
> "Well . . . Lucifer was, and is, evil."
>
> He came back with, "Where did the evil come from? If God created all things, who created Lucifer? God must have

if He created all things. Then, beneath the evil of Lucifer lies God."

"Ramtha," I said, "you don't understand. This entity is evil and he seduces us to become evil to take us from the grace of God."

Ramtha said, "Where would he take you to? You say all things are God, and all things thereof are God. In other words, in the seed of Lucifer lies God and divineness."[27]

What the Bible Says About Spiritism

God's very clear, unequivocal commandment is set forth in the Bible: we must not seek to communicate with spirits and with the dead. In Leviticus 19:31 we read this admonition: "Regard not them that have familiar spirits, neither seek after wizards, to be defiled by them: I am the Lord your God."

God condemns mediums and spiritists, classifying them as of Satan and in the same wretched class with sorcerers, diviners, and witches:

> There shall not be found among you any one that maketh his son or his daughter to pass through the fire, or that useth divination, or an observer of times, or an enchanter, or a witch. Or a charmer, or a consulter with familiar spirits, or a wizard, or a necromancer. For all that do these things are an abomination unto the Lord. . . . (Deut. 18:10-12)

It is for our protection—and our salvation—that the Lord has established these guidelines. He loves us and desires that we consult with Him, for He has the answer to all our needs. The Christian needs no man-god spirit as his intermediary or guide. We can direct-dial the Great God of creation, the one and only Heavenly Father. "For there is one God, and one mediator between God and men, the man Christ Jesus" (1 Tim. 2:5).

The mind is the chief site of conflict for man's soul. It is where The Plan of Satan is instilled in the consciousness of those in the New Age who foolishly invite demons in. Satan is indeed proving that he has powers against which no man without God can prevail. But the spiritual weapons of the Christian are mighty through God, allowing us to oppose The Plan and its vain imaginings. As Paul implored us, we engage Satan and his demons by:

> . . . casting down imaginations and every high thing that
> exalteth itself against the knowledge of God, and bringing
> into captivity every thought to the obedience of Christ.
> (2 Cor. 10:5)

The New Master Race

Therefore let no man glory in men. . . . (1 Cor. 3:21)

When a man realizes his (God) identity, a race of gods will rule the universe.
(John Randolph Price, *The Superbeings*)

John Randolph Price calls them the "Super Beings," Richard M. Bucke termed them men of "Cosmic Consciousness," Elizabeth Clare Prophet says they are the holy and undefiled "I AM." To Peter Roche de Coppens they are "Christed human beings." Ruth Montgomery's guides say they are spiritually advanced "Walk-ins." *They* are said to be endowed with all the powers of the universe. Indeed, they *are* the universe. They are the seventh—the highest stratum—in a long lineage of roots races that have occupied the earth over the millennia. Their Plan is that soon they will assume leadership of the nations, unify all governments, and establish a One World Religion headed by one of their own.

Just who are *they*? The advanced race of New Age mangods. This is the secret doctrine, what the New Age calls the "Perennial Philosophy"—the Mystery of the Ages—Man *is* God. As Meher Baba, a Sufi Moslem mystic whose writings are enormously popular with New Agers, explains:

119

> There is only one question. And once you know the answer
> to that question there are no more to ask. . . . Who am I?
> And to that question there is only one answer—I am God![1]

Sir Julian Huxley wrote that the doctrine of man, the supreme being, should be the cornerstone of the new world order.
According to Huxley, "The well-developed, well-patterned, individual human being is . . . the highest phenomenon of which we
have knowledge, and the variety of individual personalities is the
world's highest riches."[2]

Scientist Arthur Clarke, author of *2001: A Space Odyssey*
and other best-selling futuristic novels, is a fervent New Ager
who predicts that consciousness expansion—superintelligence—
and human immortality will have been achieved by the year
2100. He also forecasts a wondrous future for mankind, remarking that men "will not be like gods, because no gods imagined
by our minds have ever possessed the powers they will command."[3]

All New Agers agree with Clarke that man's destiny is godhood, but few believe man will have to wait more than a few
years. Ruth Montgomery, whose supporters have bequeathed
her the title "The Herald of the New Age," has said that her
spirit guides from the dead have revealed that we are at the very
threshold of a momentous chaotic event—the shifting of the
earth. This will occur by the close of the century, her guides tell
Montogomery, and it will usher in the Age of Aquarius, also
called the New Age. Montgomery is ecstatic when she states
that a new race of man-gods is on the near horizon:

> The New Age will bring joy and happiness unexcelled since
> the days of the Atlantean era. . . . Those who survive the
> shift will be a different type of people from those in physical
> form today, freed from strife and hatred, longing to be of
> service to the whole of mankind. . . . Their minds will be
> open to the reality of one world. . . .[4]

John Randolph Price targets an even sooner date for the
initiation of man into godhood. Price has confided to his followers that "a new species of man is coming forth to lead us out of
the darkness into a new dimension. . . ."[5] He believes that
December 31, 1986, the day when the world celebrated a Plan-

etary Healing Day, was the beginning of the end for the old race man, and that 1987 is an important year of *preparation* which will be followed by a time of *consolidation*. The final period of *inauguration* will see the reappearance of the New Age "Christ" to rule earth and the triumph of Cosmic Consciousness—divinity—for collective humanity.[6]

Bernadette Roberts, a fifty-five-year-old former cloistered Catholic nun and now a New Age author and "theologian," says that man is now on a spiritual journey toward total unity with the One, which she terms the "Godhead."

"One glimpse of the Godhead," Roberts remarks, "and no one would ever want God back!"[7]

John White, another New Age "theologian" and a prolific writer of New Age propaganda, offers this simple description of how modern man is evolving into a race of gods:

> First you go *toward* the light.
> Next you're *in* the light.
> Then you *are* the light.[8]

White contends that "sooner or later every human being will feel a call from the cosmos to ascend to godhood." He rejects the Christian belief that Jesus was the only Son of God and scoffs at the assertion that Jesus died on the cross for our sins. White states that the significance of Jesus' death and resurrection "is not that Jesus was a human like us but rather that we are gods like him." White adds, "This is the secret of all ages and all spiritual traditions. This is the highest mystery."[9]

Throughout the books and writings of New Age prophets, theologians, gurus, and teachers, one finds a common thread: Jesus is not Lord, a personal God is a myth, man is his own Lord, man is God. New Age believers are falling for the oldest lie ever told a human being—the same lie Satan told Adam and Eve in the garden: "Ye shall be as gods."

The Racial Doctrine of the New Age

The evolving New Age man-god is described as a totally new species that will replace the outmoded race which until now has controlled the destiny of man and the planet. Ruth Montgomery and others maintain that every person on earth is either an

Atlantean or a Lemurian.[10] Edgar Cayce also believed in this theory, speculating the existence hundreds of thousands of years ago of two great continents and races, Atlantis and Lemuria. The Lemurian race is peace-loving and dedicated to the good of all humanity, while the less desirable Atlantean race is warlike and separative. The future is said to belong to the higher consciousness Lemurian race.[11]

According to Montgomery, the spiritually advanced Lemurians represent the fast-approaching New Age. She says mankind is being assisted into the Aquarian Age by "Walk-ins," reincarnated guides who are even now taking possession of living humans. She says that the old soul within the body is replaced by the more highly developed soul from the spirit plane. The new person or soul, called a Walk-in, is a New Age creation sent by the guides to help mankind "by instilling courage, compassion, love and cooperation."[12]

Montgomery's cheery description of a benign process of Walk-ins taking over human bodies is in reality a horrendous picture of Satanic demons entering willing humans and boldly taking possession. Sealed by Satan, the "new" person is imbued with a reprobate mind and the New Age spirit of Antichrist.

Montgomery doesn't see it that way. Walk-ins, she says are "harbingers of a new order that will bring peace on earth in the 20th century."[13] Her spirit guides tell her that there are tens of thousands of them now in physical form. "They are New Age disciples who are returning at an accelerated pace to usher us into the Age of Aquarius when we will all be as one and the biblical prophecy of the millennium will be fulfilled."[14]

The Children of Darkness vs. the Sons of One

The Collegians International Church also teaches two seed races. There is said to be a race of lower consciousness called the "Children of Darkness" and a higher consciousness race known as the "Sons of One." The Children of Darkness are described as the children of Cain:

> They may be intelligent and brimming with knowledge, but they lack wisdom. Often self-indulgent, power and wealth hungry, they may succeed again in bringing disaster to mankind.[15]

In contrast, the Sons of One are thought to be the descendants of Noah's son, Shem. These highly evolved spiritual persons are children of light; they resist harmful technology, nuclear power, pollution, and abuses of nature. Therefore, they are the race that will succeed, bringing a universal era of peaceful consciousness.[16]

The Lucis Trust and a number of other groups speak of a New Age vanguard, said to be a superior race centered in the Tibetan mountains in a place called Shamballa. There, assisted by the invisible Masters, this race of supermen awaits the dawning of the New Age. However, their representatives have now gone out in bodily form to help humans achieve higher consciousness.[17]

Christ Consciousness: A Racial Mark of Superiority?

Other New Age leaders depict the New Age man-god as a being who has achieved the supernatural state known as *Christ Consciousness* and the superior race as collectively possessing Christ Consciousness. This does not mean following Christ Jesus. On the contrary, the New Age heaps scorn on Christianity, calling fundamental Christians a "Jesus cult."

Hayward Coleman, who advocates "Christian Yoga," exemplifies the New Age concept of Christ Consciousness without Jesus Christ when he says:

> The right way of thinking is to see Christ in every human being. This may sound born-again but it isn't. Born-again Christianity emphasizes the personality of Jesus; what I call Christian Yoga sees Christ as a Consciousness.[18]

Given New Age doctrines, there is really no place for traditional Christianity in the luminescent New Age that awaits the birth of the new race of man-gods. Of what use is the God of the Bible to a race that is its own god or a Christian Messiah to a person whose theology teaches him he is his own savior? The New Age man or woman is all-sufficient, believing that the ascension of man to godhood is inevitable.

Though traditional Christianity is reviled by the New Age,

apostate Christianity, affirming the divinity of man, is heartily welcomed. Peter Roche de Cappens is one who brushes aside objections that the New Age is opposed to Christianity. De Cappens says that the divinity of man through spiritual initiation is the *Great Work* that is the central objective of the "Ageless Wisdom."[19] He suggests that if Christians were to discover the hidden messages in the Bible, they would realize that Christianity and this ageless wisdom are perfectly compatible. De Cappens further claims that:

> A "living Christian" or a "Christed human being" is really a God-Man or woman who has achieved and incarnates self-knowledge, self-mastery, and self-integration—one who can truly express the self.[20]

This is, of course, a horrible abuse of Scripture, for the Bible makes clear that man must *not* exalt himself. The Christian would never say, "I am God" or "I am Christ," but "Not I, but Christ liveth in me" (Gal. 2:20).

Isaiah cautioned us not to place our trust in man (Isa. 2:22). Jeremiah prophesied the destruction of the Babylonian man-gods worshiped by the ancient world when he stated: "Thus shall ye say unto them, The gods that have not made the heavens and the earth, even they shall perish from the earth, and from under these heavens" (Jer. 10:11). The Old Testament prophet reminded the people that the human heart is "deceitful above all things, and desperately wicked . . ." (17:9). Jesus gave a similar testimony: "For out of the heart proceed evil thoughts, murders, adulteries, fornications, thefts, false witness, blasphemies" (Matt. 15:19).

There can be only one God, only one Christ, and man was made to honor and obey Him and Him alone.

Darwin's Legacy: The Evolution of Consciousness

The New Age belief in an evolving human race of gods originated in ancient Babylon. In 1859 Englishman Charles Darwin published his *Origin of the Species,* reviving in a pseudoscientific form the old Babylonian doctrine. Darwin's theory caught on with agnostic and atheistic scientists and continues to receive support to this day. However, over the past few decades the generally accepted theory of evolution has undergone some revisions and additions.

In the late 1950s a Jesuit priest, Pierre Teilhard de Chardin, modified evolutionary theory by refining existing philosophies and adding to Darwin's theory the concept of a further evolutionary stage for mankind—evolution into higher consciousness. Teihard de Chardin wrote that man will progressively become more Christlike until humanity reaches its ultimate goal: godhood, which he called the *Omega Point*.[21]

Teilhard de Chardin has since become practically the "patron saint" of the New Age Movement. His ideas form the basis for its un-Biblical doctrines of divine man. However, Teilhard de Chardin has a popular competitor in the person of Richard M. Bucke, whose evolutionary theories actually preceded those of the heretical Jesuit priest.

Cosmic Consciousness: The Mark of the Nobler Race?

Richard M. Bucke, a Canadian psychiatrist, in 1901 first developed the theory of a superior race evolving into a godlike *Cosmic Consciousness*. His book *Cosmic Consciousness* is now a New Age classic. Similar in most respects to Christ Consciousness, Cosmic Consciousness, wrote Burke, "appears in individuals . . . of good intellect, of high moral qualities, of superior physique." He proposed that "a time will come when to be without the faculty . . . will be a mark of inferiority. . . ."[22]

Bucke also stated that "any man permanently endowed with the Cosmic Sense would be almost infinitely higher and nobler than any man who is self-conscious merely."[23]

Naturally Bucke told his readers that he himself had been reborn into Cosmic Consciousness. He also claimed that Jesus, Buddha, Plato, Mohammed, Francis Bacon, and Walt Whitman, among others, had possessed this enlightened cosmic sense.

Richard Bucke's theory of the emergence of a spiritually superior race destined to take over the reigns of leadership is a dangerously volatile idea. Yet, it has become the cornerstone of the New Age World Religion. But Satan needed one more modification to his theory of evolution to guarantee The Plan would succeed. He needed to show how an evolutionary spark could ignite the rise of man to godhood. That addition was made possible only recently.

Transformational Evolution

A recent and profound addition to the theory of evolution is the concept of *punctuated equilibria*, first articulated in the Soviet Union in the early 1970s. According to this theory, species can develop very quickly. It does not take millions of years of random selection, as Darwin proposed, for a new species to evolve. Instead, an entire new species can arise over a brief period of only tens of thousands (not millions) of years.[24]

New Agers subscribe to this theory but take it one dreamy step further. They believe that an evolutionary leap can occur *instantaneously*. This theory of spontaneous, super-rapid evolution has become known as *transformational evolution*.

New Age teachers and gurus are fascinated by the idea that modern man might be on the precipice of an incredible evolutionary leap—to a level of superhuman higher consciousness. He will then be a god.

New Age doctrine holds that as more and more racially superior human beings become aware of their divine nature and their latent powers within, a *critical mass* of energy will develop and a new *Cosmic Consciousness* will envelop the globe. Transformed into Superbeings, *Homo sapiens* will become a race of gods. Enlightened man shall rule the universe, unite with it, and he and it shall become one.

New Agers often quote Lama Govinda, an Indian Hindu mystic who taught that the entire cosmos is but an extension of the human mind. Said Govinda, "To the enlightened man . . . whose consciousness embraces the universe, to him the universe becomes his physical body, while his physical body becomes a manifestation of the universal mind."[25]

Marks of the Inferior Race

As we've seen, according to New Age doctrine there are two great *root races* in the world: one on the threshold of god-status, the other holding the first back. The latter is an inferior race of lower consciousness.[26]

What are the marks of the inferior race? Negative thinking is this race's chief identifying mark. In contrast, positive thinking is touted as typifying the person of higher consciousness. That person is spiritually enlightened and has achieved Cosmic, Christ, or God Consciousness. In a nutshell, the higher consciousness person has an appreciation for unity, love and peace; the lower consciousness person does not.

As Christians we know that our Lord Jesus Christ loved and desired the unity of all mankind. Isaiah described the coming Messiah, Jesus, as the "Prince of Peace." So the Christian, after first trusting in his Heavenly Father, also strives for unity, love, and peace. Does the Christian, then, typify that person so highly esteemed by the New Age as a being of higher consciousness?

No, the Christian is held by the New Age to be of the lower consciousness race. New Age meanings for *unity, love,* and *peace* are diametrically opposed to the way the Bible uses these same terms. The New Age despises *Christian* unity, love, and peace because the powers of darkness which rule the New Age cannot abide the Holy Spirit who embodies these cardinal Christian values. The following explanation will make this point clear. True Christianity can never be merged into the New Age World Religion.

New Age Unity

Satan's drive for *unity,* for a *One* World Religion and a *One* World Government led by *one* man-god, the puppet of the Devil, impels New Age leaders to reject Christianity. Christianity is viewed as a negative philosophy that is, at its core, *separatist.* To the Christian, Jesus is *the* way. God loves each one of us—even sinners, and the Bible is God's Holy Word. The Christian grieves for the Hindu, the Buddhist, the atheist, the Satan worshiper and men and women of all religions and all creeds who have not yet accepted Jesus Christ as their personal Lord and Savior. It is the Christian goal to help these lost sinners learn of the truth—that Jesus Christ alone is Lord.

The Christian doctrine of Jesus *only* is hated by the New Age, which maintains that it is a negative doctrine hostile to world unity. The New Age teaches that *all paths* have "light" within them. They are all acceptable. Furthermore, in New Age theology, we are all collectively "God"; thus there is no personal God who loves us. Additionally, the Bible is considered only one of many sacred books. New Age leaders say that if only the Christian would give up his "negative," "exclusive," and "separatist" views the world could race toward unity. Unity of religions and world peace would then ensue:

> . . . We are all pure light, or pieces of God. . . . We are obviously ALL ONE. . . . If you can just remember that we are all one, we are ALL GOD. . . . Your negative feelings will disappear. . . .
> Logic, reason, intuition and the esoteric literature from most world religions indicate that if you think you have the only way then your God is too limited.[27]

According to the New Age, unity requires that the Christian cease his efforts to convert the world to salvation through Jesus and recognize that man is himself divine. To think otherwise exemplifies narrow-mindedness and wrong thinking:

> This mistake and narrowness of thinking is especially evident when we try to restrict and confine God's love, compassion and forgiveness to one special group. For example, many believe that *either* you accept Jesus as your personal master, *or* you will go to hell. This limits the experience of the Christ Consciousness to only one man (Jesus) and denies the universality of God's power within each of us that has been demonstrated by many Masters before, and since, the Master Jesus. . . . Intuitively, most people realize the awkwardness of this position in the orthodoxy and either ignore it, or ignore the church.[28]

So the Christian who believes in Jesus is labeled "anti-unity." He is also a sinner! Usually the New Age rejects any notion that "sin" exists. But the concept is resurrected for Christians who refuse the "oneness" of all creation and all religions. Not only is their refusal a separatist anti-unity "sin," but it identifies Christians as being out-of-step with The Plan:

The great secret of life is unity. We are all at one in the mind of the creator. . . . Sin is the ignoring of this fact of oneness. . . . Such ignoring or ignorance leads to envy, frustration, criticism, robbery and hate. These states of mind cause illness.

If we can learn to love our fellow men (not sentimentally but in *oneness* . . . because all is an expression of God's Plan) . . . We will then become healers—of ourselves, of others, and of the world.[29]

The principles underlying the Plan teach that higher, Cosmic Consciousness—"Christ Consciousness"—ends separativeness. Collectively, the peoples of earth can bring in the New Age Kingdom and summon the New Age "Christ." As one New Age writer emphasizes, by following the Divine Plan, "each individual is reunited with the whole, and the entire world is lifted up to a spiritual dimension of love, joy, and peace."[30]

Christians are viewed as stumbling blocks to the world's being gloriously lifted into a new spiritual dimension! *Our* fears of religious and world unity, *our* sins, *our* karmic debt prevent critical mass from being achieved. Therefore, "The Plan," says John Randolph Price, "must include the elimination of fear, the dissolving of fake beliefs, and the raising of karmic debts in each individual soul . . . so that the Light can dispel the darkness and indeed make all things new."[31]

Price has recommended that every person on earth sign a covenant with the organization he founded, The Planetary Commission, pledging to end separativeness and consenting to the healing and harmonizing of the planet. The covenant includes this phrase:

I choose to be a part of the Planetary Commission. . . . I know that as I lift up my consciousness, I will be doing my part to cancel out the error of the race mind, heal the sense of separation, and restore the world to sanity. . . .[32]

The Christian, it is implied, is contributing to an *insane* world if he opposes New Age unity. By professing Jesus Christ as *the* way of salvation, the Biblical Christian is demonstrating "the error" of his lower consciousness "race mind" and opposing the will of God. ("God," you may recall, is defined by the New Age as a universal energy force.) Thus Price writes:

> The *Divine Plan* is the Strategy and the Blueprint for each individual man or woman, for the entire human race, and for the planet itself, as conceived by the Infinite Thinker. In essence, we're talking about the *will of God* . . . the infinite Good-for-all. . . .[33]

"All is one," proclaims the New Age, "nothing is separate." Any religion or person who opposes this basic, humanistic concept is a threat to peace and the brotherhood of man. Barry McWaters suggests that an aggressive spirit of separativeness because of Christian error emerged during the last two hundred years, evidently referring to the period when the United States became an independent nation founded on a Christian belief in "one nation under God, indivisible. . . ."

> All traditional religious paths are destined to lead humanity, individually and collectively, to this fundamental understanding (of all-is-one). However, during the last 200 years, the Western world has gone through a "fall," a forgetfulness, a misunderstanding of separative thought from which we are just now re-emerging.[34]

Apparently God threw a monkey wrench into the Devil's age-old Plan when he helped create the democratic United States. At that time the entire planet was composed of undemocratic kingdoms, only a handful of which allowed the practice of Biblical Christianity. Since its founding, the United States has been at the forefront of the Christian movement. Thousands of American congregations have sprung up to praise the Lord, and they have sent forth missionaries throughout the world—missionaries dedicated to a Church headed by Jesus Christ only.

New Age Love

One of the reasons the New Age attracts so many people today is its emphasis on *love*. A theology of love is a powerful aphrodisiac in a selfish world so universally devoid of true caring.

The Bible has much to say about love—pure altruistic *agape* love. John's three-word expression is superbly beautiful when he says, simply but powerfully: "God *is* love." John 3:16 expresses the ultimate in *agape* love: "For God so loved the world, that he gave his only begotten Son, that whosoever believeth in him should not perish, but have everlasting life." Paul said that the greatest attribute of man is love. Jesus taught that the greatest commandment is love—first for God, and then for our neighbors as ourselves.

Regardless of the fact that the Bible's greatest theme is love, somehow Satan has been able to persuade millions of people that Christianity is *not* the antidote for people in desperate need of the redeeming power of love.

Moreover, Satan is using New Age teachers to promote sick kinds of love. The New Age believer is taught to love everything in the world—every deed and thought, good or evil, every religion, no matter how foul its tenets may seem; all are good, all are one. He is also taught to especially love his guru or teacher.

Even Lucifer, the dragon, is to be loved, for the New Age preaches that we create an evil Lucifer when we fail to shower him with our unconditional love. John Welwood, in a recent issue of *Yoga Journal,* remarked that the failure of man to give unconditional love *creates* "dragons and dreams."[35] As Rainer Rilke puts it, "Perhaps all the dragons in our lives are princesses who are only waiting to see us act, just once, with beauty and courage. Perhaps everything that frightens us is, in its deepest essence, something helpless that wants our love."[36]

New Age masses are easy prey for cunning teachers and gurus who charm with their hypnotic powers, preaching false concepts of love. Baghwan Rajneesh, the guru who led thousands in a strange and frenzied existence in Oregon a few years ago, was one example. Another is an Indian guru known as "His Divinity Swami Prakashanand Saraswati" (shortened to Shree Swamiji), founder of the International Society of Divine Love. This group has regional centers in Philadelphia, New York, Miami, San Diego, and Santa Cruz and Malibu, California, with administrative headquarters in Philadelphia.[37]

Shree Swamiji offers to all his teaching of Divine-Love-Consciousness. He promises you will experience what he calls "Krishn love" (evidently the love of the Hindu god, Krishna) within three days by attending one of his seminars. Advertising himself as a "living saint," Shree Swamiji claims his form of meditation can remake you into a loving divinity: an "all-beautiful supreme personality of the Godhead. . . ."[38]

The New Age believer must also demonstrate his love for Mother Earth. Failure to love and serve divine Mother Earth is a mark of the *materialistic* person of lower consciousness. Christian ministers and laymen beseech lost souls to be healed through the power of Jesus Christ. New Age leaders exhort believers to heal the earth, to meditate for the earth, to protect its ecology and environment, to respect nature as God, to believe in an evolutionary universe.

Vera Alder laments that "The world today is a sick world. It needs healing."[39] Harvard University biologist Edward O. Wilson, spokesperson for the Club of Earth, stresses that mankind is destroying entire species of insect and animal life, an event second only to the threat of nuclear war.[40]

Thinking, caring Christians most certainly are interested in preserving the planet God made for man's physical habitat, but we draw the line at loving a *divine earth*. Jeremy Rifkin, for example, says that restoring the sacred status of nature is "the great mission of the coming age." Like many other New Agers, he envisions a back to nature, whole earth (holistic) campaign to treat the earth as a living organism to be revered and loved.[41]

Robert Mueller remarks, "You know and love your home, don't you. Well, you must also know and love your planetary home." Perhaps, says Mueller, "this will be the new spiritual ideology that will bind the human race. . . . We must reestablish the unity of our planet and of our beings with . . . divinity."[42]

Another type of unacceptable New Age love is that of *self-love*. Dave Hunt calls this *self-idolatry,* and it is much in vogue in the New Age scheme of things.[43] Pop singer Whitney Houston, in her number-one record, best expressed the New Age view when she belted out the unfortunate phrase, ". . . to love yourself . . . is the greatest love of all."

Self-love is so paramount a teaching of the New Age that the first question New Age minister Elizabeth Clare Prophet often asks a person who has come to her for healing is, "Do you forgive and love yourself?" Regarded by the New Age as a form of "positive thinking" that builds a person's self-esteem, this is instead highly damaging to a person's spirit. It leads unnaturally to the concept that man is a perfect being, that he is a god. It is narcissistic and negative.

In contrast, the Bible teaches that the greatest love of all is to love God. Then God will lift up our spirits so we can be filled with love for others . . . and for ourselves.

If the Christian is expected by the New Age to love, adore, and worship his guru, love a divine earth, and—foremost of all—to love himself *above* a personal God in heaven, then Christian love cannot coexist with the "love" espoused by the New Age World Religion.

New Age Peace

The Christian's failure to subscribe to the New Age's perverted doctrines of unity and love makes world peace an impossible attainment, New Age leaders believe. They see a world poised on the brink of global destruction due to the buildup of nuclear armaments and conclude that only a universal turning to cosmic planetary consciousness will save humanity from disaster. In 1975 at the United Nations, a convocation of spiritual leaders of all faiths issued this declaration:

> The crises of our time are challenging the world religions to release a new spiritual force transcending religious, cultural, and national boundaries. . . . We affirm a new spirituality divested of insularity and directed toward planetary consciousness.[44]

The solution proposed by these ecumenical-minded religious leaders is wrong. The Bible directs man to fix his eyes on God, the great I AM. He is not a "new spiritual force," but the one and only God, whom the Jews called the "Ancient of Days." God's Plan provides for true world peace to unfold as Jesus returns to preside over man's activities.

The New Age obviously has a different idea as to how world peace can be achieved. Lola Davis says that "peace can only come when we recognize the divinity in each person."[45] Edgar Cayce agreed, adding that "peace . . . must be within self." Cayce also taught that failure to recognize man's divine nature, along with "false belief" in a Satan, can actually harm the cause of world peace and lead to other tragedies.[46] Cayce advised that

"We should not view the devil as the cause of our troubles and make him the scapegoat." Why? Because, Cayce stressed, believing in Satan "can create fear, confusion, disharmony, murders, and wars—the direct opposites to the fruit of the spirit."[47]

Jesus recognized and cast Satan's demons out of oppressed human beings and commanded the evil one, "Get thee behind me, Satan." In so doing, did our Lord, as Cayce suggested, create fear, confusion, disharmony, murders, and wars? God forbid!

Man's thirst for world peace can only be quenched by Jesus Christ. No Christian can support a world peace founded upon a denial of Jesus' divinity and the affirmation of man's divinity. Nor will the true Christian relinquish his conviction that Satan is alive and is the archenemy of peace on earth and goodwill toward men.

The Dangers of the New Age Racial Doctrine

In the New Age view, their concept of unity, love, and peace marks Christians as members of an inferior race. It doesn't take much foresight to recognize the dangers in a doctrine that artificially creates two races and sets one up as superior. Hitler's poisonous racial theories were not far afield from those of the New Age extremists. The Aryan race was to become the man-god race of a thousand-year Reich founded by Hitler and his monstrous SS troups. It is no coincidence that, like those of New Age leaders today, Hitler's theories were grounded in the occult and in the teachings of Theosophy and Hinduism. Furthermore, like Alice Bailey, Hitler, too, believed in the Masters of Shamballa and in the superiority of a Tibetan occultism.

A world view of a polluted racial doctrine that distinguishes one race as noble and godlike and the other as barely above the level of animals cannot bring to humanity the moral authority needed to solve world problems. Two-race doctrines brought us the World War II holocaust and the recent genocide by the Khmer Rouge in Cambodia. Today it is partly the Hindu racial caste system that leaves India seething with violence as sect wars against sect and Hindus go head-to-head against their Moslem neighbors in Pakistan. In recent years India has seen its prime minister assassinated while the nation's military has armed itself with nuclear bombs to frighten its would-be religious foes abroad.

In his excellent primer on New Age philosophy, David Groothuis concludes that its world view makes the New Age unfit to lead:

> The new cosmic humanism of the New Age threatens to become the consensus. This should cause us to shudder in horror. The pantheistic consensus in India has perpetuated the country's poverty, misery, and hopelessness for thousands of years. Any world view at odds with the truth of God and His creation can only wreak havoc wherever it plants roots. "Unless the Lord builds the house, its builders labor in vain." (Psa. 127:1)[48]

The Fate of the Christian

If Cosmic Consciousness is to be ushered in on a global scale, if unity, peace, and love are to succeed in tearing down the walls that separate the world's religions, the Christian must first be dealt with. He must not be permitted to thwart the reappearance on earth of the New Age "Christ" and his hierarchy. The Plan must be fulfilled. What, then, does the New Age have in store for the Christians?

ELEVEN

The Dark Secret: What Will Happen to the Christians?

And when he had opened the fifth seal, I saw under the altar the souls of them that were slain for the word of God, and for the testimony which they held: and they cried with a loud voice, saying, How long, O Lord, holy and true, dost thou not judge and avenge our blood on them that dwell on the earth? (Rev. 6:9, 10)

Those who survive the shift will be a different type of people from those in physical form today, freed from strife and hatred, longing to be of service to the whole of mankind. . . . The souls who helped to bring on the chaos of the present century will have passed into spirit to rethink their attitudes.

(Ruth Montgomery, *Threshold to Tomorrow*)

Only one thing stands in the way of Satan and his Plan today: the true Church of Jesus Christ. Up to now God has not allowed Satan to move aggressively to destroy the earth's Christian believers. But leaders of the New Age World Religion see their coming triumph over traditional Christianity as inevitable. A new, superhuman race of man-gods led by a New Age "Christ," they believe, will fashion a peace-loving kingdom of heaven on earth and unite all religions and peoples.

When will this new race, supposedly already emerging, complete its evolutionary metamorphosis and usher in a One World Religion and Government? New Agers say this will only come after the earth has been fully cleansed of negative forces—such as traditional Christianity—which today are obstacles to the new world order.

The question is, what will happen to the Christians? What do New Age leaders mean by "cleansed"?

The Dark Secret

The Plan most definitely includes ominous provisions for Christians. Now, I say this with due caution for, even if they exist, it would be difficult—perhaps impossible—for us to gain access to the actual documents that reveal outright a hideous, hidden intent to persecute, purge, or kill all the Bible-believing Christians at some point in the future after the Antichrist ascends to dictatorial power. Furthermore, our human minds cannot read the warped mind of Satan. Still, the leaders of the New Age—Satan's earthly representatives—have given the world unmistakable indications of the horrors that undoubtedly lie in store for Christians.

Jesus gave us these encouraging words, which we should take to heart in these precarious days:

> Fear them not therefore: for there is nothing covered, that shall not be revealed; and hid, that shall not be known. . . . And fear not them which kill the body, but are not able to kill the soul: but rather fear him which is able to destroy both soul and body in hell. (Matt. 10:26, 28)

Whatever fate awaits us, we need not be alarmed. Instead, we should be joyful that every day is another day we can live for the Lord.

Bible prophecy tells us that God's people will be sorely tested in the last days and will suffer for His name's sake. Satan's latter-day World Religion will be "drunken with the blood of the saints, and with the blood of the martyrs of Jesus . . ." (Rev. 17:5, 6; also see Rev. 19:11-21).

Are the Last Days Imminent?

Are we today racing toward Armageddon? Are the days of Christians numbered?

Over the past few years, as I studied the New Age World

Religion and sought to understand fully its aims in fulfillment of Satan's end-time Plan, I began to draw some frightening conclusions. If this is the revived Babylonian religious system of Revelation 17—and much evidence points to this—then Christians will soon be compelled to endure a harrowing period of unparalleled persecution and strife.

My own firm conviction is that the New Age *is* the last age. I encourage you to make up your own mind, just as I have done, and base your decision on the evidence.

Farewell to Jesus: The End of the Piscean Age

The New Age says that mankind is about to enter the Age of Aquarius—the long-awaited era of universal peace, love, and joy. The fading Piscean Age, which brought man such heartache and tragedy, was the Age of Jesus and the Christian Church. Aquarius is to be the Age of Lord Maitreya and the Universal Church.

Matthew Fox, the New Age Catholic priest, writes that God was angry when the Israelites set up their golden calf in the wilderness and worshiped a false god only because they were not in accord with the New Age Moses had ushered in:

> What were they doing? They were whoring after the Past Gods! They were worshipping the religion of the previous age, the Age of the Bull. They refused to face the new spiritual consciousness that Moses ushered in, that of the Age of the Ram.
>
>   So we, too, on the verge of breaking into a new spiritual age, need to beware of the gods of the past. . . .[1]

To what "gods of the past" is Fox referring? To the gods of the Piscean Age—to Jesus and His Father in heaven. So, in effect, using the most sacrilegious and derogatory of terms, Matthew Fox warns us not to go "whoring" after Jesus! Jesus' age is past.

Marilyn Ferguson has said that the dark, violent Piscean Age can be replaced by a millennium of love and light—a time of the "mind's true liberation," but *only* if New Agers first can find the necessary courage to *destroy* the few remaining vestiges of the Old Age. "If we have the courage . . . to expose the incompleteness, the rickety structure," she remarks, "we can dismantle it."[2]

What New Age leaders are telling their disciples is that the Piscean era of Jesus and Biblical Christianity was riddled with error and negativity and has now lost its momentum as the new evolutionary energies generated in support of the new Aquarian Age take hold.

> Negativity from the Piscean Age, and all that is corrupt in the existing system, gained power at a time when evolutionary energies were not strong enough to challenge that momentum. Endeavors which remain plugged into the dying battery of the old world will increasingly have nothing to draw from.[3]

The Cleansing of Mother Earth

The Piscean Age is on its last legs, say the Aquarian prophets, but the old world still has vestiges that need to be removed and cleared away—cleansed and purified—before it is possible for the New Age Kingdom to be built in its place. Those of lower consciousness who refuse to bow down to the gods of the New Age must be purged. Moira Timms explains that the *Planetary Initiation* of humanity and earth by the Masters is not yet possible. "Such attainment," she warns, "appears hampered by certain emotional energy which has not been spiritualized— possibly in the form of war and/or the complete purging of all back karma."[4]

In other words, what Timms calls the "New Order of the Ages" is being delayed until those who oppose its manifestation are disposed of. Thus, Timms and others predict a coming period of bloodshed and suffering, or "purification," leading to initiation and a new order. "The earth will be purified . . . for that she is being prepared," proclaims the Association of Sananda and Sanat Kumara.[5]

One frighteningly lucid statement of the purification and cleansing process was transmitted to David Spangler by a "communication from an angelic source." Spangler says that the "angelic source" advised that the redemption of the earth is near and that:

. . . Earth seeks and is given this redemption in a vast initiatory process occurring throughout the total body and life of the Solar Father. . . .

Now a vast work of purification is upon us to cleanse and beautify Earth as one would beautify a bride before her marriage; in this fashion, we greet Earth in her time of joy and accomplishment. This event seeks its expression through your hearts and minds and your dedication.[6]

The cleansing of earth is necessary, says Barry McWaters, because of the negative, self-centered acts of humanity that have harmed sacred Mother Earth. These acts, he laments, are "a cancerous tissue in the body of GAIA (Mother Earth)."[7] Similarly, G. I. Gurdjieff writes that humanity has made a number of errors that have seriously impeded the evolutionary process toward higher consciousness.[8]

Gurdjieff and McWaters would categorize traditional Christian believers as the most important group—the cancerous tissue—impeding the evolutionary process. McWaters very obviously refers to negative Christians when he complains that much of human consciousness is still caught in a "separative, alienated condition."[9]

Are Christians Fit for the New Age Kingdom?

Perhaps the chief "sin" of the Christian believer is his insistence that every human being who believes not in Jesus is in need of salvation. Therefore, McWaters brands the Christian as unfit for the New Age when he says, "We now enter a period wherein the goal of *individual salvation* is no longer appropriate. Our *guidance* calls for a *collective transformation*."[10]

From whom has McWaters received his "guidance" that "individual salvation is no longer appropriate"? Evidently, his guidance comes from the same source as the guides that inform Ruth Montgomery and the angelic spirits that have revealed The Plan to David Spangler. This source can only be Satan, who is spreading the lie that individual salvation is out and a belief in unity, in the "One," is in.

According to New Age spokesmen, the Christian's failure to trust in the One will be fatal; it will mark him as unfit and unprepared for godhood. Moreover, Timms emphasizes that those "life forms" who are not attuned to the spirit of the New Age *won't survive*. What is needed is to be "of One Mind, to attune to the Master within, the Christ Consciousness. . . ."

> Spiritual preparedness is what is needed for ultimate survival. . . . So let us state it very clearly: those who embody the consciousness of the New Age and are performing greater services to humanity will receive divine protection. . . . The good shepherds know their sheep and the light in the spiritual eye in the forehead identifies those on the journey home. The stormy channel from this age of sorrows to the New Age cannot be navigated by life-forms of unrefined vibration. This is the Law.[11]

"Life-forms of unrefined vibration" to whom Timms refers are quite likely the very same group of people whom the Maharishi Mahesh Yogi, the grand guru of Transcendental Meditation, says are targeted for extinction. In a chilling remark that reminds us of Darwin's brutal evolutionary theory of the survival of the fittest, and echoing Timms's commments about "the Law," the Maharishi stated:

> There has not been and there will not be a place for the unfit. The fit will lead, and if the unfit are not coming along there is no place for them. . . .
> In the Age of Enlightenment there is no place for ignorant people.
> Nature will not allow ignorance to prevail. It just can't. Nonexistence of the unfit has been the law of nature.[12]

Apparently, Christians, "life-forms of unrefined vibration," do not deserve to even exist!

The Maharishi's threat that the unfit must pass into "nonexistence" and Timms's statement that it may take "war and purging" to cleanse, purify, and ready the earth for the New Age Kingdom are paralleled by the writings and speeches of many other New Age authorities. Ruth Montgomery's "guides" have predicted a World War III and a catastrophic shift of the earth's axis, causing floods and other natural disasters.[13]

However, Montgomery's demon "guides" say that all the chaotic events they predict will be merely "a cleansing process for Mother Earth."[14] Evidently, Biblical Christians won't survive this cleansing process. Survivors, the guides say, will be attuned to the one world philosophy of the New Age, and the guides predict that following the cleansing and purifying process, "The new race will engage in peaceful pursuits and the uplifting of spirits. Their minds will be open to one world so that they will easily communicate with those in spirit . . . beyond the grave."[15]

Christians Will Pass into Spirit

So the man or woman of New Age consciousness will inherit the earth. Christians and other less-enlightened souls will not be able to inherit the cleansed earth because of negative attitudes.

> Those who survive the shift will be a different type of people from those in physical form today, freed from strife and hatred, longing to be of service to the whole of mankind. . . . The souls who helped to bring on the chaos of the present century *will have passed into spirit to rethink their attitudes* . . .[16]

Will the cleansing process really doom people to death so they can "rethink their attitudes"? Interviewed by *Magical Blend* magazine in 1986, Montgomery clarified this key point:

> Millions will survive and millions won't. Those that won't will go into the spirit state, because there truly is no death.[17]

"There truly is no death"? The Bible assures us that there is, in fact, a death that eventually awaits those who reject God's plan of salvation: "The wages of sin is death" (Romans 6:23). What Montgomery means is that after millions of persons unfit to live in the New Age *die physically,* they will go on in spirit where they can be reeducated and rehabilitated. Simply stated, after they die physically and pass into spirit, they'll be given a chance to change their attitude. Then and only then will they become eligible to return.

Where will Christians and other unfit persons of lower consciousness go to rethink their attitudes? David Spangler suggests that individuals who do not wish to "reach out for the rock of the new world" will be sent to places called "the inner worlds." In these inner worlds, "they can be contained and ministered to until such time as they can be released safely into physical embodiment again."[18]

The horror of what Montgomery, Spangler, and others are proposing comes fully to light when we read another of Spangler's suggestions. He cynically notes that the many people who are to be physically terminated and sent in spirit to an "inner world" remind him of the fate that the God of the Bible has assigned to the Devil:

> There is a suggestion of this in the Bible when it speaks of Satan and his minions . . . being bound for a thousand years and then being released again. Thus these ones could be withdrawn into an inner realm that would be their home while the consciousness attuned to the New Age was active in building the new world physically and psychically.[19]

In an astonishing reversal of roles, Spangler blasphemously assigns these future Christian martyrs to the same fate that the Bible assigns Satan, his demons, and his unsaved human followers. The Christian and others deemed unfit for the New Age are to be bound in the pit—the "inner realm—for a thousand years while above, Satan and his followers desecrate the earth by building their corrupt kingdom.

Is the Christian the Antichrist?

Spangler's proposing that Christians be banished to the hell reserved by God for Satan and his minions is typical of efforts by other New Agers to twist the Scriptures. It gives Satan great pleasure to take God's Word and attempt to turn it inside out. To attack the Christian believer by mocking the Bible is a common device of New Age leaders.

The abuse of Scripture takes on especially dark overtones when New Age leaders even seek to label Christians and others of "lower race consciousness" as the Biblically prophesied Beast or Antichrist. It is also common for the New Age to threaten that the plagues and tribulations prophesied in the Bible will be visited on Christians as retribution for their stubborn failure to adopt New Age attitudes.

An example of this is found in the book *Prophecies and Predictions: Everyone's Guide to the Coming Changes,* in which author Moira Timms, using the concepts of evolution and Hinduism, solemnly warns that:

> . . . the plagues of Revelation are special packages of karma
> visited upon the obstinate that they might awaken to their
> wrong attitudes . . . animals that don't adapt become extinct.
> Remember? Survival today means understanding and
> responding to change within the context of the internal
> "revolution."[20]

Timms also brings the message heard from so many elitists in the New Age hierarchy that in the New Age Kingdom on earth, those with obstinate attitudes "will graduate on to planes of existence more suited to (their) unfoldment."[21] This is a thinly veiled commitment to wipe off the face of the earth those who worship God and His Son only and who deny the New Age man-god doctrine.

Another example of the New Age plan to rid the earth of Christians is found in the attempt of John Randolph Price to define the Antichrist as:

> Any individual or group who denies the divinity of man . . .
> i.e., to be in opposition to "Christ in you"—the indwelling
> Christ or Higher Self of each individual. . . .[22]

The Bible has a definition for the Antichrist far different than that of the New Age. It's found in 1 John 4, verses 2 and 3:

> Hereby know ye the Spirit of God: Every spirit that
> confesseth that Jesus Christ is come in the flesh is of God:
> and every spirit that confesseth not that Jesus Christ is
> come in the flesh is not of God: and this is that spirit of
> Antichrist. . . .

Not only is the person who does not confess Jesus as Lord of the spirit of *Antichrist,* but he is also a *"deceiver"* (see 2 John 7). Man is no god, though Price and other deceivers in the New Age make seductive claims to the contrary. We are told by James to "humble yourselves in the sight of the Lord, and he shall lift you up" (Jas. 4:10). Peter testified that the saved person should have "a meek and quiet spirit" (1 Pet. 3:4).

Price's venomous attitude toward Christians was made crystal-clear in his book, *The Planetary Commission,* in which he vented his wrath at those who opposed the New Age Movement and its belief in the divinity of man. Price snapped, "There are some groups who continue to cling to the absurd idea that man is a miserable sinner and worm of the dust."[23]

Two other New Age leaders who attempt to link Christians with the Antichrist are LaVedi Lafferty and Bud Hollowell, founders of the Collegians International Church. They would have us believe that the plagues mentioned in the Book of Revelation refer to diseases and pollution caused by the spiritually inferior who desire "materialism." (The materialistic person, in the New Age view, does not profess unity of all religions and the sanctity of Mother Earth.) They define the Antichrist as all those individuals who possess a lower state of consciousness. What's more, they assert that:

> The Battle of Armageddon is not a war fought with weapons, it is a battle of consciousness—Christ (cosmic) consciousness against the Antichrist (Earth/material) illusions.[24]

According to Lafferty and Hollowell, the conflict between the New Age throng of believers and their lower consciousness opposition will be victoriously waged and won by the New Age. The result will be a "Yogic Kingdom of Heaven on earth."[25]

Woe to those who oppose the New Agers: ". . . if earth is unsuitable for them, they will go on to other worlds. The Yogic Kingdom will be coming to pass for this planet."[26]

So those unfit for the "Yogic Kingdom" will go on to "other worlds." Alice Bailey's demon master, Djwhal Khul, is quoted as saying that two-thirds of humanity will advance into the New Age Kingdom. The other one-third "will be held over for later unfoldment."[27] This one-third of humanity obviously includes Bible-believing Christians, as well as Jews who refuse to deny a personal Jehovah. They are "unsuitable."

What the New Age Bible Commentary Has to Say

Perhaps the worst example of Scripture twisting is a series of publications by the New Age Bible and Philosophy Center in Santa Monica, California. This group has published six volumes of commentaries purporting to interpret the Scriptures for the New Age. These books, titled *New Age Bible Interpretation*,[28] constitute an all-out assault on the Bible, mangling every passage to conform to the lies of Satan.

In these perverse New Age Bible commentaries, the reader is led to believe that Satan is one of God's messenger angels and that all the "root races" except the New Age super-race comprise "the Antichrist." Heaven is defined as the "realm of the gods" (plural). The "dragon" is said to be men whose minds function on lower planes of consciousness. The Beast of Revelation is not a single being or church, but people who embody all the evil of past incarnations and life cycles. The Beast's number, 666, is the number of inferior-consciousness man. The mark of the Beast is placed on the forehead and right hands of the masses who are "negative" in their thinking. Mystery Babylon is said to be the regeneration of man's soul as he enters the joyous and spiritually advanced New Age. The Apostle John is described as an "initiate" into the Mysteries who recognized the fruits of practicing "white magic."[29]

These Devil-inspired Bible commentaries are widely read and studied by those active in the fast-growing New Age World Religion. But the doctrines they express are not new. They are based on the occult and Mystery writings of the Masons, Rosicrucians, Gnostics, and other anti-Christian sects and groups. First copyrighted in 1935, these hardcover publications have been revised several times since, most recently in 1984. Proclaiming her works to be "an exposition of the inner significance of the Holy Scriptures in the light of the Ancient Wisdom," the writer, Corinne Heline, states in the Preface:

The reception given these interpretations has been of such encouragement as to make this work a most joyous labor of love. They are unmistakably meeting a deep spiritual hunger of countless souls. It is this need that has called them into being. . . . So it is the hope and prayer of this writer that these interpretations will prove helpful in meeting the present pressing need to restore the Bible to its rightful place. . . .[30]

Corinne and Theodore Heline are also authors of many other New Age books, including those with such revealing titles as *America's Destiny, Mystery of the Christos, Mythology and the Bible, Occult Anatomy and the Bible,* and *Supreme Initiations of the Blessed Virgin.* But these, sick as they are, pale in comparison to Heline's Bible commentaries. I've culled out several meaningful passages to give readers an idea of their scope and intent. My own comments follow the quote from *New Age Bible Interpretation.*

Revelation 6:1-8 (John sees the vision of the four horsemen of the Apocalypse after one of four angelic "beasts" invites him to "come and see"):

One of the four beasts, which says "come and see" is Aquarius, Lord of Air, summoning the Initiate to look upon the type of new race men who will qualify to meet Christ in the air when he comes again.[31]

Corinne Heline is saying in the above passage that an entity named "Aquarius, Lord of Air" is the heavenly angel who summons John to view the four horsemen. This Aquarius is no angel, for we don't have to guess who the real "Aquarius, Lord of Air" is. In Ephesians 2:2 Satan is identified as "the prince of the power of the air." Moreover, the name Aquarius is not Biblical, but refers to the astrological sign of the New Age: the Age of Aquarius.

Also, John is falsely described by Heline as an "Initiate" into the New Age Mysteries. John was an apostle, a prophet, a Christian, but he most certainly was not a Mysteries initiate.

Finally, Heline's reference to "new race men" clearly demonstrates the New Age obsession with racial doctrine and their belief in the evolution of man to god status.

Revelation 13:11-18 (the Beast with the number 666):

The collective evil of mankind has built a great form of evil, the Antichrist, described in the fifth vision of John as the beast with seven heads and ten horns. This is the concentrated evil of all the great Root Races.[32]

Here the author of *New Age Bible Interpretation* attempts to get around the wording of Revelation 13:18 which unequivocally states that the Beast is a man and *his* number is 666. Portraying the Beast as a collective group which embodies the "concentrated evil of all the great Root Races" is simply a tactic to characterize all those who are considered spiritual inferiors (i.e., Christians, Jews, and other New Age unbelievers) as the Antichrist.

Mind was a gift of the gods to man and was to be used as a rainbow bridge whereby he might pass from earth and heaven.[33]

This error by Heline reflects the common Hindu and New Age philosophy that "the gods," plural, gave man the "gift" of mind. It also refers to the evolution of man's mind as the key to his becoming a god and entering the New Age Kingdom. The rainbow is a popular New Age symbol which signifies initiation into godhood.

Revelation 15:3-8 (the seven angels with seven plagues and the seven golden vials full of the wrath of God):

Taurus, Lord of Earth and one of the recording Angels, metes out to man just retribution for deeds done while upon earth. The seven last plagues . . . refer . . . to the suffering that comes upon man as the result of following material law. . . . He has made his birthright disease, sorrow, poverty and death instead of health, happiness, plenty and immortality. These latter will be the heritage of the New Age race.[34]

Heline's comments here are bone-chilling, because "Taurus" is the astrological Taurus the Bull. Nimrod, the King of Babylon, was idolized as a bull. The massive Gate of Ishtar, through which visitors entered the City of Babylon, was decorated with murals of bulls and dragons. The Babylonians were also the inventors of the psuedo-science of astrology and its zodiac signs, such as Taurus and Aquarius.

When Heline refers to "material law" and to the "race," she is alluding to the New Age doctrine that the superior race of New Age man-gods will be rewarded, while men of the lower consciousness race (material consciousness) will undergo punishment and retribution in the coming Tribulation period.

Revelation 16:12-14 (the great River Euphrates was dried up that the kings of the East might come across. Three unclean demon spirits, like frogs, beckon the kings of the world, gathering them to the Battle of Armageddon):

As man learns to "lift" himself into a gradually ascending state of consciousness . . . the dragon and the beast will cease to exist. All evil is transitory; it is man's creation and he himself must dissolve and transmute it. . . .

A . . . cleansing will take place when the Christ returns . . . mankind may assist in this work and thus prepare the way for the "Kings of the East."[35]

Heline tells us that with the dawning of the New Age, an evil Satan, who does not really exist at all, will vanish from man's memory. The Beast—Christians unfit for the New Age—will also cease to exist. It (they) will be wiped off the earth by the New Age "Christ." Ominously, she states that this cleansing will prepare the way for the kings of the East, which she views as a positive event. The Bible prophesies that these literal kings, traveling toward Armageddon with a vast army of two hundred million, will slay one-third of the earth's inhabitants.

Revelation 21:10-27 (describes the New Jerusalem descending out of heaven and describes its inhabitants as those whose names are written in the Lamb's Book of Life):

The seventh vision of John pictures the pioneers of the New Age whose names are written in the Lamb's Book of Life.[36]

Those names written in the Lamb's Book of Life are not, as Heline states, the names of "New Age pioneers," but those who believe on the Lord Jesus, repent of their sins, and are saved by His blood.

Revelation 22:1-5 (out of the throne of God and of the Lamb proceeded a pure river of the water of life and also the tree of life, and the Lord God shall give the light):

Through the powers of the Christ . . . all nations will be welded into one vast fellowship. . . .
    The brand upon the head of Cain was *separativeness*. . . .[37]

These comments reflect the New Age Plan to unite all the world's religions and governments into one. Christians, because they are separative and against religious unity, are symbolically compared with Cain, a murderer.

Special Code Language of the Mind Destroyers

As we've seen, the New Age has made an art of twisting Scripture. Its leaders have its own unique meanings for such terms as *purification* and *cleansing* and for such phrases as *washing away karmic debts* and *pass into spirit*. Satan, the real master of the New Age, delights in mysterious code words and phrases because they allow his agents, when questioned, to escape public censure by hiding behind a verbal mirage. History has given us many examples of this. Hitler had his "final solution to the Jewish problem." Modern-day killers use such intentionally confusing terms as "neutralize," "waste," and "terminate with extreme prejudice" to indicate a person is to be murdered.

I believe that the New Age is shrewd to the point of being diabolical in using dark code words to mask its true intentions. I am reminded of the outrage after the Nazis were defeated and the atrocities of the concentration camps became public knowledge. The meaning of terms that Hitler had expressed in his book *Mein Kampf* was suddenly understood.

In April 1945, as British troops liberated Begen-Belsen Concentration Camp in Germany, they were awe-struck at what they saw. The foul stench of rotting and burned corpses filled the air, and dead bodies were stacked like cordwood. Emaciated, sore-infested inmates looked up at them with hollow cheeks. A British news correspondent accompanying the liberators was moved to report: "It is my duty to describe something that is beyond the imagination of mankind."

Satan's Hollow Victory

Jesus told His disciples that they could expect to be called devils: "The disciple is not above his master, nor the servant above his lord. . . . If they have called the master of the house Beelzebub, how much more shall they call them of his household?" (Matt. 10:24, 25).

Though we as Christians may be reviled by the New Age, our response must be love and forgiveness. We should, of course, hate the dark spirit of Satan that is causing some in the New Age to label Christians as the Beast and the Antichrist. And we must persevere in contending for the faith. As we'll see in the following chapter, Satan has the power to temporarily cause suffering and hardship for Christian believers. The Plan tells us he'll use that power to wrest control. But his victory will prove hollow and fleeting, for just beyond the veil of time, millions of angels are ready to shout and proclaim the coming of the Lord.

TWELVE

New Age Zeal . . .
New Age Aggression

*. . . they behaved, they acted as gods. We victims could
not look into the faces of gods, the faces of the killers. I
could only remember the eyes of the victims.*
(Elie Wiesel, Noble Peace Prize recipient,
Nazi concentration camp survivor)

*The Shamballa force is destructive and ejective . . .
inspiring new understanding of The Plan. . . . It is this
force . . . which will bring about that tremendous crisis,
the initiation of the race into the mysteries of the ages.*
(Alice Bailey, address at the Arcane School Conference,
Geneva, Switzerland)

Man's evolution to god status and the realization of Cosmic Consciousness are the
primary goals of the New Age believer.
The New Agers are fanatical in their dream of the world making
the leap to evolutionary consciousness. They strive for a One
World Religion and for a cultural revolution, desperate in their
mistaken notion that unless mankind achieves this evolutionary
leap, the world is doomed to suffer hunger, war, ecological
disasters, and unequaled calamity. Higher consciousness, they
contend, is the only path to salvation. They believe that only its
attainment transforms man into gods who desire unity, world
peace, brotherhood, and sharing of resources. Only when men
are gods will they protect Mother Earth and recognize her
sacred nature.

The New Age believer is convinced that Christians, Jews,
and others who believe in a personal God *cannot* inherit the
coming millennia of peace and prosperity. By refusing to accept

their own divinity, Christians and Jews are destined to remain at a lower level of consciousness. An inferior species, they are a threat to the universal blessings of peace, happiness, and love that will arrive once the New Age dawns.

Once New Agers ascend to world power, they will undoubtedly consent to the plans of the Antichrist to rid the world of the inferior "rabble" that prevents universal Cosmic Consciousness. Inspired by this supernatural Antichrist and armed with high-tech tools of terror, the New Age "Gestapo" would undoubtedly be unleashed to purge the world of Christians and other "sinners" who threaten peace and security and prevent human harmony. This was the same excuse the Roman Emperor Nero gave for persecuting early Christians, Mao offered for his murdering of millions of Chinese "capitalists," and Hitler gave for his "cleansing" of Germany by "solving the Jewish problem."

I have had occasion to discuss theological and world issues with fanatical New Age believers. On the surface, many are calm, even loving. But I have seen their mood become vicious and angry when the names of fundamentalist Christian leaders arose. Billy Graham, Jimmy Swaggart, Hal Lindsey, Jerry Falwell, and other evangelical ministers and laymen are scoffed at. Christians who profess that Jesus is *the* Way are termed "ignorant."

To hard-core New Agers, *anyone* who believes the Holy Bible inerrant is viewed as a mortal enemy. An exclusive belief in Jesus Christ as Lord and Savior is, by New Age standards, a mark of spiritual immaturity.

You Could Be a God If Only Those Horrible Christians . . .

New Age leaders tell the average New Age believer that it is only the negativity of devout Christians and Jews that prevents the world from being magically transformed into the New Age Kingdom. The New Age believer is told, "You could be a god in the next instant if only those horrible Christians weren't around with their poisonous attitudes."

It's easy to develop a sense of frustration and anger toward someone who's holding you back from becoming a god! Jack Underhill recently wrote that if all humanity would come together and accept the New Age, there would be *nothing* people couldn't do:

They can turn off the sun and turn it back on. They can freeze oceans into ice, turn the air into gold, talk as one with no movement or sound. They can fly without wings and love without pain, cure with no more than a thought or a smile. They can make the earth go backwards or bounce up and down, crack it in half or shift it around. . . . There is nothing they cannot do.[1]

Yes, Underhill stated, you can do all this. But only if everyone on earth will "come together as one." In sum, you can only become a god and do miraculous, godlike things *if* the world moves into the energies to be available in the New Age.

Is it possible New Age leaders will realize, before it is too late, that Christians love the New Agers and that we want only good for them? Can they be made to understand that man cannot transform himself into divine status? We must remember that Satan's demons have been invited into the minds of millions of New Age believers, and at a certain point their mind is no longer their own.

The Love/Hate Duality of the New Age

Those in the New Age often seem to possess dual personalities—almost a love/hate complex. For some, their emotions may initially be sympathetic and kind, but from within Satan reproves and disciplines his own. For others, the external mask of love is only a veneer which, when removed, reveals the depth of hatred that lies within.

Love/hate is common to believers in the Hindu and Buddhist faiths which undergird the New Age World Religion. In a letter from Brooklyn, New York's Lisa Moore, published in a recent *Yoga Journal,* Lisa wrote that her original notion, when beginning her life in Zen Buddhism, was that the practice of the religion brought the "cultivation of a sweet gentle personality." But, she added, "My experience in Zen practice has been the discovery of my strength, creativity, sexuality. . . . My actual practice, actual experience has been a tremendous upsurge of bottled, stored energy, including *deep rage.*"[2]

Moore's "bottled energy" and "deep rage" is an inevitable

by-product of devotion to self and to a demonic religion. Her remarks are similar to those of Miriam Starhawk, the high priestess of The Church of Wicca (Witchcraft), who has found a home in New Age circles. Starhawk has told New Agers: "We become whole through knowing our strength and creativity, our aggression, our sexuality, by affirming the self, not by denying it."[3]

Another real-life example of the New Age's seething spirit of agression is found in Kurt Koch's book *Occult ABC,* in which the Church of Scientology, a New Age cult, is briefly discussed. Koch tells of a letter received by a person who had been "treated" by a Scientologist in New York and was billed for $350. When the young man refused to pay because the treatment had been unsuccessful, he received a frightening letter from a Reverend S. Andrew Bagley of The Founding Church of Scientology which read in part:

> If you want to start a donnybrook, buddy, wail away. To use the argot of the streets, I'll just start my people to work on you, and then before long you will be broke and out of a job and broken in health. Then I can have my nasty little chuckle about you. . . .
>
> You won't take long to finish off. I would estimate three weeks. Remember: I am not a mealy-mouthed Psalm-canting preacher. I am a minister of the Church of Scientology! I am able to heal the sick and I do. But I have other abilities, which include a knowledge of men's minds, that I will use to crush you to your knees.[4]

The Extremist New Age Doctrine

Are these isolated examples? Certainly they appear extreme. But the New Age ideology lends itself to extremes, causing a person to first wax sweet, then vengeful when the demons stir up the aggressive traits latent in every man who does not have Christ within.

The extreme nature of New Age doctrine promotes aggression, hatred, violence, chaos. The demon spirit who used David Spangler as his medium saw no room for compromise with those who oppose the New Age World Order:

You cannot heal a corpse, nor do we have any wish for you to do so. The old must pass away. . . . It . . . must now make way for a new, more expanded and more fruitful manifestion.[5]

Alice Bailey, in an address at the Arcane School Conference in Geneva, Switzerland, over a decade ago suggested that the "Shamballa force"—the force from the invisible dimensions led by the Lord Maitreya—will be "destructive." It will also, she said, eject unbelievers from the earth:

The decision to release the Shamballa force during this century into direct contact with the human kingdom is one of the final and most compelling acts of preparation for the New Age.
    The Shamballa force is destructive and ejective . . . inspiring new understanding of The Plan. . . .
    It is this force . . . which will bring about that tremendous crisis, the initiation of the race into the mysteries of the ages.[6]

Bailey's comment that this destructive force would precipitate a crisis and lead to the initiation of the race into the "mysteries of the ages" is foreboding. All who refuse the Luciferic Initiation into the New Age will be adjudged to be unfit for the New Age. This will ensure a crisis period as the earth is cleansed and purified.

This cleansing could be reminiscent of the fate that befell those in Babylon who refused to partake of the Mysteries or, worse yet, *revealed* the Mysteries *after* initiation. The Mother Goddess of Babylon was a deity both of love and revenge. As Hislop's research demonstrated:

The goddess who was revealed to the initiated in the Mysteries, in the most alluring manner, was also known to be most unmerciful and unrelenting in taking vengeance upon those who revealed these Mysteries; for every such one who was discovered was unsparingly put to death.[7]

The New Age World Religion has its roots in the Babylonian Mystery Religion in which, through initiation, the worthy individual could join a race of man-gods. This is the same doctrine the New Age is promoting today, a doctrine it wishes to enthrone as the cornerstone of its world religion.

It is a doctrine in keeping with the love/hate duality of the New Age. This same doctrine is found in the Hindu religion, many concepts of which have been adopted for the New Age. Referring to the Hindu doctrine of karma and reincarnation, New Age leaders say that if the coming period of world crisis and purification results in suffering and death for unbelievers, so be it—their karma is being worked out. In other words, Christians, Jews, and other unbelievers *deserve exactly what they're getting.* Indeed, it is suggested that pain and suffering are unavoidable. They are part of universal law and serve as preparation for eventual godhood.

Christians and Jews must pay back the karmic debt they have incurred because of unbelief in world religious unity. Only then will they be fit for reincarnation into the New Age Kingdom.

In the *Bhagavad Gita,* we find all the justification the Antichrist would need to order Christian and other spiritual rebels put to death. In these heathen Hindu scriptures so revered by the New Age, the devout are taught that both life and death are illusions (maya), that the Mother Goddess's karmic wheel catches all men up into a revolving-door cycle of reincarnations. The New Age believer rejects the Christian doctrine of judgment as "negative-thinking," maintaining that man will return again and again in an endless stream of life and death.

So, killing a person can be a righteous act to help the victim work out his karma. He can thus be reborn in a later reincarnation as a happier individual.

Will the Murder of Christians Be an Act of Love?

The Antichrist will convince the world they are doing the Christian—that pitiful unspiritual, unenlightened member of a racially inferior species—a favor by sending him on to another dimension or to the next incarnation where he will be more happy. The wholesale massacre of Christians may well be justified as a humanitarian and creative act of love.

LaVedi Lafferty and Bud Hollowell tell their followers, "death is not something to fear, but only a new beginning."[8] They further state that during the Piscean Age, now passing, many people accumulated large amounts of karmic debt, the result of which is persecution, suffering, and death, which washes away karmic debt and prepares man for advancement:

> Suffering, by counter-balancing karma . . . can serve greater purposes than are apparent. We should never, from our human viewpoint, *assume* that any situation or circumstance is BAD, just because we do not understand why it must be experienced.[9]

Rivaling these words of New Age "wisdom" are the teachings of Sue Sikking, a California-based New Age minister. In *Seed for a New Age* she explains:

> So many signs for the times are called evil but they are man learning the lesson of his God-Self. This is the preparation for the advancement of mankind.[10]

This is the same horrendous idea that Christian Scientists have swallowed. Mary Baker Eddy, its founder, said: "No final judgment awaits mortals. Man is incapable of sin, sickness, death."[11]

The confused New Ager has come to believe the Satanic lie that suffering *is by choice of the victim,* that the unyielding law of karma demands suffering. James Sire, a Christian editor, explains:

> Karma is the Eastern version of what you sow you reap. But karma implies strict necessity. If you have "sinned," there is no God to cancel the debt and forgive. The sin must be worked out and will be worked out. . . . Karma demands that every soul suffer for its past "sins," so there is no value in alleviating suffering.[12]

As Sire points out, to the believer in karma and reincarnation, all suffering is "illusion" anyway. The only reality is ultimate reality, Brahaman (oneness), which is beyond good and evil.

In the New Age scheme of things, self is king, and since self is king, lord, god, and judge, why worry about ethics? If the self is satisfied, then all is right and nothing is wrong. This error in thinking permits and self-justifies the grossest cruelty. Alexander Pope expressed the bizarre nature of this type of thinking when he poetically wrote:

> All nature is but art, unknown to thee;
> All chance, direction which thou canst not see;
> All discord, harmony not understood;
> All partial evil, universal good;
> And, spite of pride, in erring reason's spite,
> One truth is clear, *Whatever is, is right.*[13]

Man is the only judge. Even if murder, rape, and other crimes could be measured on some type of moral scale and found to be "bad" or "evil," these events are necessary if karma is to be worked out: It's all just part of the theater of life:

> Who is at fault? Who is the criminal? Who really dies? Nobody! It has all been produced and staged in the physical theater for the growth of our souls.[14]

In some kind of "Twilight Zone" way of reasoning, the New Age is suggesting that we are all actors in a never-ending stage production. David Spangler calls life the "Cosmic Drama." Thus suffering and death are of little consequence. It's all just part of a Cosmic Drama.

This truly monstrous doctrine was expressed by Shirley Maclaine in her best-selling books about reincarnation and the channeling of spirits. Her television miniseries, *Out on a Limb*, includes several examples of the dangers of this un-Biblical doctrine. In one segment of the miniseries, while driving over the mountains in Peru during a visit to an ancient Inca religious site, Shirley Maclaine and friend David see the wreckage of buses that had careened off the treacherous, narrow road and had crashed to the rocks far below, killing all passengers. Emotion-less, David tells Shirley that there was a good reason why every one of those people were on those buses. "There's no real death anyway, so there are no victims."

In *Toward a New Brain,* authors Stuart Litvak and A. Wayne Senzee discuss the New Age confusion of love and hate, good and evil. They explain that its advocates sincerely believe that:

> . . . for humankind the material world is only a severe workshop essential to the forging and refining of the spirit.
>   Therefore, they suggest that even "good" and "evil" are relative. Good is whatever accelerates evolutionary consciousness, evil whatever decelerates it.[15]

The Rapture and Persecution by Antichrist

If the material world is only a "severe workshop essential to the forging and refining of the spirit," and good and evil are relative, then the New Age need feel no guilt in removing the major impediment to the achievement of world evolutionary conscious-ness: Bible-believing Christians. We are the only obstacle to the total control and domination of humanity by Satan. Still, the Devil cannot touch a hair on our heads unless God allows it.

Many, many Christian writers, pastors, and theologians be-lieve that just before the Great Tribulation, as Satan's Antichrist is preparing to attack Christians with an unparalleled wave of persecution and terror, all Christians will be lifted up—rap-tured—by Jesus. The Bible says Jesus will descend from the clouds with a shout. In the twinkling of an eye, the living who are in Christ Jesus will rise, meeting the dead in Christ in the air (see 1 Cor. 15:50-52; 1 Thes. 4:13-18; Matt. 24:37-41).

It is evident that the Satanic impulse surging through New Age believers and the transmissions being received from the Masters and the spirit guides (demons) are preparing the carnal world for the momentous staggering events to come. These events include the disappearance of Christians, the mass kidnap-ping and elimination of those who turn to God after the Rapture takes place, and the coming persecution of all who will not bow down and worship the Antichrist, who refuse his mark and who refuse initiation into the mysteries of the New Age World Reli-gion.

The Plan: Ascension of the New Age Root Race

What New Age evangelists are teaching their converts is that their "God" (the demon hierarchy) has a Plan. This Plan will result in the ascension to power of the superior root race composed of New Agers with higher, Cosmic (Christ- or God-) Consciousness. Men will at that point become gods, and the Antichrist, the Great Teacher, will inaugurate his wondrous reign of planetary unity, peace, and love.

This poisonous racial doctrine was the very same occult theology that captivated Hitler. The Führer supposed that he was to be the New Age Christ and that his Reich would last for a thousand years. The Aryan race, the highest expresson of man's evolutionary progress, would, Hitler believed, inaugurate the world into its new higher state of consciousness.

Compare Hitler's sick reasoning and his Aryan supremacy theory with that of the current New Age, as explained in explicit detail in the *New Age Bible Interpretation:*

> Not every pupil makes equal use of his ability nor does he take full advantage of his opportunities. . . . Consequently, there develops marked differences in progress. . . . The Anthropoids are failures of the human race. They failed to develop mind and are, therefore, man-like in form only. They are animal-like in consciousness, standing behind even the most advanced members of their kingdom. . . .
>
> Man will be emancipated from Race Spirit direction when he has evolved the divine powers within himself to the point where he becomes master of his own course.
>
> Seven Root Races succeed one another in the racial evolution on a planet during a world Period. . . .
>
> Aryan (is) the term applied to the Fifth root race.[16]

The New Age is teaching a doctrine of seven root races. The Aryan—Hitler's chosen race—was the fifth. The highest race order that may currently be attained by human beings on earth appears to be the sixth; but the New Age "Christ," the Lord Maitreya, is said to be a member of the exalted seventh root race. He is a spiritized being full of light who can manifest in the flesh at will. All New Agers strive to achieve this same exalted status:

> Seven is the number of perfection and completion. . . .
> Civilization is now at the sixth state of evolution, the
> polarization point between matter and spirit, light and
> darkness. The seventh stage of evolution will burgeon when
> the necessary period of purification has passed. . . .[17]

New Age doctrine teaches that as soon as enough men on earth awaken to the god within—to their Higher, Divine Self— and after the inferior root race has been eradicated from the earth, the superior root race will vault into a fourth dimension. This new dimension—the New Age Kingdom—is alleged to be the New Jerusalem:

> The New Jerusalem, the new heaven and new Earth, are
> invisibly present. They await us as the New Reality, a world
> in which we are about to be reborn when we have created
> our new bodies of light.[18]

The lower consciousness root race, including the obstinate Christian believers, is to be banished to another world, also described as another dimension and as the inner realm. Bluntly stated, *Christians will die physically and pass into spirit as the two worlds move apart and become separate.* David Spangler's demon spirit mockingly lifted phrases from the Bible and pretended to be God when he explained it this way:

> My power has been liberated and all now move swiftly
> toward their appointed destinies as their consciousnesses have
> chosen. Your world shall become—and swiftly it shall
> become—two worlds. You will call one light and one dark.
> . . . Their world (of darkness) is under the law and shall
> disappear.
>   Increasingly, the worlds will move apart in consciousness
> until they are absolutely separate and perceive each other no
> more. For it is written that two are at work in the vineyards;
> one shall be taken and the other remain. I shall snatch you
> up to me. This I have promised and this I am doing. . . .[19]

Satan's demons are passing the word: The Plan calls for Christians and others of lower race consciousness to vanish so the New Age Kingdom can be revealed. The sudden disappearance of millions of Christians will be seen as a confirmation of New Age doctrine. Global Cosmic Consciousness will have been realized. The Antichrist will declare an international holiday. Man will finally have achieved his ultimate potential. Collectively, he is God.

The Aftermath: No Room for Pity and Remorse

However, some will miss their brother, sister, husband, wife, or other loved ones. In their grief, they will turn to the ministers of the New Age gospel for answers, and they will get soothing reassurances: "All is well. The Plan is being worked. No ultimate harm has befallen your lost loved ones. Live for today, as gods."

The doubters will also be reminded of the prophetic words of Spangler's demon guide, "Limitless Love and Truth":

> In revealing a New Age . . . I can be a sword that divides and separates. You must be prepared to accept this and not resist it if such separation occurs.[20]

Resistance will be a sign that the individual has regressed to a lower Race Mind. Those who continue to resist, as well as those who turn to Jesus Christ for salvation, will be dealt with harshly by the Antichrist and his police state.

As the purges are carried out, the masses will be told it is the destiny of those being arrested to be dispatched in spirit to another world *for their own good*. Reference will be made to the laws of karma and reincarnation, which instruct the initiate that man's spirit is in bondage until he learns sufficient wisdom to become a man-god. Passage from this world into the next is therefore an event to be welcomed.

One can almost imagine the voice of the Antichrist speaking to the people of earth via satellite on television and radio. In a mesmerizing, hypnotic voice, he tells his listeners that they can sing praises that their departing loved ones will now learn the meaning of peace and unity in the invisible realm they are entering.

As his audience sinks into a relaxed trance-state, the Antichrist will reassure them that any suffering that is being experienced is for the glorification of man, that it has been foreordained that suffering and separation would occur. They must not be fearful and anxious over the loss of the old world, nor pity those who have been and are being targeted for purification and removal. Instead, his listeners throughout the world are to be One, to attune to the divine concepts of peace, love, and truth. They must see all that is occurring as natural and perfect, as a triumph of Light.

Incredibly, this greatest of man's speeches has *already been prepared and rehearsed in advance.* Listen to what "Limitless Love and Truth" has already told the New Age world as recorded in David Spangler's New Age classic, *Revelation: The Birth of a New Age:*

Release them to me, no matter where their destiny leads them . . . all responses must flow from the higher level of Love, Light, of Truth, of Joy, and of Wisdom.

Whether the old is what you see on your television, whether it is within your family or within the suffering of mankind, you must see it impartially. You must see it in its perfect state. You must not allow your personality to interfere in fear, in anxiety, in pity. You must allow yourself to relax and see it in its new and perfect state. . . .

Let your awareness flow out . . . and realize that by building the new you are giving power to those thought-forms of Peace, of Love, and of Truth which must ultimately triumph upon the earth.[21]

The Christian POW'S

What will happen to Christians? What is to be the fate of those the New Age has already branded as the Beast, the Antichrist, the evil root race that needs to suffer plagues and suffering if its karma is to be worked out? "Limitless Love and Truth," that smooth and seductive demon of the New Age, says there is a place prepared for us. The Plan provides for Christians, Jews, and other "heretics" to be contained in this other world and become helpless prisoners of war (POW's).

David Spangler says the fate of New Age unbelievers might

tempt one "to speak in terms of a day of judgment, a time of separating the chaff from the wheat,"[22] were it not for other statements of "Limitless Love and Truth." But, Spangler comments, the unbelievers will not be destroyed after their earthly demise, but just put away where they will do no further harm. And there, under watchful eyes, they'll stay. Cynically, this Satanic demon announces:

> I am in both (worlds). . . . Shall I forsake those who even now drift apart into a destiny of their own? I am their shepherd as well. I am with you and I am with them. . . . None are saved. None are lost.[23]

Those whose loved ones have vanished will believe that their loved ones are being shepherded by the spirit hierarchy somewhere in another dimension. They will be unaware that the dead in Christ will be with the Lord in paradise! Though to Satan we are counted as sheep to slaughter, God is our Protector and our Redeemer.

In believing the Great Lie of the serpent, the New Age masses will also neglect to heed the prophecy of Timothy who some nineteen hundred years ago predicted that in the latter times men would be deceived by devils:

> Now the Spirit speaketh expressly, that in the latter times some shall depart from the faith, giving heed to seducing spirits, and doctrines of devils. (1 Tim. 4:1)

THIRTEEN

A New Culture,
A New Barbarism

*And he shall speak great words against the Most High,
and shall wear out the saints of the Most High, and
think to change times and laws: and they shall be given
into his hand. . . .*   (Dan. 7:25)

*. . . And that no man might buy or sell, save he that
had the mark, or the name of the beast, or the number
of his name.*   (Rev. 13:17)

*I see the beginnings of a new barbarism . . . which
tomorrow will be called a "new culture." . . . Nazism
was a primitive, brutal and absurd expression of it. But
it was a first draft of the so-called scientific or pre-
scientific morality that is being prepared for us in the
radiant future.*

(Erwin Chargaff, Nobel Prize winner, in *Future Life)*

In my book *Rush to Armageddon,* I envisioned a
future world in which mankind was a pawn in
the hands of a Satanic Antichrist. I also described
the dangers of the man-centered philosophy embodied by the
New Age, warning that this end-time religious system threatens
humanity with catastrophe. I also noted that "the new barbarism
comes cloaked with respectability, cleverly disguised as the *only*
rational religion for twenty-first-century man." It comes not as
an evil religion but as a glowing entity of love, peace, and world
harmony.

Regardless of its positive world image, the New Age Plan for
a One World Religion and a one world political order is exposed
by the Bible as nothing less than a scheme for a totalitarian system
calculated to enslave every man, woman, and child on earth.

In this chapter we'll take a close-up view of the grand society planned for all of us in the fast-approaching New Age. The gurus and Masters of the New Age are promising an era of world peace and religious unity, of brotherhood and universal joy. What we are presented with is nothing less than The Plan for a heaven on earth. And best of all, the New Age offers every human being on earth the opportunity to be a god on this heavenly planet.

Billions of earth's inhabitants will fall for these glowing promises of a Utopia populated with human gods. But they will discover they've been deceived by the greatest liar the universe has ever known. The New Age heaven will have become a hell, and God's fearful judgment will fall upon it and its inhabitants.

Exactly what does Satan have in store for humanity in this Utopia to come? More specifically, how will he organize this wondrous New Age society? Just how will he create his own perverse, ecumenical religion? What means will Satan use to spread his gospel?

The Origins of the New World Order

One of the most remarkable New Age documents I have come across outlining the New Age Plan for a one world political and religious order is the book, *When Humanity Comes of Age*, by Vera Alder. First published in Great Britain by The Aquarian Press, this book is used as a handbook by many New Agers intent on fostering a One World Government. It has been reprinted repeatedly in the United States, being most recently published and distributed by Samuel Weiser, Inc., a New York publisher specializing in New Age and occult publications. Samuel Weiser displays on this book as a company logo the Egyptian ankh, a perverted cross which has at its uppermost focal point the Satanic circle. Also on the cover of this book is an evil-looking serpent coiled around a white dove and a drawing of the Egyptian Sphinx.

When Humanity Comes of Age provides an incredible blueprint for the New World Order, described as the "Divine Plan" or "Ideal World Plan." This Divine Plan is derived from the lesson humanity has learned "through a long series of incarnations upon earth."[1] These lessons, Alder explains, reveal that man has been going through an evolutionary process that will ultimately cultimate in a World Order, or government.

According to Alder, this World Order can only be made possible if man uses the knowledge that has been made available to him over the millennia. "Is there," Alder asks rhetorically, "a heritage of wisdom which we can seize and claim upon whose foundations we can move forward with a clear purpose and a strengthened will, to bring a new Civilization and a Golden Age into being?" Her answer is, Yes, there is such a wisdom, residing in the Temple Mystery Schools and secret fraternities that have coexisted uneasily with the major religions since the early days of man. "The origin of all such (Mystery) knowledge all over the world is buried in the mists of time and usually stated to have been given to mankind by 'the Gods.' "[2]

Alder goes on to explain that in the "old civilizations"—evidently a reference to ancient Babylon. Sumeria, Assyria, and Egypt—there was a system of high priests, astrologers, and magicians (or Magi). Rulers were expected to have reached these exalted religious positions only after a long period of initiation into the Mystery Teachings or Ancient Wisdom. Buddha and Jesus also were intitiated into these Mysteries, she claims.[3]

The early Christian Church is said to have begun to subject those of the "truth faith" who believed in these Mystery Teachings to fierce persecution. Fortunately, Alder writes, the high priesthood was able to survive this persecution:

> The Mystery Teachings were cherished and kept alive in various ways and under various guises. Freemasons, Rosicrucians, Alchemists, Kabbalists, Yogis and many other such were all keeping some aspect of the Teaching alive, in more or less uncorrupt form. These people gave their lives to this precious work because such knowledge was believed to be man's key to Godhood and to his true destiny.[4]

The early Christians did in fact recognize the evil that lay in the Mystery Teachings. So did the devout Jews of that era. The Old Testament is replete with warnings against these anti-God practices, which included necromancy (communication with familiar spirits), witchcraft, sexual perversions, astrology, psychic forecasting, divination, the worship of idols, and the upholding of men as deities. Yet the Jews persisted, and their ungodly practices so angered the Lord that He brought them into captivity in Babylon and later, in 74 A.D., allowed the Roman general Titus to totally decimate Jerusalem, destroy the Temple, and disperse the Jews throughout the world. The very Mystery Teachings that Alder says form the basis for the New Age are those which God hates.

Alder reveals to us that these Mystery Teachings, kept hidden for centuries by an elite priesthood, are now being released "in a form suitable for the present day" as a result of the work of Theosophy founder H. P. Blavatsky, "who was one of the foremost to resurrect the Ancient Mystery Teachings."[5]

Alice Bailey, founder of the Lucis Trust and The Arcane School, is owed a special debt, Alder says, because she received instructions from her spirit guide, the Tibetan Master Djwhal Khul, consisting of specific guidelines amplifying the ancient Mystery Teachings regarding a Plan for humanity.

Why has the Tibetan Master come at *this* particular juncture in history? As Alder explains it:

> Humanity is considered (by the Hierarchy) to have moved forward to the point where the theories and ideals of the Mystery Teaching may soon be put into practice in the life of the community as a whole, because a sufficiently large number of people are now so advanced as to make this possible. The ancient writings all claim that a Golden Age is indeed due to follow the death of the present Dark Age.
>
> It seems unquestionable that a time has now arrived in history where an attempt to rebuild civilization will—and must be made. . . . Plans and hope for world reconstruction are now universal and permeate all strata of the community.[6]

Robert Mueller is also a follower of the demon Master Khul. Accordingly, Mueller also advocates a Mystery Religion which embodies "universal" or "cosmic" laws. "Most of these laws," he writes, "can be found in the great religions and prophecies, and they are being rediscovered slowly but surely in the world organizations."[7] Mueller encourages a dramatic speed-up of the uniting of all religions. He says we must recognize "the unity of their objectives in the diversity of their cults." Mueller also remarks:

Religions must actively cooperate to bring to unprecedented heights a better understanding of the mysteries of life and of our place in the universe. "My religion, right or wrong," and "My nation, right or wrong," must be abandoned forever in the Planetary Age.[8]

Mueller speaks of a "design," a "pattern" for the New Age. Reading Alder's book and other New Age materials, we discover that the details of this Plan are shockingly precise. Satan has unquestionably gone to great lengths to minutely design a master blueprint for the construction of a world system led by the Antichrist. Everything prophesied by the Bible is included— nothing of importance is omitted. Let's examine the essential details of The Plan for a New World Order.

The Four Great Principles

The Plan embodies four foundation stones. First, the one world system must be formed upon the premise that is "found at the roots of all the great world religions": that man is destined "to progress toward a state of *Godhood* translated into terms of a living human civilization."[9]

Second, the framework of the one world designs must include *unity,* the concept that "Both man and his planet are living organisms and that the love of man must include an understanding and love of our planet, *as a living being,* and of all the kingdoms in nature."[10]

Third, the planet earth and man (including all animal and plant life) combined will make up a *World Body* to be governed by an elite group of twelve wise men. Collectively known as *The World Mind,* this body will constitute a *World Government* which will act for the good of all humanity.[11]

Finally, The Plan will confer to this World Mind of elite rulers sufficient power and authority so it can synthesize or unify all aspects of life, including religion, art, and science.

The Dictatorial Authority of the World Mind

We see, then, that The Plan calls for the organic unity of the planet. The World Mind will exercise total control over every aspect of life on earth. It is man's *duty*, Alder intones, "to perform all the acts of his life in accordance with 'The Plan.' "[12] The ruling elite who compose the World Mind will not be ordinary men but statesmen the people can trust, men of spiritual integrity. These superior intellects will be "composed of highly spiritual and dedicated life, drawn from all races and religion. Through the practice of meditation and by reasons of their very nature they could . . . conduct world affairs in step with the natural process of evolution."[13]

"The People will gradually be educated to the point where they will unerringly nominate such men to the ranks of government."[14] This indoctrination of the New Age citizen will be a major preoccupation of the totalitarian dictatorship in the coming New Age Shangri-La on earth. Robert Mueller sacrilegiously proposes that New Age educators instruct people regarding the "holistic" teachings of Jesus.[15] What Mueller has in mind are the un-Biblical New Age teachings that all is God and thus man is God. In this teaching, man is exalted and God is forgotten. As Mueller explains:

> I have in mind the spiritual values, faith in oneself, the purity of one's inner self which seems to me is the greatest virtue of all. With this approach, with this philosophy, with this concept alone, will we be able to fashion the kind of society we want. . . .[16]

New Age man, thoroughly indoctrinated, will *unerringly* nominate men of spiritual integrity and superior intellect. However, if as Mueller has suggested the New Age will be a "world spiritual democracy," surely there might exist differences of opinion as to who deserves to be crowned with leadership. How will the citizenry discern among the candidates? What is meant when Alder says that "the people will be educated gradually"?

The Education and Indoctrination of Mankind

We get an appalling clue to the answers in the book *Gods of Aquarius* by Brad Steiger, a popular New Age writer on psychic and occult phenomena, and in *The Armageddon Script* by Peter

Lemesurier, a New Age pyramidologist and "expert" on prophecy. Each author presents to us a terrifying vision of a Satanic high-tech world in which, as Lemesurier puts it, "All individual human minds and wills could eventually be merged into one vast world-wide megapsyche."[17]

Originally the brainchild of Tom Bearden, what is depicted is the brains of all humans directly linked by wearing skullcap radio receivers. Presto—a New Age world of harmony and peace! "At a stroke," says Lemesurier exuberantly, "most of man's major problems would be solved":

> Since all would have instant, universal feedback, there would no longer be any feeling of "us" and "them." No longer would human beings regard each other as enemies to be competed against. No longer would nations even need to exist as such. Every human being would become a man-cell of the greater body which is man himself.[18]

Lemesurier emphasizes that the technology to create such a universal thought system is nearly here and that satellite telecommunications could be the forerunner of the World Mind.

While Lemesurier says that such a system would not be compulsory, Bearden talked about *enforced* use.[19] As I discussed in both *Rush to Armageddon* and a second book, *Robotica*, the technology needed to link the human mind directly to computers and robots *is already a reality*. The age of the biologically grown microchip (called the biochip or biocomputer) that can be surgically implanted in the human brain is on the immediate horizon, and other startling technological advancements are as little as a decade away.[20]

A chilling Orwellian *1984* world of monstrous proportions may be the fate of mankind if some future New Age dictator employs the nightmarish tools of oppression that will soon become available. For example, a system could be devised in which persons wearing an electronic belt or apparatus on their foreheads would be subjected to frightening and hideous mental images indistinguishable from reality *if their thoughts were unacceptable to the men controlling the thought machine into which they were forcibly linked.*

As Englishman Jonathan Glover discussed in his thought-provoking *What Sort of People Should There Be?*,[21] totalitarian governments have long desired to rule by fear and torture. But forced physical brutality is usually messy and imprecise. Soon electronic techniques will exist to make people *want* to behave in the desired way.

New mind control and brain-altering drugs currently being researched will provide yet another avenue of control. The "proper education" of New Age man will not present a problem for a future New Age hierarchy desiring absolute compliance with a World Mind.

The Perversion Process

The Plan does not call for an *instant* revolution throughout the world, but a gradual *process* of education and reorganization. Only after full preparations will the "Christ" and the Ancient Masters of Wisdom—the spirit hierarchy—take their place on the world throne of power. The New Age Messiah and his disciples will then slowly extend their octopuslike tentacles to envelop government, education, science, the arts, medicine, law, economics, and religion.

Alder explains that "spiritual councils" will be set up in every town, village, and city and in every workplace to monitor the new system. All aspects of life will be examined to inspire conformance with the New World Religion. The final arbiter for all of man's activities—governing his every thought—will be the *New Age Bible,* containing the Great Mystery Teachings of the ages, given to the world by the "Christ" who reigns as the New World ruler.[22]

If these visions of a New Age Kingdom come to fruition, man's mind and soul will fall under the total dominion of Satan incarnate.

Alder assures us that the masses will not find this control over their daily lives objectionable. The Plan she presents calls for a Council of Education and Psychology to indoctrinate the world's citizens to enthusiastically accept "an ideal conception of their own destiny and development."[23]

Properly trained, people will begin to see that the New World Order is merely "the Church in action, the Church taking its true and rightful place as the guide and motivation of all activity." Thus, Alder remarks that:

. . . the right frame of mind would be evoked through . . .
meditation. All Christians would believe that they are
producing conditions in which Christ could guide and lead
them in their efforts.[24]

Christians and others had *better* adopt "the right frame of
mind," as Alder phrases it, because the Plan is for the World
Government to assume total control over the nations' economies. Money will supposedly "come to be considered as crystal-
lized power or spiritual energy."

Money as such would revert to its original token value.
As . . . individual needs would largely be supplied on the
ration-card system, the need for handling of money would
dwindle. There would, of course, be a universal currency the
world over. There would be a central bank. . . .[25]

This provision of the New Age Plan is particularly frightening. It would bring to pass the prophecy of Revelation 13:16, 17
regarding the Antichrist's extensive control over the economy:

And he causeth all, both small and great, rich and poor, free
and bond, to receive a mark in their right hand, or in their
foreheads: and that no man might buy or sell, save he that
had the mark, or the name of the beast, or the number of his
name.

In *Rush to Armageddon,* I discussed new technological advancements in lasers and computer science that could enable the
Antichrist to control each and every financial purchase. A "ration-card" can now be maintained in a central computer's memory banks and annotated each time a person makes a purchase at
a store or shop or by telephone. Tiny computer chips the size of
a pencil dot can now be programmed and inserted under the
skin of a person's hand or forehead with a hypodermic needle or
other device. A laser or infrared beam is then focused momen-
tarily on the spot where the chip is located, revealing on a
computer terminal screen whatever information the chip reveals,
such as the individual's Social Security number or other identify-

ing information. These are examples of how modern science and technology might be abused by a World Government bent on tyranny.[26]

Man's Behavior and Lifestyle in the New Age

The Antichrist and his cohorts will control politics, the economy, and all other aspects of society. Satan will author an unholy New Age Bible, with no restrictions on man's desire to enjoy a licentious lifestyle. Almost anything evil that man finds pleasure in will be encouraged by the religious teachers ordained to oversee New Age society. Here are some of the characteristics of the ideal lifestyle envisioned for mankind.

Families. Alder suggests that monogamy—marriage to one mate—might be deemed "too possessive and separatist."[27] Thus, the traditional family may be broken up and laws passed prohibiting marriage.

Crime. Society will be soft on criminality in the radiant New Age:

> A criminal or an idler will be recognized as a sick individual offering a splendid chance for wise help. Instead of being incarcerated with fellow unfortunates in the awful atmosphere of a prison, the future "criminal" will be in much demand. The finest types of psychologists or religionists will offer him sanctuary and earnest help. . . .[28]

Sexual Behavior. The most perverse sexual practices will have legal and cultural sanction. For example, according to Alder, "the idea that an unmarried person of either sex should have to remain childless will seem far-fetched."[29]

Social Prohibitions and Fixed Beliefs. Vestiges from the past, when man believed in Christian principles, will have to be eradicated:

> The sages of the East, such as the famed Zen Buddhists, contradicted everything that their students knew and believed in until there was nothing left. . . . We should search ourselves very carefully to see if we have any fixed ideas, any

great shyness or self-consciousness. If we have, we *must* seek freedom.[30]

The Penalty for Disobedience. In the New Age culture, every person will be his own judge of what is right and wrong, with this key exception: *disobedience* to the Antichrist by worshiping the true God will result in severe punishment. Revelation 13:15 tells us that the Beast will decree that "as many as would not worship the image of the beast should be killed."

Robert Mueller set the tone for the future in his book *The New Genesis* when he suggested that once the Kingdom of Man is set up under a World Government and after the One World Religion is established, "God" could go away forever, leaving man to be his own god. Mueller's book paints a picture of a God who, after the New Age Kingdom is in place, looks down upon the earth and says:

> Farewell, my grown-up children. At long last you are on the right path, you have brought heaven down to earth. . . . I will now leave you . . . for I have to turn my attention to other troubled and unfinished celestial bodies. I now pronounce you Planet of God.[31]

A Bright New Future . . . A New Culture

This, then is the bright new future being prepared for those here when the New Age Antichrist ascends to the throne of World Government. What we can expect is a tight-fisted theocracy with the technological means to make us "want" to obey. We can also expect a freedomless, sin-stained world in which carnality and bloody criminal behavior explode in a rampage. Erwin Chargaff, the Nobel Prize-winning biologist often called the father of bioengineering, has said that he already sees "the dark beginnings of a new barbarism . . . which tomorrow will be called a 'new culture.' "[32] Few Christians can doubt the wisdom of Chargaff's keen assessment of where man, without God, seems to be headed.

FOURTEEN

The Unholy Bible of the New Age World Religion

All Scripture is given by inspiration of God, and is profitable for doctrine, for reproof, for correction, for instruction in righteousness. (2 Tim. 3:16)

We can take all the scriptures and all the teachings and all the tablets and all the laws, and all the marshmallows and have a jolly good bonfire and marshmallow roast, because that is all they are worth. (David Spangler, *Reflections on the Christ*)

Any religion that has as its chief aim the goal of becoming the *only* World Religion needs a bible, its own sacred scriptures. Its bible must incorporate the major doctrines of the religion, provide guidance to believers for daily living, and include guidelines for organizational structure. Currently the New Age World Religion has a multitude of writings that are acknowledged as bibles, but it leaders recognize the need for a single bible to unify all New Age believers. *They are already making plans for this bible and have mapped out the major elements it is to contain.*

The Formation of a One World Religion

The first and most important order of business for the new World Mind will be the establishment of a One World Religion. A research panel will assist these world rulers in studying "man's knowledge of the divine Plan of creation throughout the ages."

Again taking Alder's blueprint as a guide, their study of The Plan will be carried out in this way:

> The ancient wisdom, as it existed in all old civilizations, will be sifted, pieced together, correlated and synthesized with the finding of modern scientists and the developments in religious fields.[1]

"The ancient wisdom" refers to the Mystery Teachings, the idolatrous practices and teachings of cultures associated with the Babylonian harlot system (including those of the ancient Egyptians, Greeks, and Romans). These repugnant doctrines and rituals will be blended with the findings of science and new revelations received from demon spirits.

Miriam Starhawk well expresses the New Age concept of what form and shape the World Religion should take when she states:

> We need to create a religion of heretics who refuse to toe any ideological lines or give their allegience to any doctrines of exclusivity.[2]

When the New Age preaches against "exclusivity," they are really talking about Christianity. In the New Age World Religion, worshipers will be allowed to believe anything they wish as long as it isn't based on what the New Age calls *separativeness*, the notion held by Christians that Jesus is *the* way.

The Unity of Church and State

The doctrine for the New Age World Religion "will be used as a test against governmental activities,"[3] which means that the state will enforce the doctrine throughout society. This becomes more clear when we read that the new Divine Plan or set of doctrines will:

> . . . be given out to mankind in the form of a Spiritual World Teaching or Religion. It will enable all men gradually to vision

the nature of God's Plan for this earth and the part they will play therein. It will imbue them with a sense of purpose, of responsibility, and of spirtual security and maturity.[4]

The World Mind, the twelve-person council of world rulers, will impose on the world's population the "new gospel" that Paul warned the early Church about: a gospel of Satan. Acceptance will not be optional; the government will force people to obey. As The Plan so aptly and politely puts it, "Progressive simplification and unification will . . . have taken place in the religious field."[5]

The New Age gospel will soften up the world for the appearance on earth of the fake "Christ" and his disciples, the Masters of Wisdom. The World Government, also known as the World Mind, will give way to the Antichrist and his chosen hierarchy of demon-possessed men:

> There will thus be the Spiritual Cabinet of twelve whose rightful head would be none other than Christ himself. . . . He whom the Christians know as Christ, the Jews know as Messiah, and the Orient knows as Maitreya may eventually be recognized as one and the same Being. In this way could a "World Religion" develop quite naturally, and in harmony with a World Government.[6]

Alder's book even describes in great detail the work of the New Age "Christ" and his twelve-person (mimicking Jesus' twelve disciples) Spiritual Cabinet, who will see that The Plan is translated into reality on earth. They will not actually administer world government—subordinates will handle the mundane. Instead, the "Christ" and the Masters of Wisdom will supervise new developments in science and psychology, insuring their "spiritual purity." *All* of society will be homogenized into one Master Mind as provided for in the Divine Plan.

> Religion would no longer be an "aspect" of human living but the almost unconscious foundation of every activity. Men would have become aware of the purpose and presence of God in every part of creation and themselves to such an

extent that they would be incapable of separating "religion" from science, education, or government. The integration would have become complete.[7]

The new society that results from this "integration" Alder ecstatically describes as heaven on earth. But any God-fearing Christian who has read the Biblical prophecies can see that this New Age Kingdom is really a *hell on earth*. This becomes most clear when we discover what is planned for currently existing religions in Satan's New Age Utopia.

Alder informs us that in carrying out the Plan, the New Age "Christ" and his Spiritual Cabinet "will represent a World Religion in which every denomination, creed and type of belief would find its place fully appreciated and without fear or favor."[8]

This pledge rings hollow when we find out what doctrines will be acceptable in this New Age system. Under The Plan, every belief is acceptable *only as it agrees with the Mystery Teachings*. Every iota of religious teaching must conform to the New Age Bible that will be published by the New Age "Christ."

The New Age Bible Is Developed

The New Age "Christ" and his spiritual aides are to develop "the new Bible of a World Religion which will be the basis of future education." People will theoretically be free to practice the particular religion to which they previously gave allegiance. But in practice, the Bible of the New Age World Religion "will become the framework for them all, assisting in their interpretation, stimulating them to move with the times and to cooperation amongst themselves."[9]

The Antichrist will initially appear to respect many parts of the Christian and Jewish traditions as well as those of other religions. But eventually he will require all religions to conform to the New Age World Religion, even decreeing that all churches, temples, and synagogues are to become centers of the new One World Religion.

Here's how Lola Davis describes this "conversion process" of world religions:

What will happen to present-day religious groups? . . .
Religions of today probably will continue to function initially
much as they do now. . . . As concepts of the world religion
are scientifically validated, learned and spread about, present
religions will begin to make changes and evolve into centers
for the world religion.[10]

In the Antichrist-led New Age era, anyone who defies the
Mystery Teachings of the mandatory World Religion or who
uses a Bible other than the official version will be considered a
danger to the state.

The New Age has long sought to destroy the Bible of the
Jews and the Christians. Alice Bailey has accused the God of the
Old Testament as being unworthy of man's worship. In 1947 she
wrote that "all sane, sincere, thinking people should repudiate
the Old Testament and its presentation of a God full of hate and
jealousy." She termed the Christian belief in heaven and hell
unacceptable doctrines designed to "keep people in line with . . .
fear and threat."[11]

Universal contempt for the Holy Bible among New Age
leaders is convincingly demonstrated by David Spangler who has
stated, "We can take all the scriptures, and all the teachings, and
all the tablets, and all the laws, and all the marshmallows and
have a jolly good bonfire and marshmallow roast, because that is
all they are worth."[12]

While the New Age has placed a low value on the Jewish
and Christian Scriptures, Satan recognizes that a bible is needed
to control the masses. Thus, the development of a New Age
Bible is among his top priorities. Robert Mueller, who calls
himself a "good Catholic," has called for the publishing of a
worldwide bible which would both implement the divine commandments of the Bible and "show how the United Nations is a
modern biblical institution." Mueller says this should be done
for the Christian, "as well as all great religious or sacred books,
such as the Koran, the Grant Sahib, etc."[13]

What the New Age Bible Will Contain

What will be the teachings and doctrines in the New Age Bible?
New Age leaders agree on its format and composition. Lola

Davis has written that, in addition to the existing Bibles in all religions, there is now *new knowledge* available that can be included in the New Age Bible:

> In this century religious data previously unavailable has been found or released. Among these are the Dead Sea scrolls; the vast treasures of religious writings found in the Potola in Tibet; Christian writings deleted from the Bible during the 4th century; writings of Teilhard de Chardin; and previously carefully guarded knowledge of the Ancient Wisdom, including the writings of the Tibetan in the Alice Bailey books; writings of mystics from various religions; the materials offered by the Rosicruicians; and many books on Buddhism and Hindu philosophies and practices. . . .
>
> Probably much of this knowledge could be advantageously used in synthesizing the major religions with a World Religion for the New Age.[14]

The Collegians International Church, a self-styled "Church Universal of the New Age," suggests many of these same sources for New Age disciples searching for the Mystery Teachings, promising that they will bring instantaneous "Purified Enlightenment":

> Humanity today is ready for the (mystery) inner teachings. . . .
>
> Your search for these inner teachings is likely to take you to both the historic and esoteric literature of mystery schools. For centuries these teachings have been preserved and the inner knowledge discreetly passed on. Some of the movements which have kept these teachings alive in the West throughout the centuries have been Gnosticism, Freemasonry, Kabbalism and Rosicrucianism.
>
> To broaden our perspective we should . . . add the esoteric literature that is behind most of the world religions. This literature includes books like the *Bhagavad-Gita, The Tibetan Book of the Dead,* and the writings of (theosophist) Alice Bailey. Put it all together, and combine it with a study of the *Kabbala* (underlying most Western mysticism), add a touch of soul, bake under pressure for many lifetimes, and PRESTO . . . Purified Enlightenment.[15]

The New Age Bible will contain countless lies and blasphemies. It will be distributed to the masses, who will be expected to pattern their lives after its dictates. This Satanically inspired bible will include such un-Biblical doctrines as reincarnation and karma, both of which are universally found in the Mystery Teachings. It will also encourage man to believe he is a deity—though spiritually inferior to the New Age "Christ." A central theme will be the teaching that man can develop great psychic powers that will make him prosperous and keep him healthy.

The Penalty for Polluting God's Holy Word

Peter advised us that God's Word is like a light that shines in a dark place, for Scripture comes direct from God (2 Pet. 1:19-21). But this "new Bible" will spew out only the false doctrines of Antichrist.

John, in Revelation 22:18, 19, warned men against adding to or subtracting from the Bible:

> If any man shall add unto these things, God shall add unto him the plagues that are written in this book: and if any man shall take away the words of the book of this prophecy, God shall take away his part out of the book of life.

Peter also cautioned: "there shall be false teachers among you, who privily shall bring in damnable heresies, even denying the Lord that bought them, and bring upon themselves swift destruction" (2 Pet. 2:1).

What Do the Mystery Teachings Reveal?

Since the New Age has pledged to develop a world Bible based on the Mystery Teachings, it is important that we ask, what are these teachings? And second, what—or whom—is their source?

Alexander Hislop wrote that in the wicked Babylonian Mystery Religion:

> All knowledge, sacred and profane, came to be monopolized by the priesthood who dealt it out to those who were initiated in the Mysteries exactly as they saw fit. . . . Thus

the people, wherever the Babylonian system spread, were bound neck and heel to the priests. The priests were the only depositaries of religious knowledge; they only had the true tradition, by which the writs and symbols of the public religion could be interpreted; and without blind and implicit submission to them, what was necessary for salvation could not be known.[16]

What was true in Babylon is true today in the New Age World Religion. The gurus, the Mystery Teachers, the chosen leaders and psychics to whom demon spirits transmit mystical messages and "Bibles" from beyond—these are priests and priestesses to whom the New Ager must turn for enlightenment.

Master Da Free John is one such high priest. New Age writer Ken Wilber (*Up from Eden*) has acknowledged Da Free John's teaching as "unsurpassed by any other spiritual Hero, of any period, of any place, of any time, of any persuasion."[17] Presumably this includes Jesus. Wilber also hails Da Free John's work *The Dawn Horse Testament,* as "the most ecstatic, most profound, most complete, most radical, and most comprehensive *single spiritual text* ever penned." This presumably includes the Bible.

Other New Age authorities agree that Da Free John and his bible are wonderfully profound:[18]

The teachings of Da Free John, embodied in an extraordinary collection of writings, provide an exquisite manual for transformation. . . . I feel at the most profound depth of my being that his work will be crucial to an evolution toward full humanness. (Barbara Marx Hubbard, The World Future Society)

A gift of unparallel importance. It very likely marks the beginning of a new tradition, a new culture, a new vision of what it means to be a human being transformed. (Herbert Long, Th.D., former dean of students, Harvard Divinity School)

Who is Master Da Free John and what marvelous teachings do we find in his writings? Da Free John was born in 1939 on

Long Island, New York. After he graduated from Columbia University, he attended several Christian seminaries but dropped out. He then practiced Yoga under several Yogis, studying the full range of psychic and mystical phenomena. He now lives an eccentric life in the Fiji Islands with a small group of devotees, writing books and making videos that are sold and shown across the United States.[19]

Da Free John states that the "Way" he describes "can be realized by you if you will understand The Secret and realize The Mystery of You and Me." What is this Way? Simply the same old New Age line: That you and I are evolving gods who just need to realize our divinity; we and the universe are one; being gods, we can enjoy life to the hilt without worrying about some old Father God in the sky telling us what to do.

Of course, like all Mystery Teachings, Da Free John's works mention such mysterious, elitist-sounding phenomena as "transcendental reality," "consciousness," "enlightenment," "Divine Reality," and something called "Radiant Bliss." But these are just icing on the cake. At the core of any and all Mystery religions and cults is the same old chorus: man is a god. As William Kingsland has remarked in his study of Gnosticism:

> The final goal, the final objective of all the *Mysteries,* was the full realization by the Initiate of his divine nature in its oneness with the Supreme Being—by whomever name called—who is the Universe in all its phases and in its wholeness and completeness.[20]

The New Age deceivers would have the masses believe that only the hidden wisdom in the Mysteries provides answers for man's purpose in life. They wrap their "man is god" teaching inside mystical mumbo jumbo and often make the disciple on the quest for wisdom pay dearly with his money—and his soul— for the "key" that will unlock the Mysteries.

Nevertheless, millions are flocking to New Age leaders who have acquired reputations as Mystery Teachers. In 1985 Randall King, ex-husband of Elizabeth Clare Prophet, head of California's Church Universal and Triumphant, alleged that Prophet and the church used devious tactics to get people's money. As King explained it:

You wanted to get them hooked into the organization's belief system . . . you wanted to get them decreeing, which was the programming technique. You get a little bit more control over these people by having them repeat these things (hypnotic chants) over and over.

They would be so caught up that, well, they would give us all their money, sell their houses, hock their jewelry, sell everything. They would give us a hundred thousand dollars and then wind up on our doorsteps in their sleeping bags and be willing to sleep on the floor, if we would just show them "the way."[21]

Prophet, who claims to be "Mother of the Universe," has denied King's allegations but claims she has "the way." The Ascended Masters, says Prophet, constantly talk to her, and guide her ministry, and help her perform healing and other miracles. Randall King believes that Prophet, his ex-wife, *is* in touch with these spirits and that the Mystery Teachings she reveals result from extraworldly transmissions.[22]

Beware the Great "Mysteries" Hoax!

As is historically true of mystical cults, Mystery Teachings hide the true intentions of cult leaders from the uninitiated. Once a person is brought into the fold, it's often too late to fully exercise free will. This is why in late 1985 the Church of Scientology became enraged when *The Los Angeles Times*, in an exposé, revealed hidden "scriptures" of that New Age church. One Scientology minister angrily remarked, "These scriptures are not even available to members of the church until they have progressed to a higher state of spiritual enlightenment."[23] Ironically, L. Ron Hubbard, the founder of Scientology, once trumpeted his teachings as "the road to total freedom."

Unlike authentic Christianity, which through the Holy Bible reveals to anyone who seeks knowledge the answers to the ultimate mysteries of life, New Agers worry that outsiders might find out the truth behind their facade of lies and deceit. I recommend you beat a hasty retreat when anyone offers to reveal inner secrets or "Mystery Teachings," for they are of the Antichrist.

Be especially wary if someone tells you that initiation into the Mysteries is necessary for spiritual advancement. This is a favorite trick of New Age teachers. A prime example is the false teachings of psychologist M. Scott Peck, best-selling author of *The Road Less Traveled*. Peck, ostensibly a Christian who claims that the study and practice of Zen Buddhism has strengthened his faith, presents a seminar entitled The Taste for Mystery. Since Peck's books are favorites with psychologically-oriented Christians, he has been invited to give his seminar at a number of large, more liberal Christian churches. In the leaflet describing the seminar Peck held at Riverbend Baptist Church in Austin, Texas, May 2-3, 1986, the New Age psychologist asserted: "The taste for mystery is a prerequisite which can be developed and which is essential for the further reaches of spiritual growth."

This is a lie that appeals to intellectuals and others on never-ending quests for "the truth." The Bible tells us that in the message of salvation, there is simplicity. In the walk to spiritual maturity, one need only ask for guidance from the Holy Spirit. He will reveal to His own "the way." Unequivocally, the prerequisite of a "taste for mystery" is a lying concept of the Adversary.

The True Mystery of the Ages

New Age teachers are fond of misquoting the Holy Bible, twisting its passages to mean whatever is pleasing to Satan. But there is as least one part of the New Testament that the New Age continually shys away from: the first two chapters of Paul's Epistle to the Colossians. The reason why they avoid these chapters like the plague is simple: Colossians says that Jesus Christ is the Son of God; He is "the image of the invisible God, the firstborn of every creature." What's more, in Colossians Paul told us in uplifting words that Jesus was the Creator of the heavens and the earth and of every dimension: "all things were created by him, and for him."

There's even more truth in Colossians—much more. Paul tells us that Jesus "is the head of the body, the church." He says that Jesus is "the beginning, the firstborn from the dead" and that Jesus "made peace through the peace of his cross," reconciling all men and "all things unto himself."

Then Paul writes momentous words that lay bare all the doctrines of the New Age, exposing Satan's promise to reveal the Mystery of the Ages to New Age initiates as a lie and a deception. The gospel of Jesus Christ, Paul reveals, is "the mystery which hath been hid from ages and from generations, but now is made manifest to his saints" (Col. 1:26).

What's more, the powerful truth is that God wants us to know that Jesus Christ inside His own—in you!—is "the riches of the glory of this mystery" (Col. 1:27). God wants us to serve His Son only (Col. 2:6). The Mystery of the Ages is revealed in the life, death, and resurrection of Jesus Christ, for in God the Father and Jesus His Son "are hid all the treasures of wisdom and knowledge" (Col. 2:3).

Another Bible passage which confirms that Jesus is the Mystery of the Ages is 1 Timothy 3:16:

> And without controversy great is the mystery of godliness: God was manifest in the flesh, justified in the Spirit, seen of angels, preached unto the Gentiles, believed on in the world, received up into glory.

You won't find this true Mystery of the Ages revealed in New Age books or in the Hindu scriptures. It won't be unveiled in the sermons of New Age ministers or made known in secret to initiates. And you can be sure it won't be found within the context of the New Age Bible that is even now in preparation. You find it only in the pages of the Christian Bible. This is why Satan's disciples so despise Christianity and why the New Age World Religion is so eager to have its own unholy bible.

FIFTEEN

Doctrines of Devils

*Now the Spirit speaketh expressly, that in the latter
times some shall depart from the faith, giving heed to
seducing spirits, and doctrines of devils.* (1 Tim. 4:1, 2)

*The idea of a man groveling before his God comes down
from his ancient heritage. . . . The science . . . revealed
by the Ancient Masters restores to mankind in this
age . . . the original destiny in perfection before the
expulsion from Paradise.*

(Lord Maitreya, a demon spirit said to be the
New Age "Christ," *The Science of the Spoken Word*)

The great battle of today and of the coming
crisis period will be over doctrine. If Satan is
to succeed with his Plan, he must win this
greatest of battles.

The Bible foretold that in the latter times men would give
heed to seducing spirits and doctrines of devils. The New Age
Bible will be the unholy vessel into which the Antichrist will
pour these doctrines of devils. It is important that Christians
understand these false and seducing doctrines of the New Age if
we are to salvage as many souls for Christ as we can while there
is still time.

On close examination we find that New Age dogma is expressed under nine major doctrinal cornerstones:

Mystery Teachings
Occultism and Eastern mysticism
Psychology/powers of the mind
Science and technology as revelation

Hedonism
Evolution
Pantheism
Selfism
Leadership by spiritually superior beings

We discussed the doctrine of Mystery Teachings in the foregoing chapter. In this present chapter, we will cover the other eight doctrines.

Occultism and Eastern Mysticism

The New Age Bible will affirm the "truths" to be found in Hindu, Buddhist, Sufi Moslem, and other Eastern mystical religions. Many New Agers are also enthusiastic supporters of the so-called "hidden arts"—witchcraft and the occult, which they see as compatible with Eastern teachings. The occult, they say, is a two-edged sword which can be used for white *or* black magic. But Christians knowledgeable of the occult attest that deep wounds are inflicted on those who draw that sword with naked hands. There is *no* white magic, as entrapped New Agers often find out to their horror.

The person who practices the occult arts is a *shaman*. Joan Halifax, in her book *Shaman: The Wounded Healer*, states: "Communion with the purveyors of power is the work of the Shaman. Mastery of that power: this is the attainment of the Shaman."[1] *Webster's New Collegiate Dictionary* defines *shamanism* as an Eastern religion "characterized by a belief in an unseen world of gods, demons, and ancestral spirits responsive only to the shaman."

Increasingly, New Age literature has been packed with glowing stories of visualization, spiritism, sorcery, magic, witchcraft, and earth and witch doctor medicine. Prominent New Agers often claim that Jesus was Himself a shaman and a sorcerer.

The New Ager active in occultism and Eastern mysticism believes himself to have higher consciousness and powers derived from close relationship to hidden spirits and forces. These powers are said to enable him to work wonders. It is claimed a person can use "white magic" to heal sickness, win another's love, lose weight, improve school grades, improve memory, or achieve other goals.

New Age leaders do sometimes perform miracles with the power of Satan and wield considerable psychic skills. The Bible tells us that in the last days lying spirits will be able to perform miracles and to emulate the wonders of God and His angels and prophets so well that, if it were possible, the very elect would be deceived.

Witchcraft is also a growing movement among New Agers, who claim that witchcraft is a legitimate religion which has strong similarities to the Eastern religions:

> Witchcraft is a religion. . . . Only in this century have witches been able to "come out of the closet" . . . and counter the imagery of evil with truth. . . . To reclaim the word "witch" is to reclaim our right . . . to know the lifespirit within as divine.
>
> The longing for expanded consciousness has taken many of us on a spiritual "journey to the East" and to Hindu, Taoist, and Buddhist concepts. . . . Eastern religions offer a radically different approach to spirituality than Judeo-Christian traditions. . . . Their goal is not to know God, but to be God. In many ways these philosophies are very close to that of witchcraft.[2]

The Bible warns us to avoid the dangers of practicing witchcraft and occultism. We read in Deuteronomy 18:10-12: "there shall not be found among you any one . . . that useth divination, or an observer of times, or an enchanter, or a witch, or a charmer, or a consulter with familiar spirits, or a wizard, or a necromancer. For all that do these are an abomination to the Lord" (also see Gal. 5:20 and Rev. 9:20, 21).

Karma/Reincarnation

The un-Biblical concepts of karma and reincarnation are almost universally accepted by New Agers. This is understandable, for all Eastern religions likewise embrace these dreadfully poisonous doctrines.

The law of karma demands that individuals suffer and pay in this life, or in a subsequent reincarnated life, for one's shortcomings. However, the Christian New Testament makes clear that while we do reap what we sow, nevertheless Jesus' sacrifice on the cross redeemed us and removed the stain from original sin. Furthermore, Paul taught us that salvation is a gift from God, "lest any man should boast" of his good works. We also know that bad things often happen to good people, as was proven in the case of Job and martyrs among the early Christians.

Many New Agers believe in the concept of national, racial, or group karma as well. They reason that the Jews must have had "bad karma" for Hitler and the Nazis to persecute them so vilely. This concept of group bad karma is a malevolent thing, for it can be used to justify such evil acts as mass torture, incarceration of a particular ethnic, racial, or national group, and genocide. The law of karma suggests that whatever an "inferior race" gets, it deserves!

A future Antichrist would certainly find the concept of bad karma useful in dealing with those who refuse to take the mark of the Beast or who stubbornly display a "low level of consciousness" by professing belief in either Jesus as Christ or a personal God.

In addition, the Bible instructs us of the eventual *resurrection* of the dead but labels reincarnation as a falsehood. "The wages of sin is death." Reincarnation (also called rebirthing) implies eternal existence, or immortality. But immortality is a gift from God available only to those who receive salvation through the redemption offered by the suffering of Jesus Christ.

Replacing the Biblical teaching of a heavenly paradise ruled by God the Father and His Son, Jesus Christ, many New Agers substitute the Eastern doctrine that enlightened men, through higher consciousness, can achieve godhood. New Agers believe that until this state is achieved, when a person passes away he is usually *reincarnated* into another body. (However, he may remain a spirit indefinitely if he or his spirit guides and superiors dictate.)

Reincarnation and the existence of some type of shadowy spiritual ruling order are definitely antithetical to Christian belief. As to achieving a state of higher consciousness tantamount to godhood—a kingdom of God, or heaven, on earth—Scripture guides us to the truth that "flesh and blood cannot inherit the kingdom of God" (1 Corinthians 15:50).

Psychology/Powers of the Mind

Psychology and the belief that all men can unlock magical forces in their minds to perform miracles will be among the doctrines included in the New Age Bible.

The emphasis on psychotechnologies and the mind sciences by New Age advocates reflects their preoccupation with self. Satan's goal is to separate man from God's love. Therefore, the New Age World Religion focuses on the individual. Its seductiveness and attraction lie in its promises to make believers divinely powerful and give them absolute control over their lives. The individual is held up as either a god or a potential god whose latent, godlike powers can be unleashed through self-help application of psychological techniques such as Transcendental Meditation or the use of LSD and other psychedelic drugs to alter one's consciousness and release the powers of the mind.

The New Age believer is convinced that through diligent self-help and by invoking spirit guides, he can link his own psyche to the Universal Mind. In this way he can create his own reality. Health, wealth, and happiness are thought to be self-created.

New Age psychologists and teachers successfully appeal to many potential members with a "psychology gospel" and claim that man can attain godlike mind power. A number of New Age healers and ministers practice psychic healing and claim to demonstrate other supernatural phenomena. "Anyone can do it" is the bait that lures people.

Science and Technology as Revelation

For centuries Satan has inspired scientists and pseudoscientists to label Christianity as unsophisticated and behind-the-times. Many of these atheistic, agnostic, and secular humanist arguments will become part of the New Age Bible. The bible that is developed by the Antichrist will be applauded as fully in keeping with a high-tech age. Furthermore, New Age citizens will be told that the New Age scriptures can be *changed* whenever new scientific discoveries suggest revisions are needed.[3]

Much of the New Age science is ancient Hindu and Babylonian doctrine given a fresh coat of paint with the "revelations" of new technology. New Agers promoting Hindu philosophies rarely inform the new recruit that a touted scientific "discovery" is of ancient Hindu origin. An example of this is the ad shown below, just as it appeared in the *Austin American-Statesman* (January 10, 1986). Note that nowhere is the public told that "Vedic Science" is actually doctrinal Hinduism. At the core of this fake science is the Hindu practice of Transcendental Meditation.

Science or Pseudoscience?

Below I have listed a few quotes from scientists, technologists, and others who have endorsed the New Age, believing its precepts consistent with modern science and technology.

It would be wise in view of New Age claims of scientific authenticity to consider the words of Paul in 1 Timothy 6:20: "O Timothy, keep that which is committed to thy trust, avoiding profane and vain babblings, and oppositions of science falsely so called."

A New Age world religion is needed to synthesize scientific knowledge with spiritual teachings and to unify mankind. (Lola Davis, *Toward a New Age World Religion*)

If there are those who claim a conversion experience through reading scripture, I would point out that the book of nature (science) also has its converts. (Heinz R. Pagels, *The Cosmic Code*)

We need not make a pilgrimage to India or Tibet to become enlightened about . . . Eastern thought. . . . The East and West could blend in exquisite harmony. Do not be surprised if physics curricula of the 21st century include classes in meditation. (Gary Zukav, *The Dancing Wu Li Masters*)

As we approach the 21st century . . . religion, art, and science are encountering each other anew and are molding a new consciousness that will transcend all three. (Stuart Litvak and A. W. Senzee, *Toward a New Brain*)

The parallels to Eastern mysticism are appearing not only in physics but also in biology, psychology and other sciences.
Western science is finally . . . coming back to the views of early Greek and the Eastern philosophies. (Fritjof Capra, *The Tao of Physics*)

Today we are at the threshold of a new era. All signs point to this fact. . . . We look toward a transformation into a New Age using, however, the insight and wisdom of the ancient mystics. This new world view is emerging because there has been a recent correlation between modern physics and the mysticism of Eastern religions. (Henry Clausen, Sovereign Grand Master of Freemasonry, *Emergence of the Mystical*)

Hedonism

The New Age Bible will definitely allow for hedonism, based on the belief that no act is sinful. This is music in the jaded ears of a mass murderer, a rapist, or a child molester.

Jesus came because of man's sin:

> He that committeth sin is of the devil; for the devil sinneth from the beginning. For this purpose the Son of God was manifested, that he might destroy the works of the devil. (1 John 3:8)

In John's day, there were also hedonists who claimed that sin was a fiction. But John cut straight through their lie when he boldly stated: "If we say that we have no sin, we deceive ourselves, and the truth is not in us" (1 John 1:8). This Biblical passage is neglected by the New Age. The only "sin" that the New Age will admit to is that committed by men who fail to become god-conscious. Here are some examples of their twisted hedonistic thinking:

> There is no authority superior to the guidance of a person's inner self; the universe is of good intent; evil and destruction do not exist. (from "Seth's Teachings," Seth Center, Austin, Texas)

> If . . . what Christ represents demands suffering, repentance, and self-negation, then this needs to be seen clearly, in contrast to the New Age which represents abundance, love, upliftment of the individual, collective well-being. . . . (David Spangler, *Revelation: The Birth of a New Age*)

> The Bible was not intended to be interpreted literally in all its parts. . . .
> The idea of "original sin" is totally false. . . . The High Religion has nothing to do with sin, only the spiritual development of man.
> Evil exists only in our minds—it is a human creation. (John Randolph Price, *Superbeings*)

Everybody has the truth. Jesus had his truth; I got my truth. I can't use anybody else's. . . . You are all beautiful. You are God. That is it, baby, you are having a time, and that is life. (Terry Cole-Whittaker, *Magical Blend* magazine)

You are the supreme being . . . there isn't any right/wrong. (Carl Frederick, *Playing the Game the New Way*)

No one is guilty. We are all innocents. (Leo Buscaglia, *Personhood*)

What we know about the universe is so amazing! There are a hundred billion galaxies out there; no generation before ours has known this! And what does 99 percent of religion in the West do? It tells people to think about their sins. (Rev. Matthew Fox, *Yoga Journal*)

Evolution

The unified government led by the Antichrist will certainly make the teaching of transformational evolution a principal part of public and private school and college curricula. Students at all levels will be taught—and ministers will be required to teach—that man is capable of godhood through god-consciousness.

The New Age Bible will outline the concept that all evolution began and is controlled by a higher intelligence emanating from within the material universe. The Babylonian worship of the Sun God will be revived under a scientific-sounding guise. New Age leaders have already paved the way for this new scientific "revelation." Their contention is that the sun created basic life-forms on earth so they would evolve into human life. The sun is therefore man's god and creator.

Elizabeth Clare Prophet is a leader in this New Age philosophy that places a Sun God in man's spiritual orbit. She has told readers of her magazine, *The Coming Revolution*, that:

The healing of the nations begins with the healing of ourselves. We must draw forth from the Great Central Sun—the highest concentration of spirit in our universe, the Great

Source of light and energy—that eternal Light with which we were anointed from the beginning.[4]

The modern-day, New Age Sun God is called the Solar Logos (Word) by Alice Bailey, who in her book *The Rays and the Initiations* reveals him not only as a fiery planetary body but as *Lucifer*. Bailey talks of the Central Spiritual Sun as being the "universal energy force" that is the source of power for Lucifer, man's *planetary initiator* into the New Age to come. Lucifer is to oversee man's evolutionary march toward divinity.[5]

The arrival of the Solar Logos was announced in a full-page ad in *Newsweek* which stated in part:

At this very moment, our world is undergoing an enormous change comparable to the dawning of the day itself. We are facing the reality of a gigantic Force of Life such as mankind has never experienced before, which is called the spiritual "Sun of the New Age."[6]

Pantheism

The evolution doctrine of a Sun God and a Solar Logos fits in nicely with the ancient pagan belief system called *pantheism*. Pantheism will also be a core teaching of the New Age Bible. Pantheists deny the existence of a personal God, maintaining that the universe itself and everything in it is "God." Man, the New Agers believe, is both a piece of the whole and the whole itself.

As Ruth Montgomery was told by her spirit guides:

. . . We are as much God as God is a part of us . . . each of us is God . . . together we are God . . . this all-for-one-and-one-for-all . . . makes us the whole of God.[7]

The absurdity of pantheism requires a fantastic imagination. In J. D. Salinger's short story "Teddy," a sharp-minded youngster recalls his experience of the immanent, pantheistic God while watching his little sister drink a glass of milk: "All of a sudden, I saw that she was God and the *milk* was God. I mean, all she was doing was pouring God into God."

If for New Agers there is no personal God, and if man is himself God, there can be no place called heaven where God and His Son Jesus and all of His mighty angels reside. Yet, Jesus taught His followers, "Our Father, which art in heaven, hallowed be thy name. . . ." The Bible makes clear that there *is* a heaven separate from this planet (see Col. 1:12-29; Eph. 1:20; Acts 7:49).

As to the lie that God resides in all matter, in Isaiah 45:12 we find this proclamation by God: "I have made the earth, and created man upon it: I, even my hands, have stretched out the heavens, and all their host have I commanded." In Ecclesiastes, we are instructed, "For God is in heaven, and thou upon earth. . . ." In Acts 7:48, Stephen announces that God does not reside in idols or in earthly habitats: "The Most High dwelleth not in temples made with hands. . . ." Further evidence is found in Hebrews 9:24: "For Christ is not entered into the holy places made with hands . . . but into heaven itself, now to appear in the presence of God for us."

Satan's Master Plan cannot work unless people accept the fiction that there is no personal God who loves and cares for them. So he has sent forth his ambassadors to push in the West the strange but currently popular doctrine so long accepted in the East: pantheism.

Eckankar is a group teaching pantheism. Listen to what its advocates say:

> God is worldless. . . . God is then everything and in all things but unconcerned about any living thing in this universe, or throughout the cosmic worlds.
> He is detached and unconcerned about man. . . .[8]

Once a person swallows the odd theory of pantheism, he is handed a complementary theory: since God is in everything, everything is God. Therefore, the sun is God, Mother Earth is God, the moon, stars, and galaxies are gods. They are alive. And if the planets and stars are living gods, man is subordinate to them. It is therefore his sacred duty to revere these divine, living beings. The New Age's revolutionary theory of a Sun God and a

Solar Logos (Lucifer) as Master of humanity becomes a required tenet of religious belief.

Vera Alder informed us in *When Humanity Comes of Age* about these strange new nature teachings that will be incorporated in the New Age Bible. She says that the Antichrist and his "Spiritual Cabinet" will assist our understanding that *the pagans were right all along:*

> It will come to be realized that the habit of older civilizations and of intuitive primitive peoples of investing the earth, the sun, and the forces of nature with the character of deities and worshipping them as such, was not one of ignorance.
>
> It will occur to people eventually that the fact of acknowledging one God over all should not necessitate denying the existence of all the major and minor deities whom many believed that He created in order to develop and run the universe and who are mentioned under various names in all Bibles.[9]

Worshiping the Heavens

This belief in a divine sun, earth, and moon leads many New Agers to worship these planetary bodies as deities. The full moon ritual is especially popular, as is the passing of seasons. Meditation in general is thought to be beneficial, lending peace and harmony to earth. A report from one New Age group, the Academy for Peace Research, has seriously issued a preliminary report which asserts:

> It's clear that the combined thought power of several million people is continuing to affect the solar and geomagnetic activity. The Academy is involved in a three-year scientific research project to test the hypothesis that people praying or meditating together on a global basis can decrease solar activity and the Earth's magnetic field and thereby bring more harmonious conditions on earth.[10]

Jesus said, "I am the way, the truth, and the life: no man cometh unto the Father, but by me." God's commandment is,

"Thou shalt have no other gods before me." But according to The Plan, it is holy and proper to worship the earth, the sun, and other forces of nature as gods, as did the pagans.

Selfism

Get man to believing he is the only god there is, teach him self-love and self-worship, and he'll forget all about the true God in heaven. This is the Devil's Plan, and it is working magnificently. *Selfism,* one of the Commandments in the coming New Age Bible, won't be viewed as a strange doctrine, because it is already fervently practiced by millions today both in the New Age World Religion and in the Secular Humanism community.

Today's New Age leaders are emphatic about the man-centered focus of their religion, attributing to man a divine dimension. Most readily and arrogantly proclaim that at the very heart of their heretical doctrine is the teaching that man-is-a-becoming-god. This is the essence of selfism. Swami Muktananda, a guru highly praised by EST's Werner Erhard and by Master Da Free John, tells his listeners: "Kneel to your own self, honor and worship your own being. God dwells with you as you!"[11]

Benjamin Creme says that in the New Age men will invoke (command) things into existence, this being possible for men who have become deities. Creme assures us that "prayer and worship as we know it will gradually die out and men will be trained to invoke the power of deity."[12] Allan Cohen writes that man will understand the ultimate meaning of personhood only when he realizes, "I am God, there is no other."[13]

The seductive concept of selfism aligns New Age religion with contemporary lifestyles. "Be all that you can be," a U.S. Army TV commercial promises. "Look out for Number One," demands a best-selling nonfiction book. Psychologists, fashion experts, beauty advisors, and inspirational speakers—some of whom are ordained Christian ministers—exhort us to put self first, to love ourselves, and to seek, before all else, to be smart, beautiful, self-sufficient, rich, successful. The attainment of "self-esteem" is touted to be the primary and most important ingredient in a contented and happy life.

In my Bible I find that the two greatest commandments are

first to "love the Lord thy God with all thy heart, and with all thy soul" and *then* to "love thy neighbor as thyself" (Matt. 22:36-40) Nowhere do I find that we must love ourselves *before* we can love others, nor is the concept of self-esteem mentioned even once. Instead Jesus and the great spiritual leaders of the Bible counseled that we *deny ourselves* and that we seek God not as man-gods puffed up with self-love, but with a humble heart and a spirit of meekness.

The rise of selfism was prophesied by Paul, who wrote that the last days would be perilous times:

> For men shall be lovers of their own selves, covetous,
> boasters, proud, blasphemers, disobedient to parents,
> unthankful, unholy . . . despisers of those that are good.
> (2 Tim. 3:2, 3)

Not everyone who preaches self-love is necessarily a New Ager, but those who espouse this anti-Christian philosophy inevitably find themselves in the same camp with ardent New Agers because self-love is an essential part of New Age belief.

It is no wonder New Age religion has been successful in drawing new members. It calls for no change in behavior and no humbling oneself before the true God. And it proposes to take under its rainbow-colored umbrella people of all religions and faith groups.

Leadership by Spiritually Superior Beings (Satan and His Demons)

The doctrine that man is an evolving god, but that *he must be obedient to superior evolved man-gods* will be an important feature of the New Age Bible. This teaching will ensure the dominance of the Antichrist and his demonic aides. Perhaps the major drawing card of the New Age World Religion is its seductive flattery that man is a deity. But ironically man will find that in seeking to be his own master, he has become the slave of one far greater in intelligence and supernatural power.

Have Doctrines of Devils Infiltrated the Christian Church?

Jude's epistle warns us about people who have "crept in unawares" into the very tabernacle of God: infiltrating His body, the Church. Charles Bullock, pastor of Christ Memorial Church in Austin, Texas, aptly describes these apostate unbelievers as "religious creeps."[14] Pretending to be believers, their undercover purpose is actually to subvert the truth. In the following chapter we'll discuss the treacherous work of these apostate men and women and see just how The Plan seeks to undermine and destroy the Christian Church from within.

SIXTEEN

Apostasy: The New Age Plan to Take Over the Christian Church

Let no man deceive you by any means: for that day
shall not come, except there come a falling away first,
and that man of sin be revealed, the son of perdition;
who opposeth and exalteth himself above all that is
called God. . . . (2 Thess. 2:3, 4)

Teaching ritual and the history of the Goddess religion
to priests, ministers, nuns and Christian educators was
a new experience but deeply rewarding. I found the
students very receptive to new ideas, hungry for new
forms of ritual and very creative. . . . I am very glad to
discover such strong movement within Christian
churches that is sympathetic to the Pagan Spirit and
willing to learn from the teachings of the Old
Religion. (Miriam Starhawk, *Circle Network News*)

The Plan of the New Age is to take over every Christian church and every Jewish temple in the world and to turn these great and small architectural structures into centers for the New Age World Religion. This is an absolute fact.

If this grandiose goal of The Plan does not astonish you, then hear this: New Age leaders are convinced that they will vanquish and destroy the Christian churches of America and the West *without so much as a whisper of protest* from the tens of millions of Christians in those churches. What's more, they believe that their takeover of Christianity *will be welcomed by most Christian ministers and laymen.* Their victory, these New Age leaders say, will come as Christians abandon their current out-moded doctrines en masse and enthusiastically adopt those of the New Age!

The orthodox Jewish faith is also a target, with its belief in God Almighty and the primacy of the Old Testament.

The New Age truly believes that its current campaign of subtle subversion and quiet undermining of Christian doctrine will result in total victory. It will not be necessary to stage a direct, frontal assault on Christianity. No. What is planned is an insidious, veiled attack. The horrible intent of the leaders of the New Age is to invade and conquer Christianity much as bacteria do a living organism. The end result will be to leave the Christian body a rotting corpse, full of worms and eaten away from within.

Marilyn Ferguson reveals in *The Aquarian Conspiracy* some of the ideas being circulated about how New Agers can use subtle means to infiltrate churches and other organizations. Ferguson recommends against frontal attack, explaining it "hardens their position." Better, she says, are such strategies as that of John Platt, who advises that any minority that understands the power of the seed crystal, of amplifying an idea, can quickly assume influence beyond its numbers. Another strategy is offered by Matt Taylor who suggests, "You can steer a large organization with subtle input."[1]

Such tactics may be the reason avid New Age writer and intellectual William Thompson has said:

> The new spirituality does not reject the earlier patterns of the great universal religions. Priest and church will not disappear; they will not be forced out of existence in the New Age, they will be absorbed into the existence of the New Age.[2]

Dictators learned long ago that willing acceptance by a people is far preferable to forced repression. To threaten Christianity with open destruction is not Satan's style. He knows that it only invites counterattacks, and he does not wish to awaken and alarm those who might oppose him. Satan plays the game dirty, with trickery and treachery. He makes inside moves. His is the tactic of the Trojan horse.

The Three-Pronged Plan to Take Over the Christian Church

The leaders of the New Age have a sophisticated Plan to replace Christianity and Judaism with their own World Religion. The three phases of this scheme are to *discredit, infiltrate,* and *deceive.*

Objective: Discredit Jesus and the Bible

How can the Christian Church best be strangled and rendered lifeless? Satan knows that all he has to do is to first undermine belief in Jesus Christ and, second, discredit the Bible.

The New Age war on Jesus and the Bible is vile and vicious. Some New Agers seek to portray Jesus as just a man, a man who studied at the feet of his spiritual superiors—Tibetan, Egyptian, and Indian priests, priestesses, and gurus. Others attempt to label Jesus a rich man's son, as a teacher whose supposed miracles were faked, or even as a powerless disciple who was raised from the dead by the Lord Maitreya, the New Age "Christ," in an occult manner. By some New Age accounts, Jesus' mother, Mary, was a Temple prostitute and Jesus Himself had an extramarital affair with Mary Magdalene.

Perhaps the most prevalent lies by New Age leaders are accounts of what happened to Jesus during the so-called "lost years" between His boyhood and the beginning of His ministry. Since these eighteen years are omitted from the accounts in the Gospels, the New Age has, like a ravenously starving vulture, moved in with dispatch to fill the gap. Kevin Ryerson, the demon channeler for Shirley Maclaine and other celebrities, says his spirits have told him that "the man Jesus studied for eighteen years in India before he returned to Jerusalem. He was studying the teachings of Buddha and became an adept Yogi Himself."[3]

Elizabeth Clare Prophet claims to have come across documents from deep in the Himalayas which describe what Jesus did and said in India, Nepal, and Tibet. Her book, *The Lost Years of Jesus,* "reveals" that the youth Jesus joined a caravan headed for the East, where he studied under wise men who taught him mysticism.[4] Reverend J. Finley Cooper, a priest in the Episcopal Church of the United States, has said of Prophet's book: "I am indeed grateful to Elizabeth Clare Prophet. . . . I commend the book to all of God's sons and daughters."[5]

Edgar Cayce's demon guides gave him the revelation that Jesus traveled extensively in Egypt, India, and Persia. In Persia, said Cayce, Jesus learned from Mystery Religion teachers about the truth of Zu and Ra, two Babylonian gods. In Egypt, as an initiate of the Mysteries, He was tested at the Great Pyramid, earning membership into the exalted White Brotherhood of Masters.[6]

These heretical accounts of Jesus' travels and of His being initiated into the Satanic Mystery Teachings are not supported by one shred of evidence. But they are made more palatable by scheming New Age leaders who claim that "Much of this information was probably cut from the Bible in the 6th century by the church, along with reincarnation, as being an 'embarrassment' and threat to the exclusiveness of the doctrines and their power over the people."[7]

Did Christ Die in Vain?

Another horrendous attempt to strip Jesus of His unique status as the Son of God is the assertion that Jesus' death was not sacrificial, was staged by plotters, or was arranged by the Lord Maitreya, the New Age Christ-pretender.

Denying Jesus' sacrifice on the cross is common among New Agers. Elizabeth Clare Prophet, the fount of so many lies regarding Jesus and the Bible, writes:

> . . . the erroneous doctrine concerning the blood sacrifice of Jesus—which he himself never taught—has been perpetuated to the present hour, a remnant of pagan rite long refuted by the Word of God. God the Father did not require the sacrifice of His Son Christ Jesus, or of any other incarnation for the sins of the world. . . .[8]

That Jesus died on the cross as an atonement for our sins is indelibly stamped throughout the Old and New Testaments. Here are just a few passages: John 1:1, 14; 3:16; Matthew 1:18-25; 20:28; Galatians 4:4, 5; Philippians 2:5-11; 1 Corinthians

15:3-8; 2 Corinthians 5:21; Hebrews 4:14-16; 1 John 2:1, 2; Romans 4:25; 5:18, 19; Isaiah 53:6. In the face of such voluminous evidence, Prophet's statement that God did not require the sacrifice of His Son, Jesus, is exposed as a bold lie unsupported by the Scriptures.

Peter Lemesurier, an occult pyramidologist and prolific New Age writer, has an even more blatant account of Jesus' death. He suggests that Jesus was a member of the Essene sect, a radical Jewish group that sought the overthrow of the Romans and the throning of Jesus as king. Lemesurier proposes that the Essenes snatched Jesus off the cross before He physically died, and this is why His tomb was empty.[9]

That Jesus' resurrection was arranged by a psychically powerful spirit other than God is the claim of Benjamin Creme. Creme says that the resurrection happened this way:

> The Christ (Maitreya) resurrected the body of the disciple Jesus. When the body was laid in the tomb, the Christ, Maitreya, entered on the third morning. His consciousness once again entered into the body of the disciple Jesus and brought it back to life—as he had done before with Lazarus. . . . This . . . has happened quite often since, and before. But resurrection is a very special thing technically. It is a great occult happening.[10]

Creme and others also tell Christians not to pray to Jesus because Jesus is not God but a disciple of Lord Maitreya. Even the Apostle Paul, now called "the Master Hilarian" in the spirit world, is ahead of Jesus in the hierarchy: ". . . Christ is not God. He is not coming as God. . . . He would rather you didn't pray to Him but to God within you."[11]

The New Age elite also says there will be no real Second Coming of the Lord. This untruth goes hand-in-hand with the New Age doctrine that Jesus is not Christ. Emmett Fox, formerly a prominent liberal Christian minister whose books are very popular among New Agers, has written:

> The Christ is not Jesus. The Christ is the active presence of God—the incarnation of God—in living men and

women. . . . In the history of all races the Cosmic Christ has incarnated in man—Buddha, Moses, Elijah and in many other leaders. . . . However, in his New Age, the Cosmic Christ will come into millions of men and women who are ready to receive it. This will be the second coming of Christ for them.[12]

This same idea is taught by Lavedi Lafferty and Bud Hollowell of the Collegians International Church:

The second coming of Christ does not refer to the man Jesus but to the manifestation of the Spirit of the Cosmic Christ in the hearts and minds of all humanity. The "cloud" Jesus said he would appear as, refers to the dimensional level of mind or consciousness.[13]

It is important to the New Age that Jesus' divinity be discredited, that He be demoted from Godhood to manhood. Jesus the man will not return as God to rule humanity. That role is reserved for the Lord Maitreya. This blasphemous teaching fulfills the prophecy of Saint Peter:

. . . there shall come in the last days scoffers, walking after their own lusts, and saying, Where is the promise of his coming? for since the fathers fell asleep all things continue as they were from the beginning of the creation. (2 Pet. 3:3, 4)

New Agers insist that Jesus is practically a nobody, yet go to great lengths to tie Jesus' teaching with the unholy doctrines and practices of the New Age World Religion. Jose Silva, founder of the Silva Mind Control System, says Jesus came expressly to teach people the Silva system of meditation and communication with "spirit counselors." Paul Twitchell tells initiates of Eckankar the Jesus' words, "Come, follow me," were the Lord's invitation to men that they meditate and travel out-of-the-body to the astral plane.

Is the Bible Riddled with Errors? The Plot to Discredit the Bible

The New Age teachers are also quick to quote, or rather, misquote, the Bible when it serves their purpose. On one hand, they maintain the Bible is flawed and of very little use. On the other, they claim the Bible confirms the New Age world view. They twist and distort Scripture to make it say exactly the opposite of its true literal meaning.

One New Age authority who attempts to cite the Bible for evil purposes while insisting it is riddled with errors is F. Aster Barnwell. The cover of his book *The Meaning of Christ for Our Age* is decorated with drawings of Buddha, the serpent draped over a cross, and a skull superimposed on a winged rod. The contents are even more hideous than the cover.[14]

Who is F. Aster Barnwell? Formerly an economist with the Canadian province of Ontario, Barnwell says that in 1979 he abandoned his job and began to devote his life to the study of astrology, psychology, Eastern philosophy, comparative religion, Yoga, and mysticism, leading him to realize that the Judeo-Christian Bible isn't what it appears to be.

Barnwell claims there are many myths, errors and inconsistencies in the Bible. He recommends that we don't accept the Bible and Jesus as literal truth but instead, we see Jesus in a *psychological context* as opposed to a factual, historical one. He specifically cites the "myth" of the virgin birth, suggesting that this is legend rather than miracle. Also mythical is Jesus' sacrificial death and resurrection.[15] Barnwell informs us that "many Eastern concepts and doctrines have heretofore gone unrecognized in the teachings of Jesus."[16]

To Barnwell, we need to reinterpret Scripture using New Age concepts. For example, "salvation" is not an event but a life-long process of "breaking down psychological barriers." The "Name of Jesus" or the "Blood of Christ," says Barnwell, "is more understandable if we think of these phrases as meaning 'an agency of activation'—something inside a person that works to promote consciousness and growth."

"It is doubtful," adds Barnwell, "that the apostles could have meant anything more by the 'name' of Jesus than a sort of psychological focusing."[17]

Barnwell criticizes the traditional view that Jesus is the "only name under Heaven" by which salvation can be attained by man. We must, he insists, go beneath these literal words in the Bible to understand their hidden Mystery meaning, and so discover that Jesus is not the only way. Therefore:

> When a Christian accepts . . . that the name of the historical person, Jesus, is the "only name under Heaven" by which salvation can be attained by man, he may actually hinder the cause of Christ rather than promote it.[18]

The author of *The Masters of Wisdom,* John G. Bennett, goes even further in a Satanically generated attack against the Biblical accounts of Jesus. He rejects the idea that Matthew, Mark, Luke, and John authored the Gospels and sees them as Mystery writings. Their authorship, according to Bennett, must be attributed to Mystery schoolteachers and to disembodied spirit (demon) Masters:

> The four gospels were compiled by four different schools of wisdoms, each entrusted with a different task. . . . St. Luke's gospel was written to connect Christianity with the Great Mother tradition through the Virgin Mary. . . . St. John's gospel is an interpretation based on the Gnostic tradition. . . . St. Matthew's is preeminently the gospel of the Masters of Wisdom.[19]

The Gifts of the Spirit: Are They for Everyone?

Again and again, we see in action this conspiracy to undermine the Scriptures. A favorite stratagem is to pretend that the gifts of the Spirit described by Paul in 1 Corinthians are not exclusive to Christians, nor, it is said, are they gifts from a personal God. *Anyone* can freely access the universal forces and beome a healer, a psychic, a prophet, or a worker of other miracles. *A Course in Miracles,* given to a New Ager by a demon through automatic writing, emphasizes: "Miracles are natural. When they do not occur, something has gone wrong."[20] Another New Age source remarks:

You don't have to be a born again evangelist or a Filipino (psychic healer) miracle-worker to heal people. All of us possess the power to be psychic healers. . . .[21]

Satan is indeed giving some of his followers extraordinary occult powers. In exchange, he wants and gets their souls.

Jesus said that in the last days there would be those who do wondrous works in His name; but, said Christ, they will not be His sheep:

Not every one that saith unto me, Lord, Lord, shall enter into the kingdom of heaven; but he that doeth the will of my Father which is in heaven. Many will say to me in that day, Lord, Lord, have we not prophesied in thy name? and in thy name have cast out devils? and in thy name done many wonderful works? And then I will profess unto them, I never knew you: depart from me, ye that work iniquity. (Matt. 7:21-23)

Revising the Bible: The Devil's Foul Strategy

A devious strategy that seems to be paying off for the New Age is that of revising—or updating—the Bible to make it more "meaningful" to modern times. This strategy takes several paths. One is the drive to create a *unisex Bible*. Radical feminist groups and liberal churchmen, encouraged behind-the-scenes by New Age leaders, have ardently campaigned for several years now that the Bible's language is sexist and exploitative. The National Council of Churches has long demanded that the words "Lord" and "King" be replaced with "Sovereign." This group also wants the word "God" to be changed to "Our Father and Mother." Even the term "Son," which refers to Jesus, the Son of God, isn't good enough for the National Council of Churches, which insists that "Son" should be removed in favor of the neutral term, "child."[22]

The revised National Council of Churches lectionary, which contains recommended Biblical passages for pastors to read during worship services, arbitrarily slices some words and adds other terms to the universally recognized translations of the Bible. John 3:16, for example, becomes: "For God so loved the world that God gave God's only child, that whoever believes in that child should not perish, but have eternal life."[23]

It is likely that this new, monstrous rewording of John 3:16 and the recommended use of the terms "She" and Her" to refer to God is a preliminary to reintroducing the ancient Babylonian concept of the Mother Goddess to Christian congregations. Satan's motive in sowing Scriptural confusion and discord in the Church becomes clear once we understand the obvious parallels between the perverse Mystery religious system of Babylon and the present-day doctrines of the New Age.

Does the Bible Contain Hidden Mystery Teachings?

Yet another effort to revise the Bible is the New Age push to reinterpret the Bible to unveil and discover its hidden Mystery Teachings. New Age scholars hope to reinterpret the Bible in light of the occult teachings of Eastern mysticism. This is the reason for *The New Age Bible Interpretation* and for the recent publication of a score of books that offer a "fresh look" at the Scriptures.

Those pushing Satan's Plan for a One World Religion are working hard to pollute Christianity with Eastern teachings. Peter De Coppens, editor of a series of books on New Age theology published by Llewellyn, a company specializing in astrology and occult publications, suggests that a "universal brotherhood of human beings" can be achieved by Christians who practice a "Yoga of the West." "If the final *planetary synthesis of the Eastern and Western spiritual traditions is to be realized*," he writes, "Eastern mysticism must be incorporated into traditional Christianity."[24]

De Coppens praises the creation of a New Age theology in which Christianity is horribly mixed with almost every anti-Christian philosophy that ever existed. He mentions the quest for wisdom by those who earnestly study "Eastern religions and Yoga, the new psychologies, the old Sacred Traditions and Esoteric Brotherhoods of Mysticism, Occultism, Magic, and Alchemical Schools as well as Theosophy, Anthrosophy, and Rosicrucian Societies, not to mention ancient witchraft, modern parapsychology, and the many Western cults that have emerged."[25] After listing these Satanic religions and philosophies, he states that "all religions, all races, all societies" have always had the same living source of revelation and spiritual guidance, and that to find Truth, the Christian need look no further than *within his own self*, for each of us is God:

> What we are interested in is not the calcified, institutional shell we are most familiar with, but Christianity as a true and living adventure, as the . . . "Ageless Wisdom" whose central objective has always been and will always be the incarnation and full realization of the Great Work—Spiritual Initiation through union with God, who . . . is none other than our true Self.[26]

De Coppens encourages Christians to believe in the development of "Christed human beings," whom he defines as "a God-man or -woman who has achieved and incarnates self-knowledge, self-mastery, and self-integration—one who can truly express the Self."[27]

De Coppens further says his research showed that the roots of Christianity can be traced back to the Chaldean, Egyptian and Greek Mystery traditions, as well as the Hermetism, Qubalah, Alchemy, Druidic, and Rosicrucian traditions. Thus, it is not necessary for those in the West seeking "a viable, livable, and effective process of psychospiritual transformation" to depart the Christian faith. Instead, a sincere and devout Christian may find in his own tradition and church "the answer to his deepest and most authentic spiritual needs and aspirations."[28]

In essence, de Coppens tells us that we need not make a pilgrimage to Tibet, New Delhi, or Mecca to seek guidance from the gurus. All that's necessary is that we "discover" within our present Christian faith Eastern and occult meanings and *reinterpret the Bible accordingly.*

Other New Age authorities echo de Coppens. "In the Gospel of Jesus Christ," says Barnwell, "there is a hidden 'blueprint' showing the way that a human being becomes divine." Corinne Heline's *The New Age Bible Interpretation* contends that "the entire Bible is written so that it has one meaning for the masses of the people and another for occult students."

Will Christians be gulled into believing the claims of New

Age leaders? As the New Age's Lola Davis so proudly exclaims, "Within the last two decades there has been an increasing awareness of mysticism among Christians. Many are studying meditation and reading esoteric books." The next step, already taken by many, is to view the Bible as just another esoteric book of secret Mystery Teachings, whose true meanings can only be deciphered by those to whom the "spirits" provide revelation.

Paul wrote that he was careful to avoid fancy words and argument in his sermons lest the simple but powerful message of Jesus and salvation be obscured. The Bible, then, is not a book of hidden Mystery Teachings to be explained for us by some New Age guru, but a revelation of Jesus Christ and a clear and simple guide to every aspect of our lives.

Fake Gospels

In an attempt to reduce the growing influence of early Christianity, the Jewish Essene sect, the Gnostics, and other heretical groups created a number of fake bibles and Gospels (including the Gospel of Peter and the Gospel of St. Thomas). Invariably these books include details that contradict the Bible, including lies about Jesus teaching reincarnation and karma. Predictably, New Age spokesmen quote such passages as "proof" of their un-Biblical doctrines.

Fake Gospels are also turning up that are said to be *new revelations* given by angels or spirits to modern-day prophets. The *Book of Mormon* is an example, as are the abominable versions of the Bible published by the Jehovah Witnesses and the Christian Scientists.

A "Gospel" that is widely quoted by the New Age is *The Aquarian Gospel of Jesus the Christ*. Supposedly transmitted verbatim to an American from Ohio named Levi in 1911 through a vision by an angelic presence, the *Aquarian Gospel* depicts Jesus studying with the Yogis in India. Consider this passage in which Jesus and a friend ponder about the "truth" of reincarnation:

> 9 One day Ajainin sat with Jesus in the temple porch; a band
> of wandering singers and musicians paused before the court
> to sing and play.

¹⁰ Their music was most rich and delicate, and Jesus said, Among the high-breed people of the land we hear no sweeter music than that these uncouth children of the wilderness bring here to us.

¹¹ From whence this talent and this power? In one short life they surely could not gain such grace of voice, such knowledge of the laws of harmony and tone.

¹² Men call them prodigies. There are no prodigies. All things result from natural law.

¹³ These young people are not young. A thousand years would not suffice to give them such divine expressiveness, and such purity of voice and touch.

¹⁴ Ten thousand years ago these people mastered harmony. In days of old they trod busy thoroughfares of life, and caught the melody of birds, and played on harps of perfect form.

¹⁵ And they have come again to learn still other lessons from the varied notes of manifests.²⁹

Outright Lies

When it is not possible to discredit the Bible and its teachings of Jesus and godly doctrine by means such as the production of fake Gospels, New Age spokesmen sometimes go on the offensive, directly challenging the Scriptures and the writers of the books of the Bible. Thus, Benjamin Creme attempts both to slam Christianity and exalt The Plan by holding Paul up to a bad light:

> Christianity was really built by St. Paul . . . and St. Paul made a number of mistakes. He distorted Christianity considerably. He is now one of the Masters of Wisdom . . . humanity suffered through Paul's mistakes, but The Plan eventually won out. The Plan is ideal.³⁰

Creme's ridiculous assertion is that after his death Paul was informed of his mistakes by the Lord Maitreya. Paul has since been assigned by Maitreya to a position as a Master of Wisdom.

John Randolph Price also challenges and reinterprets Scripture. He says that Deuteronomy 6:5-9 ("and thou shalt love the Lord thy God with all thine heart, and with all thy soul, and with all thy might") means that we are to love our own Higher Self. We also find the following statements made by this high-ranking leader of the New Age:

> The Divine Plan for you does not have a special section on suffering . . . you are not here to endure hardships.[31]

> In truth . . . you never fell from grace, and you certainly were not tossed out of some garden and told to till the ground until you dropped dead.[32]

Objective: Infiltrate the Christian Church

Infiltration—subversion of the Christian Church from within—is already far advanced. Marilyn Ferguson warned in 1980 that:

> Formal religion in the west has been shaken to its roots by defections, dissent, rebellions, loss of influence, diminishing financial support. . . . If they cannot find new roles in a rapidly changing society, they may go the way of the railroads—without Amtrak.[33]

The New Age does not seek to have Christianity "go the way of the railroads." It suits the Devil's purpose to keep the Christian churches intact. What Satan wants is the hearts and minds—the very souls—of the living members of Christian churches. Christian pastors who bring blasphemous New Age-oriented messages and lay witnesses who teach new Christian converts that the Bible is flawed and that the New Age doctrine and the Bible are compatible are examples of what Satan has in mind for the future of Christianity.

Evangelist Jimmy Swaggart has wisely said that the Christian cannot be sure he's in a local *Christ-filled* congregation just because he's a member of a certain denomination or that the shingle on the door of his church indicates a particular faith group. Apostasy and heresy seem to be sweeping Christianity.

The New Age is heartened and encouraged by Christianity's growing apostasy. New Age leaders now often advise their followers *not to leave* their churches, but instead to work for changes *from within.* The New Age plans to seed the churches with what Elissa McClain has called "Cosmic Christians"—people who pretend to be Christians, but are in fact disciples of Satan sent to disrupt and destroy.

New Wave, Cosmic Christians

There is a New Wave of "Christians" flooding our churches today, bringing with them the idolatrous and blasphemous doctrines of the New Age. Calling themselves "spiritual," some support social welfare goals and pacifism but deny the power of Jesus. Others profess a belief in the New Age prosperity gospel.

Norman Boucher, in *New Age Journal*, enthusiastically reports that "after rejecting the belief of its fathers, an entire generation is reclaiming religion—and changing our churches and temples in the process."[34]

The New Wave Christian leadership and laity is eager to learn of the ideas and doctrines of the New Age. For example, New Age psychic and medium Ruth Montgomery says that for years she has received support and invitations from both Catholic and Protestant churches:

> When I reluctantly wrote *A Search for the Truth* in 1965, I feared ostracism by the religious community. Instead, I was flooded by invitations from Protestant ministers to speak from their pulpits, and from Catholic academia to address their student bodies.[35]

As mind-boggling as it is sad, even witchcraft and Satanism are finding favor inside a few Christian churches. Miriam Starhawk, perhaps the world's best known witch propagandist, has been invited by Christian groups to speak about her goddess witchcraft religion. In *Circle Network News*, a newsletter for witches, she stated that she "found the students very receptive to new ideas, hungry for new forms of ritual and very creative." Starhawk concluded: "I am very glad to discover such strong movement within Christian churches that is sympathetic to the Pagan Spirit and willing to learn from the teachings of the Old Religion."[36]

The success of Satanic witchcraft in infiltrating Christian

churches has spurred the Church of WICCA to escalate their efforts at achieving recognition and respect. The Christian Information Bureau, a Dallas, Texas, ministry wonderfully dedicated to shining some light on the growing apostasy, recently published in its newsletter a story about a witches' organization which asked its members to "contact Christian allies: Put us in touch with sympathetic Christian clergy and lay people . . . who will write letters on behalf of us and the WICCAN religion, which we can pass on. . . ."[37]

The mixed-up Christian leaders and congregations who are now desecrating their churches by bringing in occultism and listening to New Age heralds and teachers, or worse, demons, are the vanguard for Satan's New Age One World Religion. For years we have seen a tidal wave of heresy and apostasy as some churches ordained homosexual ministers and even sanctioned marriages between members of the same sex. We've seen a growing number of churchmen spread lies about our Lord and about the Bible. Below are just a few recent examples.

Denial of Biblical Accuracy

In Great Britain, Right Reverend David Jenkins, the Anglican Bishop of Durham, prides himself on his heresies. *Newsweek* magazine reports that Henkins denies the miracle of Jesus' resurrection. "No concrete event underlies the doctrine," says the bishop. He also denies the virgin birth and claims that the description of Biblical tongues of fire at Pentecost is just colorful phraseology. However, Jenkins's boss, the Most Reverend Robert Runcie, smiles at his heretical underling, remarking, "There's room for everyone in the Anglican Church."[38]

Politicization of the Church

Long-time members of mainline denominations are becoming increasingly frustrated at the heretical turn their Church's leadership is taking. Nikolai Lenin, the first Communist ruler in the Soviet Union, once urged his followers to politicize the Church if they wished to neutralize its influence. His advice is now being adopted by a growing number of Presbyterian, Methodist, Episcopal, Lutheran, Baptist, and other Churches in the United States.

The leadership of the Presbyterian Church (U.S.A.) repeatedly has branded the U.S. government a warmonger. Its Advisory Council on Church and Society recently published a study which promotes pacifist resistance to the government and calls on its members to withdraw from military-related occupations and refuse to serve in military service. Opinion polls show that rank-and-file Presbyterians strongly disapprove of their Church's stance, but its activist hierarchy has seized control and continues its broadsides against America.[39]

The Presbyterian Church has also adopted the title "New Age Dawning" for its Five-Year Plan for Evangelism in the Presbyterian Church (U.S.A.) To critics who opposed this, including many Presbyterians, Robert Meneilly, chairman of the committee that chose this slogan, retorted, "Those who oppose the New Age movement would likely oppose what the Presbyterian Church (U.S.A.) already is doing and saying."[40]

The United Methodist Church also has a number of pastors in high places who appear to have become pawns of the New Age. In one recent issue of the *United Methodist Report* alone, several Methodist laymen wrote Letters to the Editor pleading with the Church to return to its long-standing traditions of loyalty to the Bible and to God.[41] Here are a few selected, actual comments from the published letters of Methodist laymen that perfectly characterize what seems to be happening at-large inside the denomination:

Letter No. 1:
"The . . . changed self-concept of today's minister is provoking and troubling. . . . I reject the notion a minister's *personal life* offers the sole opportunity or context in which he can express his real self."

Letter No. 2:
"It gets harder each year to sell the (church) . . . when the hierarchy promiscuously abuse the system with what appears to be very little concern for the folks back home.
"Boards such as the General Board of Global Ministries and its high-handed approach . . . disregard(s) the need for missionaries. . . . Instead they support . . . schools and rebellious groups promoting violence—definitely not Christian

in any way, shape, or form, at the expense of the Gospel.

"On top of that, the church has within its structure such groups as the Commission on the Status and Role of Women . . . that hires self-avowed practicing lesbians. . . ."

Letter No. 3:

"The creeping spiritual rot that destroys our church continues. Among other incidents, I have endured a pastor who prayed to 'our heavenly Mother,' a district superintendent who . . . announced he was voting in favor of the ordination of homosexuals, and a United Methodist missionary to Japan who torpedoed a missions conference with this statement: 'I teach English and would never presume to convert a Shintoist. They have their way.' "

Church Unity and Ecumenicism

One of Satan's greatest lies is that unity guarantees purity and goodness. He seeks to unite all Christian Churches—indeed all religions—in an inseparable bond of un-Biblical ecumemicism.

Pastor Thomas H. Trapp, campus pastor for Wisconsin Lutheran Chapel and Student Center at the University of Wisconsin in Madison, last year wrote an article taking to task those who call for unity but push for a gospel other than Jesus:

Jesus is the starting point for discussion on spiritual unity. But ecumenical organizations, like the World Council of Churches, frown on those who insist on the Christ of Scripture. Members of the modern ecumenical movement say or imply that it's "narrow" or "unloving" when we insist that Jesus is the only way. . . . These critics, in effect, deny the Christ of Scripture who personally insists that He is the *only* way to God. (John 14:6)[42]

Pastor Trapp's decrying of a false unity is Biblical, for Peter (2 Pet. 2:1) and other Bible writers cautioned us to beware of false prophets and apostasy in the last days. In regard to the World Council of Churches (WCC), these prophesied warnings have come to pass. In recent years key articles in *Readers Digest* exposed the terrible misdeeds of this politically-oriented apostate group. The WCC has given millions of dollars to Marxist groups and terrorists around the world fighting pro-Western governments. The WCC has refused to criticize Soviet atrocities in Afghanistan and elsewhere, and averted its eyes when countries such as Ethiopia massacred its citizens, persecuted Christians, and closed Christian churches.[43]

The most convincing indictment I have seen of the WCC comes from Edmund W. Robb, chairman of the Institute on Religion and Democracy in Washington, D.C., and his journalist daughter, Julia Robb. In their extremely well-documented exposé *The Betrayal of the Church*, they lay bare the apostate conduct of the WCC, the National Council of Churches, and the mainline Christian denominations that support these groups. "The World Council of Churches is blatantly and unashamedly opposed to the free market," the Robbs report, "and makes full use of its U.S. funds to combat the free enterprise system."[44]

Might the WCC, either unwittingly or knowingly, someday throw its support behind a One World Government led by the New Age "Christ?" The Robbs show how, in its battle against free enterprise, the WCC has called for a "world economic order or have advocated some sort of international control of the earth's economies." The WCC and its supporters believe "that the fortunes of the world's disadvantaged would improve if the world's economic system were under a gigantic bureaucracy."[45]

You begin to fully understand the depths to which the WCC has sunk when you learn that many New Age spokesmen are very complimentary toward this four hundred-million-member organization. Lola Davis expresses the general consensus of the New Age when she remarks that the WCC may well become the nucleus of a World Religion:

> The World Council of Churches . . . has potential to serve as a source of unity among the diversity of religions. The West is becoming more familiar with the Eastern religions because of the efforts of some of their spiritual leaders.[46]

The National Council of Churches (NCC) also has sent funds to Communist Vietnam, praised Marxist regimes, as well as terrorist groups such as the Palestine Liberation Organization (PLO), and criticized U.S. government policies. Among the largest of thirty-two denominations representing forty million Christians in the NCC are the United Methodist Church, the Presbyterian Church (U.S.A.), the United Church of Christ, the Disciples of Christ, and the Episcopal Church.[47]

Apostasy: The Roman Catholic Example

It can easily be documented that New Age practices and doctrines are rampaging within the Catholic Church also. So, while Biblical Christians rightly are alarmed about the growing trend toward apostasy within the Protestant churches, they should understand that apostasy within the Catholic Church has an even stronger foothold.

Examples of Catholic New Age apostasy are so numerous I have room for only a few.

Some Catholic priests invite demons by teaching Silva Mind Control and other meditation and invocation rituals to their parishoners. Jose Silva, the founder of the Silva Mind Control System, is a Catholic.

A number of Catholic nuns and priests are devoted believers in Zen Buddhism, Tai Chi, and Hinduism. A recent article in *The Catholic Accent* displayed photos of nuns at a Zen retreat bowing to each other, to recognize the divinity in each other.[48] Father Bede Griffiths, a monk in the order of St. Benedict, has lived among the Hindus in India for the last thirty years. He remains officially a recognized Catholic teacher of the gospel, even though his teachings are 100 percent Hindu and 100 percent New Age. Griffith says he agrees completely with heretic priest Meister Eckhart, who once said, "I pray God to rid me of God."[49]

Objective: Deceive the Christian Churches

The New Age is not having difficulty deceiving many Christian leaders and laypeople. Two examples will suffice to illustrate the extent to which some Christians have fallen victim to The Great Deception.

Peace and Love: The Empty New Age Commitment

Many Christians have been seduced by the New Age's soothing commitment to "love" and "peace." These two words pack such power among Christians that many just cannot believe that New Agers who express commitment to love and peace could be instruments of Satan. The words of Hal Lindsey on October 28, 1986, on TV's Trinity Broadcasting Network should provide an awakening: "The pursuit of *peace* by the Antichrist through the New Age Movement is how they'll take over the world."

Larry A. Jackson, president of Lander College in Greenwood, South Carolina, a graduate of Union Theological Seminary in New York, exemplifies the new view that instilling brotherly love is *the* most important mission of the Christian Church:

> The church of tomorrow will affirm a belief . . . that ultimate reality is love. . . . Love as ultimate reality will become the central message of the church.[50]

The Devil can appreciate a human love that excludes Jesus. Jackson has also implied that dropping insistence on the Lordship of Jesus while emphasizing some kind of abstract love will appeal to scholars, politicians, and business executives. This is New Age propaganda.

Does God Want Everyone to Be Rich?

An un-Biblical doctrine gathering steam in Christian churches is the "Prosperity Gospel." This unholy doctrine is a key tenet of the New Age which falsely claims that riches are marks of the truly religious person. Lola Davis explains that since God is in everything—trees, grass, automobiles, and paintings—material possessions must be the "bounties of God." "Would it not," she asks, "contribute to peace and joy on earth if we accepted material things as expressions of God and therefore, as spiritual elements? Only this way," Davis exclaims, "can mankind develop God-like qualities."[51]

Fashion and success consultant Robert Pante, who has been called the "high priest of prosperity, minister to the moneyed," scoffingly remarks, "Those who pray with a poverty conscious-ness aren't going anywhere. Lots of poor folks pray and don't get anything."[52]

Pante specializes in conducting seminars in which he berates women attendees who don't dress great—that is, who are not up to Pante's standards—with such derisive comments as, "You look like you don't get out much," and "She looks like an aging cheerleader."

Pante, the author of *Dressing to Win,* says that he is "a social worker for the rich, soon to be rich and those strongly desiring to be rich." He believes that the problem with the poor is that they don't believe they are gods. That's how he acquired wealth, Pante insists. "I was very poor. Then I found out I was god, a co-creator."[53] Riches and success ensued, Pante assures his audi-ences.

These sentiments are shared by many other New Age spokesmen. They say that not only does induction into the New Age World Religion certify a person as scientific-minded and a thinking person, but it also makes him destined to become blessedly affluent.

The New Age leader lures new converts by holding out the carrot of riches and prosperity through mind power. Man-gods supposedly *will* money to come their way. John Randolph Price thrills his followers by telling them, "You were born to be rich!" He teaches that all that's necessary is for the individual to devel-op a prosperity consciousness through willpower, which Price terms the "Will of Wealth."[54]

Was Jesus a Wealthy Man?

One New Age minister has even been able to appeal to the individual's most coarse materialistic desires while, at the same time, casting doubts on the life of Jesus. Dr. Catherine Ponder, a minister of the Unity Church in Palm Desert, California, has been described as the "Norman Vincent Peale among lady minis-ters." She teaches positive thinking and powers of the mind, asserting that a person can profit from prosperity "secrets."

Dr. Ponder's books allege that Biblical heroes were wealthy because of their spiritually advanced minds. Her book, *The Millionaire from Nazareth: His Prosperity Secrets for You* proclaims that there is gold in the gospel for you. According to Ponder, "Jesus understood, used, and taught the mental and spiritual laws of prosperity. A part of Jesus' mission was expressly to save mankind from its belief about financial limitations."[55]

Ponder further claims that Jesus practiced what he preached. He was not a poor illiterate carpenter. Jesus was a world-traveling rich man: "Contrary to what most of us have believed, Jesus certainly was not poor. Instead, Jesus was the wealthiest man who ever trod this earth."

She goes on to say that it is pagan to be poor. "The prosperous truth is that, as a child of God, it is a sin to be poor and it is your birthright to prosper and succeed."

Ponder's claims are ridiculous but contain within them a covetous message that has captivated tens of thousands of people who want desperately to become rich. Certainly if Jesus, a simple carpenter's son, had been a materially wealthy man, He would not have had to resort to the miracle of the fishes and loaves of bread. He would not have been without honor in His own city, and after His arrest, His disciples could have paid off the authorities to win His release. Instead, He went to the cross a pauper. The Roman guards attending His execution cast lots for His only worldly possession: His cloak.

The promise to deliver prosperity to its converts is the driving force behind at least some of the New Age success. Unfortunately, some Christian leaders have taken this same tack, preaching that a Christian can have Cadillacs, mansions, millions of dollars. "Just name it and claim it."

Some, like Harlem's Reverend Ike, are terribly blatant. The ministry of Reverend Ike, known as the flamboyant "money preacher" because of his penchant for diamond rings, gaudy gold jewelry, and expensive luxury cars, continues to thrive even though he preaches heresy. In early 1987, when he agreed to record a song, "Mind Your Own Business," with country music star Hank Williams, Jr., Ike snapped:

I really wanted to sing "Mind Your Own Business," because if you mind your own [curse word deleted] business, you'll have more time and energy to get rich, which is what it's all about. Get your own [curse word deleted] Rolls Royce instead of being jealous of mine.[56]

Reverend Ike may be the most crass and brazen "money preacher," but many others have joined the prosperity bandwagon in recent years. In addition to money, some ministers and TV evangelists are preaching to their listeners the horrible falsehood that giving to the Lord is a *financial investment,* that God will pay them back tenfold, even a thousandfold for their contributions. Thousands of Christians today are giving for entirely the wrong reason: only to get something back in return.

Does the Bible Support the Prosperity Gospel?

God does not promise us material riches. We know that Jesus told us it is harder for a rich man to receive salvation than it is for a camel to go through the eye of a needle. He also praised the poor widow who was only able to give an insignificant sum as a tithe, while he condemned the rich who beat their breasts and boasted of all they had given the Church. Jesus gave us this wisdom:

> Do not store up for yourselves treasures on earth, where
> moth and rust destroy, and where thieves break in and steal.
> But store up for yourself treasures in heaven, where moth
> and rust do not destroy, and where thieves do not break in
> and steal. For where your treasure is, there will your heart be
> also. (Matt. 6:19-21, NIV)

Material things are not in themselves bad, but to expect God to shower us with them *is.* God promises to take care of our financial needs sufficiently. Anything more than the basics should be deeply appreciated and the Lord given thanks and praise. But He owes us nothing. Indeed, His Son Jesus *bought us.* We are His. In His love for us, He paid the price and now He offers to us the world's richest possessions—greater than all the diamond mines in South Africa, all the gold and jewels that King Solomon ever possessed: the priceless gifts of forgiveness of our sins, contentment while on earth, and the incredibly valuable rewards that await each believer in heaven.

Christian ministers of the Prosperity Gospel are "spiritual cousins" of the New Age. They are blurring distinctions in the minds of their flocks as to the vital difference between the spiritual teachings of the Bible and the money-hungry values of the New Age. Such leaders bring discredit on God and themselves, and they help the New Age deceive men and women and keep them from the truth.

Where Apostasy Leads

The Great Apostasy is already far advanced. Satan's Plan to discredit, infiltrate, and deceive is succeeding in weakening the very foundations of the Christian Church. This is no surprise, for Peter warned of false prophets who will bring in damnable heresies (2 Pet. 2:1-3). Peter told us to "Be sober, be vigilant; because your adversary the devil, as a roaring lion, walketh about, seeking whom he may devour" (1 Pet. 5:8).

The Devil is no respecter of persons: he seeks to devour *all*. In the following chapter I'll show how Satan has designs on the most vulnerable and least protected segment of humanity: our children.

SEVENTEEN

Cry for Our Children

*But whoso shall offend one of these little ones which
believe in me, it were better for him that a millstone
were hanged about his neck, and that he were drowned
in the depth of the sea.*   (Matt. 18:6)

*I am convinced that the battle for mankind's future
must be waged and won in the public school classrooms
by teachers who correctly perceive their role as the
proselytizers of a new faith. . . .*

*The classroom must and will become an arena of
conflict between the old and the new—the rotting corpse
of Christianity, together with all its adjacent evils and
misery, and the new faith . . . resplendent in its
promise. . . .*   (John Dunphy, *The Humanist*)

C hristene Mireles was so pleased that some
classmates from school had invited her to a
party. But shortly after the fourteen-year-old
student arrived, she found that no one among the twenty-five
people at the party would talk to her. In fact, they all seemed to
be angry with her. "Some had a terrible look in their eyes,"
Christene recalled.

Suddenly a group of girls ran toward her and started punch-
ing and beating her up. Surprised and frightened, she cried out
to a nearby adult chaperone. The man just looked on, a smirk
etched across his face. Christene heard him actually encouraging
her attackers to continue beating her.

Later, from her hospital room, Christene tearfully explained,
"I didn't know they were all Satanists." The young teenager had
been beaten because she had refused to become a Satanist and
join a devil-worship group.[1]

Across America and throughout the world, Satanism has

spread its strong and evil tentacles around young men and women. The rise of the occult has become a plague among youth of all ages as well. But Satanism and the occult are only two symptoms of the disease know as New Age spirituality.

The New Age has cast its rotten net in a bold quest to destroy an entire generation. Its subversive influences permeate all of society. It is imbedded in the curricula of our public schools, infecting kid's library and comic books; it has reared its hideous head on Saturday morning TV cartoon shows and turned many popular cinema productions into celebrations of sorcery, violence, and sadism. The New Age has transformed America's largest toy companies into purveyors of demonic terror and has helped to turn rock music concerts into blood-curdling ritualistic devil-fests.

Our children have been at risk for decades now as Satan has worked The Plan, wielding his dark supernatural powers in unprecedented attack waves. His goal: to wipe out all vestiges of Christianity and the Bible from our schools and our culture and, by so doing, to win youth away from Christ.

Atheism and Secular Humanism, though extremely successful, were only crude first attempts by the Devil. In the New Age movement and religion, Satan has latched on to something far more effective and more direct. Both atheism and Secular Humanism honor man and his potential. But man does not have the spiritual resources to stand on his own. His destiny is to serve either darkness or light, God or His adversary. The New Age is designed, therefore, to take man-worship to its logical and ultimate conclusion: the exaltation of Lucifer as Lord of the Universe.

Where Does God Stand?

Jesus was not a man to tolerate evil of any kind. But of all the sinful acts a man might commit, the Lord made it abundantly clear that harming a child is one of the most despicable. Jesus loved sinners so immensely that He willingly gave His life for them. Yet He bluntly told His disciples that "whoso shall offend one of these little ones which believe in me, it were better for him that a millstone were hanged around his neck, and that he were drowned in the depth of the sea" (Matt. 18:6).

The adult who damages a child subjects himself to the terrible wrath of the Almighty. An especially frightening condemnation is reserved for the individual who harms a child *spiritually,* for, as Jesus said, "It is not the will of your Father which is in heaven, that one of these little ones should perish" (Matt. 18:14).

The child abusers of the New Age will someday be judged for what they are doing to our children. I cry aloud for the defenseless boys and girls whose tender bodies and souls are at the cruel mercy of the New Age overlords.

Why Children Are the Target

The Bible instructs us to "Train up a child in the way he should go: and when he is old, he will not depart from it" (Prov. 22:6). The mind of a young child is much like a malleable lump of clay. Satan desires to grasp and mold the precious commodity that is the clay-like mind of a child into a grotesque shape and form. Mocking God's creation, Lucifer is intent on refashioning our children into his own grim and perverse image.

New Age leaders know that if they are to bring in the New Age Kingdom, it will be necessary to snatch the new generation from their parents. William McLoughlin, a New Age political activist, believes that what he calls the "awakening" can be accomplished by the 1990s:

> The reason an awakening takes a generation or more to work itself out is that it must grow with the young; it must escape . . . the old ways. . . . Revitalization is growing up around us in our children, who are both more innocent and more knowing than their parents and grandparents. It is their world that has yet to be reborn.[2]

The Lucis Trust's Alice Bailey pinpoints the year 2000 as the Jubilee period for the New Age. Until then, she suggests that New Age disciples work especially hard to impart a new consciousness to young people. What must be done, Bailey emphasizes, is to "condition" the minds of young people, preparing them for the emergence of the New Order:

We are today vitally concerned with what is called the "new consciousness," from which new values to live by may be born as an impetus to carry humanity on into the New Age.[3]

Even a brief look at New Age literature reveals the importance given to the spiritual seduction of children. Among recent writings are such books as *Magical Child, Gift of Unknown Things, Children of the New Age, Celebration of the Child, Nurturing the Child of the Future,* and *The Conscious Child.* In such books, New Age adults are learning all the subtle and deceitful tricks they can use to persuade the young that the religion of their elders is of no value, and that instead they must worship the demon gods of the New Age.

Readers are told, for example, that children may have to be "encouraged" into exploring the new world that awaits them. Marilyn Ferguson suggests that one must not be afraid to "upset the learner." Ferguson cites one New Age spiritual teacher who commented, "True compassion is ruthless." Ferguson also approvingly quotes the poet Apollinaire, who wrote:

> Come to the edge, he said.
> They said: We are afraid.
> Come to the edge, he said.
> They came.
> He pushed them . . . and they flew.[4]

This is scary and spine-tingling stuff. Our kids are like some kind of spiritual fodder to the New Agers, to be ruthlessly pushed and mauled until, finally, they willingly accept the "truth" that the Bible is a lie, that the Son of God is a hoax, and that Lucifer the Great Initiator is the "bright and morning star" coming soon to restore each of us to wholeness.

The Plan envisions a society so saturated with occultism and New Age symbolism that children cannot escape being drawn into the clutches of Satan. As Phil Phillips so wisely stated in his exposé of occultic toys and cartoons: *"By the time the child is a teen, unless his parents have instilled Christian values in him, he will have more knowledge of the occult than he will have of God."*[5]

If you doubt for a moment the death grip that New Age

leaders have on the souls of our children, examine the current trends in each of the following areas of our culture and society:

Schools
Books
Cartoons and movies
Toys and games
Rock music

Are Public Schools the Devil's Playhouse?

Do you know what happens to your child once he or she is bundled up and sent off to school each day? Are you aware of the ideas teachers are putting into your child's head? Beneath the calm exterior of our nation's schools lies a raging volcano known as New Age doctrine and ritual. Each day, children are made to walk through the fire of this volcano so that the values of the New Age will become second nature to the upcoming generation.

The children themselves are not mature enough to know what is happening to them, and they have no frame of reference they can use to explain to their moms and dads the changes that are being induced into their hearts and minds as a result of classroom activity.

John Dunphy, an ardent New Ager who confesses a consuming interest in "folklore, history, and religion, especially ancient mystery-fertility cults and the Christian Gnostics," sounded the clarion call to battle in an award-winning essay he wrote for *The Humanist* magazine. In his essay, entitled "A Religion for the New Age," Dunphy remarked:

I am convinced that the battle for humankind's future must be waged and won in the public school classrooms by teachers who correctly perceive their role as the proselytizers of a new faith: a religion of humanity that recognizes and respects the spark of what theologians call divinity in every human being. These teachers must embody the same selfless dedication as the most rabid fundamentalist preachers.

The classroom must and will become an arena of conflict between the old and the new—the rotting corpse of

Christianity, together with all its adjacent evils and misery, and the new faith . . . resplendent in its promise. . . .[6]

The Underhanded, Deceptive Tactics of New Age Educators

Just how does the New Age propose to rid the schools of the "rotting corpse of Christianity"? The answer can be quickly seen: It is expected that deceit, treachery, and subversive lies will win the day. The influence of Dr. Beverly Galyean, who recently passed away, is still apparent in the curricula and educational practices being fostered on an unsuspecting public by New Age educators, administrators, and teachers. At an educators' conference sponsored by the Association for Humanistic Psychology, Galyean, a consultant on New Age-oriented "confluent education" for the Los Angeles City Schools, told co-conspirators:

> Around Los Angeles hundreds of people are practicing this kind of education, but fear permeates the environment because of a call for "fundamentals," discipline, control. . . .
> Our answer: . . . if your district wants discipline, tell them about programs that operate on the principle of self-control. . . . perhaps hyperactivity is a problem at your school. Use natural methods for calming over-active energies: Yoga, meditation, massage, movement, nutrition. . . . The crises now facing most school districts can be the springboard for your own humanistic experiments.[7]

Galyean's suggestions to educators call for them to inculcate in our children the belief that "We are all God, that we all have the attributes of God. . . ."[8] But in order to get this belief into our classroom without arousing the hackles of Christian parents who might object, Dr. Galyean advised discretion. Don't reveal our intentions, she cautioned. For example, when a teacher leads children into a group meditation exercise in which they visualize and make contact with demon guides, the teachers are to describe such guides as "imaginary guides" or "wise persons."[9]

Mario Fantini, formerly a Ford consultant on education, now at the State University of New York, has bluntly stated: "The psychology of becoming has to be smuggled into our schools." Marilyn Ferguson says that many New Age teachers have opted for "peaceful struggle." Esther Rothman finds it encouraging that "many teachers are already crusading rebels in the best sense of the word." "Only then," Rothman contends, "when aggression, love and power are used constructively in the classroom, can education really suceed."[10]

School supervisory personnel and administrators are even given formal instruction and training on how deceit and camoflauge can bring New Age material into classrooms. Charlotte Iserbyt, an educator who is also a Christian, has documented that subversion is rampant. Charlotte was herself given such training through federally funded programs, including the course Innovations in Education, designed by Professor Ronald Havelock. Charlotte says that this course:

> . . . instructed me on how to sneak in all the mind-bending techniques and humanistic courses and methods without getting caught, and how to identify the resisters in my community. Of course, I was a resister.[11]

Many teachers and educators promoting the New Age World Religion now blatantly and without fear slam Christianity in the classroom, while openly praising New Age principles and proclaiming the coming of the New Age Kingdom. Almost every conceivable New Age perversion is now being practiced in the classroom, offered up to our children as "constructive therapy," "values clarification," and enlightenment."

Child Abuse in the Classroom

Teachers have incredible powers for good or for evil. Unfortunately, Satan is inspiring many teachers to work at pushing an entire generation of young students over the cliff into a sea of occultism and spiritual despair. Marilyn Ferguson has devilishly noted that "even doctors, in their heyday as godlike paragons, have never wielded the authority of a single classroom teacher, who can purvey prizes, failure, love, humiliation and information to *great numbers of relatively powerless, vulnerable young people.*"[12]

Some of the many types of spiritual mayhem being carried

out by New Age warrior teachers and administrators came to light when the U.S. Department of Education conducted hearings around the country to gauge public opinion regarding the implementation of the "Protection of Pupil Rights" Amendment to the Hatch Act. Hearing examiners were startled when so many parents came forward to speak to the tragedy that has become commonplace in the classrooms of America.

Phyllis Schlafly, president of Eagle Forum, provided a wonderful service to America and to Christianity when she edited the transcripts of these hearings in the book *Child Abuse in the Classroom* (Crossway Books, 1985). This important book convincingly documents the inroads made by the New Age World Religion and its fellow traveler on the path, Secular Humanism. Below I have extracted some of the more poignant and revealing testimonies.

"My son was given questionnaires. . . . The young children are expected to fill in sentences, such as, 'The trouble with being honest is _____.' They are asked, what would be the hardest thing for you to do: steal, cheat, or lie? . . . (and) for group discussion in 3rd grade: How many of you ever wanted to beat up your parents?"

"MACOS (Man: A Course of Study) was a very subtle way of teaching our children genocide, homosexuality, euthanasia."

"Toward the end of this course last spring, my son told me what was happening in class. Mr. Davis, the teacher, would bring up a controversial moral issue such as premarital sex or homosexuality and call on members of the class to defend their positions on the issue. He would call upon those with opposite moral beliefs from Jon, thus exerting peer pressure on Jon to change his moral values. Jon was consistently called on up to 23 times per class session to defend his values. . . . When Jon mentioned to Mr. Davis that he was calling on him more than anyone else, Mr. Davis just said, 'Oh,' and continued calling on him."

"Dungeons and Dragons is a game played in many classes. . . . This game has been named as the reason for several suicides in the United States."

"In my son's 5th grade Health class . . . homosexuality was presented as an alternative lifestyle. Sexual activity among 5th graders was not discouraged."

"My younger daughter, in the 4th grade . . . started telling the happenings in her room . . . these happenings included role playing, Circle Times, and Secret Circle Times, in which my daughter was instructed not to tell anyone what was said or done, not even parents . . . my daughter has had to receive medical treatment because of this. . . ."

"A school test had this phrase dropped in—just like subliminal advertising: 'It must be lonely to be God. Nobody loves a master.' "

"On Labor Day . . . our son, Joe, committed suicide . . . when going through some . . . of his things I found some papers with notes taken in his psychology class. The notes were about psychic experiences, ESP, psychokinesis and astroprojection. . . . I began to question what was being taught. . . .

   ". . . I then asked my daughter, Theresa, who was a junior, to bring home the psychology book from the school. It was *Psychology for You,* by Sol Gordon. . . . Sol Gordon is a signer of the Second Humanist Manifesto. As I looked through it, it seemed to be a "how to" manual to the occult world. It suggested devising an experiment with a Ouija board. Pages 234 to 239 explain how to do meditation and TM and on page 313 and 314 it tells how to do Yoga."

"As we have removed prayer and the Bible from our schools, Yoga and Transcendental Meditation and other Eastern religions have crept into the classrooms . . . replacing the Judeo-Christian ethic. Mount Lebanon High School has a sign pointing the way to the Yoga room."

"I have a Future Studies publication, which was produced with the support of the National Institute of Education. The name of the publication is Future Studies in the Kindergarten through Twelve Curriculum authored by John D. Haas. The material is prepared for teachers to give them ideas. The preface suggests that the teachers infiltrate strategies into the curriculum. If this course has merit, why would a teacher be encouraged to sneak it into the curriculum? Topics suggested for the study include: Fertility Control, Contraceptives, Abortion, Family Planning, Women's Liberation, Euthanasia, New Age Consciousness, Mysticism, ESP, New Religions, Changing Older Religions, Guaranteed Income, Nuclear War, and so on."

". . . 'We teach them Yoga to attain peace, harmony and self-awareness.' 'Also,' the teacher said, 'I turn off the lights in the room and turn on moonlight, then we just lie on the floor and talk and fantasize. We also play fantasy scenes, breathing exercises and do . . . a Yoga exercise. . . . Children are to meditate.' . . ."

"Astrology books for youth were also available at that time. Children were to write their own horoscopes and make their own astrological sign."

"I met with a 6th grade teacher regarding a . . . seance that was held in her classroom. . . ."

"The children had to role-play the main character in each book, such as a warlock, a spiritist, an exorcist, and a poltergeist."

"The (school) counselors said . . . 'Yes . . . Christianity once served our country in a positive way, but now students today should seek other forms of religion to study and learn from.' Then the counselor suggested Yoga and meditation, and some of the Eastern mystic religions . . . these are little kids going up against a strong-speaking counselor."

"Our county was chosen . . . to implement the Global Studies Program. . . . The goal of Global Education is to prepare all youths to accept a world government for all systems and a global interdependence."

"In language textbooks in my own school district for grades K through 8, I found entire spelling lessons dealing with the terminology of the occult. . . . School libraries are full of witchcraft, demonic, and occult literature."

These are examples of how our children's minds are being warped and how our rights as parents are being violated. But as horrendous as these examples are, they are only the tip of the iceberg. My research has turned up hundreds of other nightmarish examples of the New Age takeover of many of our classrooms.

In Buffalo, New York, young students are required to learn the Silva Mind Control method and have reportedly "contacted" such dead spirit luminaries as George Washington and Patrick Henry.

In Atlanta, Georgia, in a case I became personally involved in, two courageous Christian women who objected to their children being forced by teachers to lie in the darkness and listen to hypnotic, mind control tapes became the retaliatory target of angry teachers and educators. Local pastors refused to "get involved."

In other schools, witches have been invited by officials to acquaint students with "alternative religions."

A literal avalanche of religious filth has entered the classroom, brought in by those responsible to protect our children.

Many of our kids are currently defenseless victims of adult men and women who are, in truth, ministers and propagandists for an alien religion hostile both to Christianity and to everything America stands for. The classrooms of America have become the breeding grounds and assembly lines for the manufacture of tens of thousands of little New Age gods.

Books Written in Hell

Young boys and girls who visit their school libraries are nowadays certain to find on the shelves a large number of books written to indoctrinate children on New Age values and ways of thinking. Here are descriptions of some of the more popular kids' books that school and public libraries have recently added to their collections:

The Dragons of North Chittendon, by Susan Fromberg Schaeffer. A fantasy story about a world constantly in a state of war because of the enmity that exists between humans and dragons. The hero is Arthur, a peace-loving dragon. Through visualization, he befriends a young man, Patrick. Patrick, who communicates with the dragon in dreams, longs for a "new age" in which dragons and men will live side-by-side in harmony and peace.

The Dragon ABC Hunt, by Loreen Leedy. For three- to six-year-olds. Depicts dragons as fun-loving, gleeful, humanlike creatures deserving love and respect by humans.

Secret Spells and Curious Charms, by Monika Beisner. This book comes fully illustrated with Satanic circles, triangles, and squares. It contains many magic spells and incantations for youngsters to practice.

King Stork, by Howard Pyle. The King of Storks helps a little boy woo a princess. In reviewing the book, even the liberal *Publishers Weekly* says it was surprised to find "such a sexy, bare-breasted lass as the princess in a children's book."

I Will Call It Georgie's Blues, by Suzanne Newton. This is a book that tells the story of a Reverend Mr. Sloan, a Christian minister whose behavior is destructive to his family. The Reverend is pictured as a master of outward pretense.

Watermusic, by Sarah Sargent. This book is an outrage. It is practically the story of a "young Shirley Maclaine," relating the mystical experiences of a thirteen-year-old girl as she talks with demons from beyond, as well as a giant white bat. It includes the playing of occultic ritual music and a confrontation with a monster, an "evil" counterpart to the "good" white bat.

Nelson Malone Meets the Man from Mush-nut, by Louise Hawes. Young Nelson borrows a huge snake from a neighbor who practices witchcraft. The young boy takes the snake to school with him for the celebration of Pet Day. The snake wins a prize as the most glamorous animal.

Dragon Dance, by John Christopher. Two young boys are thrown into an alternate world. They visit a mystical Eastern religious sect in the mountains of Bei-kun, where the priests have strange psychic powers.

Elliott and Win, by Carolyn Meyer. A story with decidedly pornographic overtones. The plot includes broken marriages and affairs, "faggots" and homosexuality, and a tough gang that rapes a young girl.

Is there any doubt the secular publishing industry is aiding and abetting the New Age conspiracy? The messages in the books mentioned are neither subtle nor veiled. They openly and forcefully focus the child's attention toward the decadent, pro-Satan theology of both the New Age and Secular Humanism. For example, notice that in some of these books, the dragon, the bat, and the snake—symbolizing Lucifer—are portrayed as "good," while the Christian minister is blasted for his sorry example as a leader.

Whatever Happened to Wholesome Movies and TV Shows?

Donald Duck, Mickey Mouse, and Pollyanna aren't "in" nowadays. New Age sorcery and devil worship *are.* If you haven't recently watched the Saturday morning TV cartoon shows for kids, do so. You'll be shocked at what you see. It's as if Satan himself produced some of these shows. Let me give you just a few examples of shows that the major networks and advertisers swear by the most:

"Thundercats." This cartoon series is chock-full of sorcery images. There's the magical eye of Thundra (which any student of ancient religions will easily recognize as the Third Eye of the Hindus and the all-seeing eye of the Egyptian-Babylonian Sun God, Horus). The main character in this cartoon frequently "talks" to his dead father's spirit. His magic sword levitates to his hand—a psychic trick often claimed by occultists and Hindu gurus. "Thundercats" also is known for Yoga exercises, serpents, and demon gods.

"The Smurfs." These lovable blue critters appear at first glance to be harmless. But New Age scriptwriters, directors, and producers have been successful in perverting the friendly Smurf show with New Age occult symbolism. Again we find levitation being practiced as well as magical chants and the occasional display of the Satanic pentagram. Papa Smurf uses enchantment to ward off evil.

"Rainbow Brite." The rainbow is a Biblical symbol that the New Age has wickedly mocked by attributing the false notion that the rainbow represents man's bridge to godhood. The "Rainbow Brite" heroine is pictured on the box of a best-selling cereal. Examine her image and you'll find a small, five-sided star (the Satanic pentagram) on her cheek.

"She-Ra, Princess of Power." This is the fantasized story of MYSTERY BABYLON, MOTHER OF HARLOTS incarnate. Ra is the ancient Egyptian Sun God/Goddess, also known as the Queen of Heaven and the Goddess of Power. In the TV cartoon, She-Ra operates within and between two planet worlds: Eternia and Etheria. (Though the show does not explain the name, the *Ether* world is the habitat where some New Agers say their New Age "Christ" and the disembodied spirits reside.) She rides on a friendly horse, "Spirit," that has the ability to transform itself into a unicorn (a New Age symbol of horned power and Satanic enmity) and has wings of rainbow colors. She-Ra is portrayed as a godlike being with supernatural powers—the most powerful woman in the universe—who constantly battles with evil.

"He-Man, Master of the Universe." He-Man is also a supernatural man-god. Children are indoctrinated into such New Age occultic symbols and practices as pyramid and crystal power, serpents, the Satanic ram's head, the skull, witches' charms and spells. The child is introduced to such characters as Skeletor, Sorceress, Beast Man, and Stratos, a half-man and half-bird.

And on the Big Screen . . .

Big screen movies don't offer much better fare for children. Movie producers seem driven to churn out one occult fantasy feature after another. By cleverly weaving together "good" and "evil" characters and themes, anti-Christian movies have managed to cloud our children's minds so they can no longer discern between the real and the unreal or between right and wrong.

A prime example is the movie *E.T.,* which grossed over $619 million. E.T., a demon look-alike, was a creature from space who had powers only a god could possess. In fact, he was patterned after Jesus Christ. E.T. healed people; he could read their minds and communicate without language; he levitated and ascended. This cinema production even included death and resurrection scenes.

E.T. is just one of many films that capture and manipulate the subconscious minds of children. Another is *Close Encounters of the Third Kind,* a Steven Spielberg production in which powers from another world communicate with selected humans on earth. Each person is drawn by *impulse* toward a meeting and union with the peaceful aliens. Many in the New Age say that they, too, are called by impulse by their spirit Masters from the invisible world.

Young boys especially love the many *Ninja* movies. Watch just one such movie and your eyes will be dazzled by the brutality and carnage represented. These include direct allusions to mental sorcery, oriental meditation, and supernatural mind powers. Also note that the Ninja warrior is skilled at wielding a unique death weapon: a Chinese star, a Satanic pentagram-shaped instrument with razor-sharp edges.

Study carefully the messages most of today's movies are sending kids and you'll soon realize the shocking truth: our children are being gradually initiated into a New Age of occultism, sorcery, and blasphemy. In *Dune,* children are given an image of a young man's initiation into godhood; the *Star Wars* sagas present a universal deity vaguely named "The Force," a cosmic energy that is incorporated in all living things. In the adventurous *Raiders of the Lost Ark* and *The Temple of Doom,* children are exposed to "powers" and then shown how to actively participate in their exercise.

What Happened to Joy in the Toybox?

Once upon a time parents could be confident that their only worry in buying toys was whether the toy was physically safe for kids. A far greater danger now lurks in the toybox: the strong possibility of irreversible damage through explicit Satanism built into the toy. Toys have become spiritual killers.

Today the largest-selling toys are dolls and figurines of licensed cartoon characters, such as She-Ra and He-Man. Incredible as it may seem, many of these toys represent demons. For example, the "Masters of the Universe" cartoon series offers children toys connected with He-Man, manufactured by Mattel. One offering is Skeletor. Read the instructions that come with Skeletor, and you'll discover that every child who follows those instructions is inviting into his mind nightmarish demons of darkness:

> When you put on your Skeletor helmet and armored belt you become transformed into an agent of evil. Use your power sword shield to combat good. With your mystical ram's head scepter you will be able to call forth the denizens of darkness to help conquer the forces of good.

Your child can get his hands on a dizzying array of similarly demented toys. He can purchase Godbox and be guaranteed a direct line to God. Little girls and boys can play with the Power Lords, a toy set with such characters as "Shaya, Queen of Power," "Raygoth," and "Gapplog." Shaya, like She-Ra, has cosmic powers and can transform her body into that of an extraterrestrial. Crystlar introduces children to a strange world where magic reigns following a cosmic demon war.

Some toy companies don't even *try* to disguise the Satanic message inherent in their toys. Yet parents seem all too eager to buy their kids toys like Skeletor, Power Lords, Godbox, and Crystlar. The same holds true for fantasy games now popular with children. That Dungeons and Dragons is an occult game endangering the souls of young players is no secret. This also can be said of a similar game, Dragonraid.

In addition to toys and games that are openly occultic in nature, there is an alarming trend among toy and game makers and comic book publishers to display Satanic and witchcraft symbolism. Some skateboards now being sold by Toys R Us, for example, have hideous dragons emblazoned on the surface. Other times this is done subtly, for maximum subliminal effect. For instance, in what is otherwise a joyful adventure story, a Satanic triangle or hexagram or an upside-down cross will appear innocuously in the background of a scene. Certainly the artist, writer, and publisher know exactly what they're doing. Most parents haven't the foggiest notion that their children's minds are being subjected to underground psychic warfare.

Rock Music

Several Christian writers have exposed rock music's preoccupation with sexism, Satanism, and occultism. However, too many parents continue to allow their children and teenagers to focus their minds on heavy metal rock music. The time has certainly come when Christian parents should put their feet down and take authority over their children. The alternative is to willingly allow the child to enter a spiritual realm of unspeakable horror.

Consider the names of some of the most successful rock groups and their biggest hits. The group Judas Priest sells out in live performances at Madison Square Garden in New York City. Their blasphemous album "Defender of the Faith" smashed all sorts of sales records. They've also released "Hell Bent for Leather," "Point of Entry," "Unleashed in the East," and "Screaming for Vengeance." In Nevada in 1985 two teenagers formed a suicide pact after listening to the Judas Priest album "Stained Glass" while drinking liquor and smoking marijuana. One died from the shotgun blast; the other is permanently disfigured for life.

The Dead Kennedys is another rock group. The offensive name is only part of their story. Their repugnant album "Frankenchrist" (a hellish combination of Frankenstein and Christ) comes complete with a poster neatly tucked into the album sleeve. The poster depicts what initially appears to the eye to be beansprouts poking out from a bed of plants. But a second glance makes one's heart sick, for the rigid, tubelike objects turn out to be not plants, but erect male sex organs.

Such atrocities are not rare in the bizarre world of rock music. I recently opened up a revealing issue of the immensely popular teen magazine *Spin,* available at most grocery stores. There I learned about the group Def Jam and its new album, "Slayer: Reign in Blood." The leadoff song on this monstrous album begins with the words, "Auschwitz, the meaning of pain." From there, the listener is taken on a roller-coaster ride straight to Hades. Along the way his mind feasts on Satanism and death.

Def Jam tells us that the brutal Nazi concentration camp doctor Joseph Mengele was the "Angel of Death": a "sadist of the noblest blood" who "toiled to benefit the Aryan race" by "performing surgery without anesthesia."[13]

Rock's Worship of Satan

I began this chapter with the true story of Christene Mireles, an El Paso, Texas, teenager unmercifully beaten after she refused to join a cult of Satan worshipers. Unfortunately, her story is not unique. Satan worship and its allied activity, witchcraft, is on the rise throughout America and the world. It is undeniable that Satanically inspired rock music is a prime contributor to this despoiling of youth.

Book retailers report that sales of Satanic Bibles have doubled in the last three years. These Bibles are bought by adults and youth alike. Satan worship groups and witches' covens have sprung up everywhere, often formed by school-age youth. The *Chicago Tribune* carried a story of a fourteen-year-old DuPage County, Illinois, boy who threatened two other youths, saying that his Satan worship cult would sacrifice them to the Devil.[14] The *Associated Press* reported that in Monroe, Michigan, a seventeen-year-old was killed in a Satanic sacrificial ritual. Police investigated at the local high school and eventually seized a black robe and hood, a dagger, a chalice, red liquid in a bottle, and other Satanic paraphernelia.[15]

In El Paso, where Christene Mireles unexpectedly encountered a band of devil-worshipers, school officials and police authorities admit that Satanic worship and witchcraft rituals have become a fad among the young. Teenagers proudly display occult symbols such as 666, pentagrams, lightning bolts, upside-down crosses, and swastikas. Also highly favored is Satanic art on T-shirts sold by such heavy metal rock groups as Black Sabbath, Slayer, Iron Maiden, Judas Priest, and Ozzy Osbourne.[16]

Florence Luke, director of El Paso Hotline, reports that some teens who have experimented with Satanism and occultism later call in to say they are gripped with fear that the Devil is trying to kill them. "The animal sacrifices and the drinking of blood is very real to these children. Most of them can't even sleep at night. Some of them have thoughts of suicide and thoughts of killing others," Luke said.[17]

From Texas, Michigan, Florida, California, New Jersey, and across the nation, reports keep coming in. Satanic symbols are found at crime scenes by police, homeowners report damages by vandals who leave behind spray-painted or scratched symbols of Satanism, the dead carcasses of sacrificed animals turn up in vacant lots near isolated farmhouses, and depressed (and oppressed) teenagers are committing suicide. Satan is at war with the youth of planet earth.

A Call to Parents

The New Age has designs on your children. The question is, What are you, a Christian mom or dad, going to do to prevent your child from being hopelessly sucked into the swirling vortex of New Age occultism that surrounds him or her?

There is much you can do. Our God is strong enough to protect our innocent children. We must put our boys and girls off-limits to the New Age and to its spiritual leader, Satan.

I was struck recently by the testimony of the elderly, articulate Irene Park.[18] Irene, today a committed Christian, was formerly the High Witch of Florida. "My mind was totally depraved and taken over by the Devil," she said. She admits to terrible deeds during her many years in the occult; for example, seducing young children sexually and introducing boys and girls to Satanist ritual. A repentant Irene now confesses that Satan had vested in her his dark powers, which she used to savage young children.

Irene said that as a witch the only children she could *not* seduce—though she greatly lusted after them—were the children of dedicated Christian parents, parents who constantly prayed over their children through the precious blood of Jesus.

There is a lesson here. We as Christians should rightly be outraged at what our schools, the entertainment industry, and others are doing to our children. But we need not be paralyzed with fear about the prospects for our children. God has the answer, and we can turn to Him with confidence.

EIGHTEEN

Dress Rehearsals for the Main Event

The Lord is not slack concerning his promise . . . but is long-suffering . . . not willing that any should perish, but that all should come to repentance. But the day of the Lord will come as a thief in the night. . . .

(2 Pet. 3:9, 10)

The Second Coming has occurred. . . . Now is the time to begin building the new earth.

(David Spangler, *Revelation: Birth of a New Age*)

We do not know at what hour the New Age "Christ"—whom Spirit-filled Christians will recognize as the Antichrist—will come. But New Age prophesiers and seers suggest that he is now living and that his appearance is imminent.

Jeanne Dixon, the world-famous astrologer with definite ties to the New Age, on February 5, 1962, had what she referred to as "the most significant and soul-stirring vision of her life." Dixon saw an ancient pharaoh and his Queen Nefertiti walking toward her. The queen held out a baby as though offering it to the world. "The eyes of the child," reported Dixon, "were all-knowing . . . full of wisdom and knowledge."[1]

Dixon watched as the baby grew into manhood. Then the image of a cross formed above him and began to expand until it enveloped the earth. "Simultaneously, peoples of every race, religion, and color, each kneeling and lifting his arms in worshipful adoration, surrounded him. They were all as one."

Ms. Dixon was convinced that this vision was of the reincarnated "Christ" who, she suggested, was born on that day. He will, Dixon predicted, "bring together all mankind into one all-embracing faith . . . the foundation of a new Christianity with every sect and creed united."

One prominent New Age group, the Tara Center, announced that the "Messiah" was ready to assume his earthly throne:

> The world has had enough . . . of hunger, injustice, war. In answer to our call for help, as World Teacher for all humanity, the Christ is now here.
>
> HOW WILL WE RECOGNIZE HIM? Look for a modern man concerned with modern problems—political, economic, and social.
>
> Since July, 1977, the Christ has been emerging as a spokesman for a group or community in a well-known modern country. . . . We will recognize him by his extraordinary spiritual potency, the universality of his point, and his love for all humanity. . . . He comes not to judge, but to aid and inspire.

The Tara Center published the above announcement in paid ads in major newspapers around the globe in 1982. The ads promised that the "Christ" would appear "within the next two months," speaking to humanity through a worldwide television and radio broadcast:

> His message will be heard inwardly, telepathically, by all people in their own language. From that time, with his help, we will build a new world.

The world has yet to meet this New Age "Christ"-figure. But Benjamin Creme, head of the Tara Center, headquartered in London and North Hollywood, California, has stated that the "Christ," whom he calls the Lord Maitreya, is now confidentially working in London and is a member of a Pakistani community in that city. The time for his appearance on the world scene did not prove to be ripe in 1982, Creme explains, insisting that the Lord Maitreya will yet appear to commence his earthly reign.[2]

God's Timetable for the Last Days

Why was the time not ripe in 1982? Why has the New Age "Christ" failed to appear? There can only be one explanation: Satan has up to now been constrained by the Holy Spirit. Though Satan is surely anxious to do his dirty work, the almighty power of God has up to now denied Satan his long-awaited opportunity to seize total control. God has a timetable for these last days, known only to Him (Matt. 24:36). Neither Satan nor any man knows when God will allow the final curtain to rise.

So for the past several decades Satan has been forced to practice dry runs for the main event. The aborted ascension to power of the Tara Center's Lord Maitreya is one example of a dress rehearsal. There have been—and may be—many others. Satan's Plan for a One World Religion and a One World Government will eventually succeed, *but only according to God's timetable.*

Let's review a few more of Satan's ill-fated failures to establish his one world system led by Antichrist. What we'll see is that Satan's power is severely circumscribed by that of our Heavenly Father. Yet, Satan's insatiable craving for absolute authority drives him on in his quest for sovereignty.

Krishnamurti, the New Age Messiah

The strange case of Jiddu Krishnamurti demonstrates that Satan has been practicing for many decades for the main event—the time when his Beast with the number 666 would acquire absolute dominion on earth.

Krishnamurti is a disciple of Theosophy and a Hindu. In 1909 Annie Besant, then head of the Theosophical Society headquartered in India, announced that through Yoga and meditation it had been revealed to her that the young Krishnamurti had been chosen to be the "World Teacher" and "Guiding Spirit of the Universe." Besant prophesied that the "Christ" spirit—he who directs the invisible hierarchy—would manifest itself by taking possession of Krishnamurti's body.

Dave Hunt, in his insightful, best-selling work *Peace, Prosperity, and the Coming Holocaust,* documents the turn of events that occurred after Krishnamurti's selection as the "Christ."[3]

Besant, Hunt noted, predicted that the new "Messiah" would combine all religions into one. Then he would create a world government.

Theosophists and many other New Age believers were convinced that the long-awaited "Christ" was finally being revealed to mankind. It was reported by those who listened to Krishnamurti speak at a Star of the East convocation in 1911 that he "spoke in the first person as a god." Nearly six thousand delegates were there, and some knelt down and worshiped Krishnamurti. Others witnessed "a great coronet of brilliant, shimmering blue" appearing above his head.

In 1926, after a tumultuous welcome in Europe, the New Age Messiah sailed off to America. As Hunt put it, "Krishnamurti needed only a favorable reception in the world's most powerful and influential nation to launch the New Age."

It was not to be. Even as his ship docked, Krishnamurti complained about the "electrical atmosphere" in New York City and America. He said that he was unable to meditate successfully. Apparently his occult powers failed him, and his spirit guide mentors were unable to function. The *New York Times* reported tht the young "Christ" heir apparent became almost incoherent during an interview aboard ship. Rather than being perceived as a powerful spiritual figure worthy of world rulership, Krishnamurti was reported to be "a shy, badly frightened, nice-looking young Hindu."

Plans for Krishnamurti to speak in New York were abruptly canceled. He sailed back to his native India a failure. The publicity which hailed him as God incarnate abated. Krishnamurti himself later disavowed that he was the "Christ." Today Krishnamurti's books sell well to New Agers, and he is occasionally interviewed for New Age publications. But no longer does anyone—not even the most ardent of Theosophists—believe that he is the "Messiah" or "Christ." New Agers now wait expectantly for the "real Christ" to be unveiled and appear as World Teacher.

Hitler, the Aborted New Age Messiah

There is abundant proof that Adolf Hitler was specially chosen by Satan for his horrid mission. It may well be that the Nazi monster was slated to be the Antichrist. However, God's time-

table of events did not agree with Satan's. Also, evidence un-
earthed since World War II indicates that Hitler disobeyed Satan
and fell out of favor with his hellish master.

It is certain that Hitler was heavily into the occult and a
Satanist and that his murderous activities were carried out under
orders from below. In 1974 theosophist Foster Bailey, Alice Bailey's husband, apparently referred to Hitler's role as Satan's disciple in carrying out The Plan when he wrote:

> Another approved hierarchical project is the uniting of
> the nations of Europe into one cooperating peaceful
> community. . . . One attempt was to begin by uniting the
> peoples living in the Rhine River Valley using that river as a
> binding factor. *It was an attempt by a disciple but it did not
> work.* Now another attempt is in full swing, namely the . . .
> European Common Market.[4]

In his excellent book *The Twisted Cross,* Joseph J. Carr
documents the depths of occultism in Hitler's Third Reich.[5] He
shows that the Nazis worshiped pagan gods, that the dreaded SS
(Gestapo) conducted Mystery initiation rites and swore blood
oaths to Satan, and that the top Nazi leaders were dedicated
students of the black magic arts and witchcraft. The Nazis also
believed in evolution, karma, and reincarnation—all New Age
concepts.

Hitler himself was an avid reader of occult literature and a
member of the occultist Thule Society. The swastika, the Nazi
symbol of a twisted cross, is itself an occult religious symbol
found frequently in ancient times on the altars of pagan gods and
still seen today on the walls of some Hindu temples in India. The
Babylonians first originated this religious symbol, Satan being
fully aware of the future death of Jesus on the cross and desiring
to distort the meaning of that event. To the Babylonians, the
swastika symbolized the Sun God, Baal.

According to Carr, Hitler was taught his occult and magical
knowledge by Dietrich Eckart, a Master Adept of the Thule
Society's inner circle. Eckart had passed the word to others in
this group that he had received confirmation from his "master"
that he would be the one to train up a "vessel for the Antichrist"
who would lead the Aryan race to great triumph and victory
over the Jews.

Adolf Hitler is known to have greatly admired his mentor and teacher, Dietrich Eckart. In return, Eckart showered praise on the popular young radical. However, the old man well recognized the source of Hitler's uncanny, almost hypnotic powers. On his deathbed in December 1923, Eckart told those nearby not to mourn him because he, Eckart, will have influenced history more than any other German. He exhorted his followers to "follow Hitler," reveling that:

> He (Hitler) will dance but it is I who will call the tune! I have initiated him into the SECRET DOCTRINE, opened his centers of vision and given him the means to communicate with the powers.[6]

In the last chapter of *The Twisted Cross,* author Joseph Carr discusses the parallels between Nazism and the New Age Movement. He concludes that while he is not yet fully convinced that the New Age is *the* Antichrist movement predicted in Biblical prophecy, it is "an Antichrist movement that could easily spawn another Adolf Hitler—and a holocaust that makes the killing of the Jews during World War II look like a minor action."[7] He also writes:

> One cannot argue against the claim that the Nazi worldview and major elements of the New Age Movement worldview are identical. They should be, after all, for they both grew out of the same occultic root: theosophy. Their respective cosmogony, cosmology, and philosophies are identical.[8]

The False Prophecy of the False "Christ"

In a previous chapter, we discussed David Spangler's New Age "Christ," who mockingly calls himself "Limitless Love and Truth." Evidently this Satanic entity has been constrained up to now by the Holy Spirit from emerging from the "inner realms of the earth," where Spangler says he now resides. In 1961 it was announced by this spirit that by Christmas Day of 1967 he would be revealed to the universe. Between the years 1961 and 1967, New Age believers waited expectantly for their "Christ" to appear as promised. "When nothing externally significant happened," Spangler admits, "there was considerable disappointment."[9]

However, Spangler cleverly explains away the failure of his "Christ's" prophecy by belatedly declaring that "Limitless Love and Truth" *did* come at the appointed time in the form of "a remarkable release of energy upon the earth."[10]

Spangler further maintains that thousands of individuals around the world felt that energy flow:

> The transfusion of energies from the old etheric to the new one had been sufficiently completed; Cosmic blessings had been placed upon earth. The Christ, imprisoned in the tomb of matter for nearly two thousand years, had ascended. . . . The New Age had been born. . . . Revelation was on the move![11]

Spangler does not fully explain his statement that the "Christ" (that is, Satan's "Christ") had been "imprisoned in the tomb of matter for nearly two thousand years" before his ascension. Apparently this refers to the fact that by His sacrifice on the cross, Christ Jesus had bound Satan in his tomb within the inner reams of the earth, severely limiting his freedom of movement and his ability to operate with impunity on earth. But Spangler is claiming that with the end of the year 1967, Satan had been loosed from his tomb of matter and is now on the move. If this be so, it was God's will that the Holy Spirit no longer restrain the evil one. The ultimate battle for control of man's soul had commenced.

As Daniel correctly prophesied, the Antichrist is to be allowed to "forecast his devices against the strongholds, even for a time," for "his heart shall be against the holy covenant; and he shall do exploits" (11:24, 28).

Still, what is significant to realize is that in 1967, contrary to Satan's ultimate Plan, God confounded the New Age by refusing to allow him to appear in his final incarnation in the flesh as the Antichrist, the Beast of Revelation. The earth operates by God's timetable, not by Satan's, and the events of the last days will be exactly as God has planned. Jesus Himself testified:

But of that day and hour knoweth no man, no, not the angels of heaven, but my Father only. . . . Watch therefore; for ye know not what hour your Lord doth come. (Matt. 24:36, 42)

In 1982, fifteen years after the New Age "Christ" had failed to appear as promised through David Spangler, another New Age leader, Benjamin Creme, announced that the time had come. As I mentioned earlier, in April of that year, in major newspapers around the globe, Creme's group, the Tara Center of London and North Hollywood, California, bought ads proclaiming the "Christ's" appearance would take place within the next two months. Again, God confounded those who plotted against His will. The Lord Maitreya, the chosen vessel of Creme's New Age group, failed to appear as predicted. The time was not ripe for his emergence.

Satan, battered but not yet defeated, came back for more punishment on December 31, 1986. On that day, at 12 noon Greenwich Mean time, tens of millions of New Age followers worldwide gathered in stadiums, convention and meeting halls, hotel rooms and private homes, and in churches to invoke the New Age. Thousands among them summoned the New Age "Christ" and his hierarchy to manifest themselves. The event was designated International Meditation Day (also called by other names, such as World Peace Day and World Healing Day). This incredible gala was sponsored by hundreds of New Age organizations in sixty nations and coordinated by the Quartus Foundation and its affiliate, The Planetary Commission, Austin, Texas.

John Randoph Price declared in advance that five hundred million New Age believers around the globe would be participating in International Meditation Day, one hundred million of these worshipers being Hindus in India. Fifty million Americans were expected to join in the meditation. As Price put it, the intent of these millions was to participate in:

A planetary affirmation of love, forgiveness and understanding involving millions of people in a simultaneous global mind-link. The purpose: to *reverse the polarity of the negative force field in the race mind,* achieve a critical mass of spiritual consciousness, usher in a new era of Peace on Earth, (and) return mankind to Godkind.[12]

Speaking to the 71st Annual International New Thought Alliance Congress on August 1, 1986, Price pledged, "Both earth and man are waking up. . . . It is going to happen, because the restoration of the Kingdom on Earth is the Divine Plan."[13]

The tens of millions of New Age religious believers who dutifully participated in this momentous "awakening" were, however, not treated to the desire of their hearts. Reciting in unison the World Healing Meditation[14] prepared by The Planetary Commission, they pleaded with the "One Presence and Power of the Universe" to deliver "peace" and "good will" to earth. They pridefully declared, "I am a co-creator with God, and it is a new heaven that comes."

Blaspheming our Father in Heaven and His Son, they flattered themselves with the pronouncement that "I and the Father are one, and all that the Father has is mine. In Truth, I am the Christ of God. . . . I am the light of the world."

Finally, the masses who congregated at locations near and far on December 31, 1986 decreed some type of magical command by affirming that "I am seeing the salvation of the planet before my very eyes. . . . It is done and it is so."

Their fervent declarations and commands were of no avail. The New Age failed to promptly materialize, and the New Age Messiah they were invoking did not appear.

This time, however, New Age leaders had cleverly prepared an explanation in advance for the eventuality that God would once more deny the fulfillment of the coming of the Antichrist and a One World Order. John Randolph Price had written that there may be those (presumably Christian fundamentalists) "who will continue to resist based on the illusion of vested interests."[15]

Price said that the Seekers and the Light Bearers (the New Age believers) would in that case need to embark on a three-stage program to 1) *construct* or build upon the spiritual foundation begun on International Meditation Day; 2) *consolidate* and strengthen the bond of Divine Love that had begun; and 3) finally, and most importantly, *inaugurate* the world into a New Age Kingdom.[16]

Price told readers it should be obvious what this third stage or phase is all about. "The word inauguration," he explains, "comes from Latin *inaugurare* which means to give sanctity to a place or official person."

> Does that mean that Jesus Himself is returning, and that this stage will usher in His reign as Lord of the world in physical form? Or does it mean the "externalization" of the Hierarchy of Spiritual Masters? Or does it mean that . . . each one of us will awaken to the Truth of our being—that the Higher Self of each individual *is* the Christ? Perhaps all three happenings and experiences will occur. . . .[17]

Here Price seems to appeal to almost every perverted New Age doctrine. First, he tells the deluded Christian apostate that the New Age "Jesus" (or rather, the reincarnated demon spirit who would come masquerading as Jesus) might return. Then he addresses the desires of those who preach the externalization, or spontaneous appearance, of the hierarchy of spiritual Masters, now said to operate in an invisible spirit dimension. Finally, he seductively implants the almost universally acclaimed New Age idea that, with the inauguration of the earth, each of us will ascend to godhood by becoming ourselves a "Christ."

Regardless of the clever machinations of such mesmerizingly talented New Age leaders as Spangler, Creme, and Price, the failure of their "Christ" to appear as predicted is persuasive evidence that these men are not prophets of God, but of the Adversary.

The Mark of the True Prophet

The Bible flatly states that, without fail, *every prophecy announced by a true prophet will come to pass* (see Deut. 18:20-22). God does not fail, nor do His prophecies. Never has even one prophecy of the Bible failed. Now contrast this incredible accuracy with that of the New Age "prophets." We have already seen that their New Age "Christ" has repeatedly failed to materialize as prophesied.

Another example of a spectacular failure of a New Age prophecy is that of Ruth Montgomery's reincarnated spirit guides. In *Strangers Among us*, they erred by predicting a "big spending Democrat" would succeed Jimmy Carter as President and that the Shah of Iran would spend his declining years in Europe. Reagan, a Republican, succeeded Carter, and the Shah died unexpectedly in Mexico of a terminal illness.[18]

Other examples of prophecies that went awry are found in the predictions of Edgar Cayce, idolized by millions of New Agers as the "Sleeping Prophet" because medical diagnoses came to him in a vision while he slept. Cayce, a Kentucky Sunday school teacher now deceased, is still greatly revered, and his many books are praised by the New Age as exemplifying the best of "Christian mysticism." Cayce was a spiritual healer who practiced telepathy, fortune-telling, and clairvoyance. Kurt Koch, world-renowned occult expert, enumerated in his book *Occult ABC* the many false teachings of this New Age prophet.[19] Among them:

1) Jesus Christ was only a reincarnation of Adam, Melchizedek, Joshua, and Zend (the father of Zoroaster).
2) God is a Mother-Father God.
3) Jesus and His mother Mary were "twin souls."
4) God does not know the future (though Cayce himself claimed he did!).
5) Man's redemption comes from his own doing; in other words, we are our own saviors.

Cayce professed to be an avid Bible reader and a dedicated Christian. He erroneously testified that his gifts came from God. As Koch so eloquently states: "We are faced here with a strange mixture of Bible study and magic. It is one of Satan's specialties to hide under a Christian disguise."[20]

The Sleeping Prophet, Edgar Cayce, had a number of prophecies which failed to come to pass. A most notable failure came in 1941 when he prophesied that in 1967 or 1968 a portion of the long-fabled continent of Atlantis would emerge from under the sea. News reports from those two years certainly do not reveal any such thing happening. Yet Cayce's prediction undoubtedly caused many people who believed in him to be led astray during the years between 1941 and 1968, because a belief in Atlantis and its mythical race of supermen is a key tenet of faith on the part of many New Agers.

When Will the Final Antichrist Appear?

Satan has been forced time and again to abandon his plans to unleash the final Antichrist on the world. However, these failures should not blind us to the truth. Satan *will* eventually produce the Antichrist, who will be an evil person outdoing any and all evil rulers who have ever lived. Even Hitler will have been a pale imitation. Just when can we expect this vile Antichrist to appear?

Paul gave us a glimmer of knowledge concerning this when he cautioned the church of Thessalonica:

> Let no man deceive you by any means: for that day shall not come, except there come a *falling away* first, and *that man of sin be revealed,* the son of perdition . . . even him, whose coming is after the working of Satan with all power and signs and lying wonders. . . . (2 Thess. 2:3, 9)

Jesus instructed His disciples that just before the terrible events of the latter days, false "Christs" and false prophets would arise and show great "signs and wonders":

> Then if any man shall say unto you, Lo, here is Christ, or there; believe it not. . . . Wherefore if they shall say unto you, Behold, he is in the desert; go not forth: behold, he is in the secret chambers; believe it not. For as the lightning cometh out of the east, and shineth even unto the west; so shall the coming of the Son of man be. (Matt. 24:23, 26, 27)

Just as our Lord prophesied, Satan continues to produce false prophets and "Christs." Maitreya, Krishnamurti, and Hitler were examples of false "Christs," and Spangler, Creme, Montgomery, and Cayce exemplify the fake prophets we were warned to expect. We can be confident that Jesus will return as the Christ, but not as a reincarnated spirit and not as a mere man. He will return with brilliant light from heaven, in fullness of glory, triumphantly appearing out of the clouds. This is a certain event that Satan will not be able to to duplicate.

So we know there will first be a "falling away" of many in

the Church and then the Antichrist will appear, whose coming is after the working of Satan. This falling away, Paul said, will leave the ungodly multitudes vulnerable to the lies of Satan's man-god, the Beast and Antichrist. Captive to sin, they will not be able to discern the truth but will believe a "strong delusion" (2 Thess. 2:10-12).

This great falling away is already far advanced. New Age doctrine is being brought into mainline denominations as well as independent Christian churches and is especially gathering strength in the Catholic Church. Combined with other signs of the last days—such as the events in Israel and the Middle East—this is a prime indication that the day is at hand when the prophetic Tribulation period will begin and the "son of perdition" will be revealed.

NINETEEN

What Must Christians Do?

*(For the weapons of our warfare are not carnal,
but mighty through God to the pulling down of
strongholds;) casting down imaginations, and every
high thing that exalteth itself against the knowledge of
God, and bringing into captivity every thought to the
obedience of Christ.* (2 Cor. 10:4, 5)

*In answer to our urgent need, THE CHRIST IS IN THE
WORLD. A great World Teacher for people of every
religion and no religion. A practical man with solutions
to our problems. He loves ALL humanity. . . .*
(The Tara Center, USA Today)

Somewhere, at this very moment, a man is perhaps being groomed for world leadership. He is
to be Satan's man, the Antichrist. His number
will be 666.

This world dictator will be looked upon by the masses not
only as a masterful political genius and leader, but as a *spiritual
teacher.* In every nation, including the United States, he will
aggressively move to replace Christianity with his own religious
system: The New Age World Religion. This one world religious
system is at the core of The Plan.

Doubters may object, this can't happen in America—Anywhere else, but surely not in the U.S.A.! Americans, who have
always enjoyed the fruits of democracy, find it difficult to believe
that their religious freedoms could ever be abridged by a future
New Age Antichrist.

The history of this planet says otherwise. The United States
and the handful of other democracies in the world are but a
small oasis surrounded by a hostile desert of totalitarian and

authoritarian dictatorships. A disastrous world war, a great economic depression, a concerted campaign by terrorists armed with nuclear weapons to overthrow the government—any of these events could within months or even minutes possibly bring to Washington a new, undemocratic regime bent on destroying the remnants of Christianity.

The end of democracy and religious freedom could also come gradually as more and more liberties are lost and an anti-Christian environment slowly develops within democratic nations. Some believe this process has already begun.

Though we do not know specifically how or when our democratic freedoms will be extinguished, what we do know is that the Bible prophesies the last-days arrival of an Antichrist who will assume dictatorial world power and move aggressively to punish Christian believers. First Peter 4:12, 13 tells us not to be taken by surprise when this occurs, but to rejoice:

> Beloved, think it not strange concerning the fiery trial which is to try you, as though some strange thing happened unto you: but rejoice, inasmuch as ye are partakers of Christ's sufferings; that, when his glory shall be revealed, ye may be glad also with exceeding joy.[1]

The New Age appears to be the instrument that Satan will use to catapult his Antichrist to power. Once he is firmly entrenched, he will unite all cults and religions into one: the New Age World Religion. When Christians refuse to be initiated into this Satanic religious system, they will be dealt with very harshly. Many will be put to death. The New Age is working hard today to set up an enviornment of hatred toward Christians and what they stand for, so the public mood will be ready when the Antichrist begins his brutal anti-Christian programs.

A New Age propaganda campaign is already at full-throttle to brand us as warmongers and separatists. We are described as the Beast, the Antichrist, a racially inferior species unfit for the New Age Kingdom. Discerning Christians see the signs and know what is happening. Billy Graham, for example, in his book *Approaching Hoofbeats: The Four Horsemen of the Apocalypse* demonstrated his discernment when he wrote: "I hear the hoofbeats of the four horsemen approaching. I hear the thundering approach of false teaching, war, famine, and death."²

The Sovereignty of God

It is significant, however, to note that after confiding to us that he hears "the thundering approach of false teaching, war, famine, and death," Billy Graham went on to say: "I see and hear these signs as a shadow of God's loving hand at work for the world's redemption. God is offering hope for those who heed the warning."³

The New Age has come so far so fast that unless we put things in perspective it is easy for us to assume that all is lost. *All is not lost.* The Word of God assures us that Satan's victory will be short-lived. The Plan will ultimately fail.

Because we are Christians, Jesus has given us freedom from worry. We know that He who is within us is greater than he who is in the world. God is our victorious, all-conquering King. Paul spoke to this in these uplifting words:

> Who shall separate us from the love of Christ? . . . I am persuaded, that neither death, nor life, nor angels, nor principalities, nor powers, nor things present, nor things to come, nor height, nor depth, nor any other creature, shall be able to separate us from the love of God, which is in Christ Jesus our Lord. (Rom. 8:35-39)

So we are not fearful for ourselves. Our joyous fate is sealed by the grace of the Lord. But we can rightly be anxious over what might befall our loved ones, neighbors, and friends—and all of mankind—who, because they do not know Jesus, do not possess eternal security.

The emergence on the world scene of the prophesied, end-time Satanic religious system can in one sense be viewed as positive, for it signals the imminent return of Jesus Christ and heralds the Kingdom of God that is soon to come. But our hearts grow heavy when as Christians we realize the harvest is drawing near and there is so little time to warn the lost and bring to them the blessed message of salvation. The New Age World

Religion should provide incentive for Christians to boldly preach the gospel and to earnestly spread the good news that the time of man's deliverance is truly at hand.

What Can You Do?

I have prayerfully asked God to reveal to me what I should say to concerned Christians who ask, "What can I do about The Plan of the New Age to destroy Christianity and put man under bondage?" The Lord has answered my prayers, and I would now like to share with you the four positive steps that you and every Christian can take in this time of crisis and turmoil.

Step 1: Read and study your Holy Bible so you will be knowledgeable of God's Word and invulnerable to New Age distortions and unholy claims.

While all around us, muddled intellectuals and mixed-up men and women are, figuratively speaking, "losing their heads," we should keep ours clear by strengthening our minds with the wisdom of the Book of Books. The warfare for man's soul involves a series of battles over *doctrine,* and if Christians are to save as many of the lost as possible, we must be girded with God's truth. Our footing must be sure as we engage the enemies of the Scripture.

Step 2: Put Jesus first in your life and make soul-winning for Christ your top priority.

When we put Jesus first in our own lives and make soul-winning our top priority, all the forces of hell cannot withstand us. Christians who affirm and commit themselves and their churches to what Jerry Falwell has called the "irreducible minimums" will serve as shining beacons of light to lost souls. Falwell says these include the primacy of the Bible as the inspired, inerrant Word of God, an unshakable belief in the divinity of Jesus Christ, and the acceptance of Jesus Christ as the only way to salvation.

Step 3: Confront and fight New Age apostasy wherever you find it, understanding that Jesus is Lord and that He will prevail. Use prayer as both a resource and a powerful vehicle to ward off God's enemies.

In the Epistle of Jude we find the admonition that we should "earnestly contend for the faith which was once delivered unto the saints." Jude told us to look for "certain men crept in unawares, who were before of old ordained to this condemnation, ungodly men, turning the grace of our God into lasciviousness, and denying the only Lord God, and our Lord Jesus Christ" (Jude 1:3, 4).

What a powerful message for today! Earnestly contend for the faith! Listen also to what James told us: "resist the devil, and he will flee from you" (Jas. 4:7). How do we go about this?

The Bible provides the answer. James told us to be soul-winners, to convert the lost: "Let him know, that he which converteth the sinner from the error of his way shall save a soul from death, and shall hide a multitude of sins" (Jas 5:20).

Be assured that in witnessing for Christ, you will be going up against the strongholds of Satan. You will also, on many occasions, be locked in battle with the evil "wisdom" of those promoting New Age doctrines and falsehoods. The Bible tells us that we must not wish men of evil Godspeed (2 John 10, 11). Theirs is a mean-spirited goal, and we must not be tolerant toward a belief system which has as its principal aim the poisoning of souls. Our right attitude should be one of "tough love": we love the individual, but we deeply regret and reject his awful message.

Confrontation with evil cannot be won without prayer. The Christian who prays constantly and meditates on God's Word will find that his actions and words are imbued with great power from the Holy Spirit. Always remember that Jesus has already proven victorious. As Pastor Charles Bullock has so profoundly said, "We're not on the winning side. *We're on the side that won!*"[4]

Step 4: Reach out in Christian love to individuals in the New Age Movement, many of whom are confused, hungry for spiritual things, and searching for truth. Show them that Jesus Christ is the answer and that He loves them.

Though Satan is the very foundation-stone for the New Age World Religion, we must be very careful about our attitudes toward New Age believers. By no means is every person involved in the New Age Movement calculatingly evil. Most people entangled in this movement are themselves victims. Some are earnestly searching for the truth and are spiritually hungry. Also, many are motivated by sincere humanitarianism; but being mentally confused, these individuals are deluded by New Age gurus and teachers. A great number may not even be fully aware of The Plan which Satan and New Age human leaders have conceived for man's future. While we abhor the un-Christian tenets of New Age believers, we must always keep uppermost in our minds the fact that Jesus died for *their* sins as well as our own.

This is why I encourage Christians to reach out to New Agers in love and to counteract this apostasy with all the spiritual weapons that Jesus so richly provides us, including prayer, reading God's Holy Word, Christian example, and—most important of all—faith.

But they that wait upon the Lord shall renew their strength; they shall mount up with wings as eagles; they shall run, and not be weary; and they shall walk, and not faint. (Isa. 40:31)

Notes

CHAPTER 1: The Plan

1. Marilyn Ferguson, *The Aquarian Conspiracy: Personal and Social Transformation in the 1980s* (Los Angeles: J. P. Tarcher, Inc.: 1980), pp. 23, 24.
2. John Randolph Price, *The Planetary Commission* (Austin, Tex.: Quartus Books, 1984), p. 32.
3. Vera Alder, *When Humanity Comes of Age* (New York: Samuel Weiser, Inc., 1974), pp. 190-193.
4. John Randolph Price, *The Planetary Commission*, back cover.
5. John Randolph Price, *The Superbeings* (Austin, Tex.: Quartus Books, 1981), p. 1.
6. John Randolph Price, *The Planetary Commission*, p. 69.
7. *Ibid.*, pp. 47, 48.
8. M. E. Haselhurst, "The Plan and Its Implementation," *The Beacon*, September/October 1975, p. 147.
9. Moira Timms, *Prophecies and Predictions: Everyone's Guide to the Coming Changes* (Santa Cruz, Calif.: Unity Press, 1980), pp. 129-131.
10. Benjamin Creme, full-page ad by Tara Center in twenty major newspapers around the globe, April 25, 1982.
11. David Spangler, *Revelation: The Birth of a New Age* (Middleton, Wis.: Lorian Press, 1976), p. 61.
12. *Ibid.*, pp. 204, 205.
13. From the promotional material of The New Group of World Servers, reprinted in Constance Cumbey's *A Planned Deception: The Staging of a New Age Messiah* (East Detroit, Mich.: Pointe Publishers, Inc., 1985), pp. 248-253.
14. Barry McWaters, *Conscious Evolution: Personal and Planetary Transformation* (San Francisco, Calif.: Evolutionary Press, 1982), p. 15.
15. *Ibid.*, p. 147.
16. Constance Cumbey, *A Planned Deception*, pp. 195-197.
17. Lola A. Davis, *Toward a World Religion for the New Age* (Farmingdale, N.Y.: Coleman Publishing, 1983), p. 189.
18. *Ibid.*, pp. 177, 178.
19. John Randolph Price, *The Superbeings*, pp. 3, 38.
20. John Randolph Price, *The Planetary Commission*, pp. 47.
21. Terry Cole-Whittaker, quoted in *Magical Blend*, Issue 14, 1986, p. 13.

CHAPTER 2: Mystery Babylon: Satan's Church, Yesterday and Today

1. Alexander Hislop, *The Two Babylons* (New York: Loizeaux, 1959; first edition published 1916 in England), pp. 287, 288.
2. I have benefited in my research from the excellent accounts of the Mystery Religion of Babylon found in Alexander Hislop's book *The Two Babylons*. Also of great use were these references: Werner Keller, *The Bible as History* (New York: Bantam Books, 1982); Henry M. Halley, *Halley's Bible Handbook*, 24th Edition (Grand Rapids, Mich. Zondervan, 1965); and Ralph Woodrow, *Babylon Mystery Religion* (Riverside, Calif.: Ralph Woodrow Evangelistic Association, 1981).
3. Miriam Starhawk, quoted in *Yoga Journal*, May-June 1986, p. 59.
4. *The Spirit of Truth and the Spirit of Error*, compiled by Keith L. Brooks (Chicago: Moody Press, 1985).
5. Kathleen Alexander-Berghorn, "Isis: The Goddess as Healer," *Woman of Power*, Winter 1987, p. 20.
6. Hal Lindsey, quoted on "Praise The Lord," Trinity Broadcasting Network (TBN), October 28, 1986.
7. Paul Crouch, *ibid.*
8. Full-page ad by New Age Activists in *Psychic Guide* magazine, September-November 1986, p. 5.
9. *Ibid.*
10. *Ibid.*
11. William Irwin Thompson, *Pacific Shift* (San Francisco, Calif.: Sierra Club Books, 1986).
12. John Randolph Price, *The Planetary Commission*, p. 46.
13. "Djwhal Khul" (channeled by Alice Bailey), "Food for Thought," *Life Times*, Winter 1986-87, p. 57.
14. Robert Lindsey, reported in the *New York Times*, September 28, 1986.
15. *Ibid.*
16. *Ibid.*
17. *Ibid.*
18. Jack Underhill, "The Second American Revolution, The New Crusades," *Life Times*, Winter 1986-87, p. 2.
19. *Ibid.*
20. *Ibid.*
21. John Randolph Price, *The Planetary Commission*, pp. 28-32.
22. Corinne Heline, *New Age Bible Interpretation*, Vol. VI, New Testament, fifth edition (Santa Monica, Calif.: New Age Bible and Philosophy Center, 1984), pp. 44-49, 213-215.
23. Peter Lemesurier, *The Armageddon Script* (New York: St. Martin's Press, 1981), p. 232.
24. *Ibid.*, p. 237.

CHAPTER 3: Toward a One World Religion and a Global Order

1. Gerald and Patricia Mische, *Toward a Human World Order* (Ramsey, N.J.: Paulist Press, 1977).

2. David Spangler, *Revelation: The Birth of a New Age*, p. 204.
3. John Randolph Price, *The Planetary Commission*, pp. 30-31, 143-147, 162. Also, *Superbeings*, pp. ix-xv, 3, 15, 38.
4. John Randolph Price, *The Planetary Commission*, p. 28.
5. Lola Davis, *Toward a World Religion for the New Age*, p. 180.
6. *Ibid.*, p. 212.
7. *Houston Chronicle*, November 3, 1975, p. G-12.
8. Robert Mueller, *The New Genesis: Shaping a Global Spirituality* (New York: Image Books, 1984).
9. LaVedi Lafferty and Bud Hollowell, *The Eternal Dance* (St. Paul, Minn.: Llewelyn Publications, 1983), Epilogue pages (unnumbered).
10. *Ibid.*
11. Jonathan Stone, *SCP Journal*, July 1977.
12. Benjamin Creme, full-page ad.
13. Jean Houston, interviewed in "Jean Houston: The New World Religion," *The Tarrytown Letter*, June/July 1983, p. 5.
14. Marilyn Ferguson, *The Aquarian Conspiracy*, p. 191.
15. Lewis Mumford, *The Transformation of Man* (New York: Harper & Row, 1972), p. 142.
16. William Irwin Thompson, *Darkness and Scattered Light* (Garden City, N.Y.: Anchor Books, 1978), p. 13.
17. Mark Satin, *New Age Politics* (New York: Dell, 1979), p. 149.
18. *Ibid.*
19. Donald Keys, *Earth at Omega: Passage to Planetization* (Boston: Branden Press, 1982), p. iii.
20. Alice Bailey, *The Externalization of the Hierarchy* (New York: Lucis Publishing Company, 1957).
21. Lola Davis, *Toward a World Religion for the New Age*, pp. iv, 167, 168, 175, 176.
22. Alice Bailey, *The Externalization of the Hierarchy*. Also see *The Reappearance of the Christ* (New York: Lucis Publishing Company, 1948) and *The Rays and the Initiations* (New York: Lucis Publishing Company, 1960).
23. Matthew Fox, *Whee, Wee, We, All the Way Home . . . A Guide to a Sensual, Prophetic Spirituality* (Santa Fe, N.M.: Bear & Company, 1981), p. 242.
24. Matthew Fox, *Manifesto for a Global Civilization* (Santa Fe, N.M.: Bear & Company), pp. 6, 43-45.
25. *Ibid.*, p. 43.
26. Robert Mueller, *New Genesis: Shaping a Global Spirituality*, p. xiii.
27. *Ibid.*
28. *Ibid.*
29. *Ibid.*, p. 126.
30. *Ibid.*, p. 28.
31. *Ibid.*, p. 29.
32. *Ibid.*, pp. 145, 146.
33. *Ibid.*
34. *Ibid.*, pp. 169-171.
35. *Ibid.*, p. 171.

36. *Ibid.*, p. 189.
37. *Ibid.*, p. 186.
38. See Dave Hunt, *The Cult Explosion* (Eugene, Ore.: Harvest House, 1980), pp. 229-234.
39. Maharishi Mahesh Yogi, quoted in Dave Hunt, *The Cult Explosion*, p. 230.

CHAPTER 4: *Conspiracy and Propaganda: Spreading the New Age Gospel*

1. H. G. Wells, *The Open Conspiracy: Blueprints for a World Revolution* (Garden City, N. J.: Doubleday, Doran, 1928).
2. Alice Bailey, *The Externalization of the Hierarchy*, p. 67.
3. Marilyn Ferguson, *The Aquarian Conspiracy*, pp. 413-416.
4. Donald Keyes, *Earth at Omega: Passage to Planetization* (Boston: Branden Press, 1982), pp. 96, 98.
5. Mihajlo Mesarovic and Edvard Pestel, *Mankind at the Turning Point* (New York: E. P. Dutton, 1974).
6. *Ibid.*
7. Marilyn Ferguson, *The Aquarian Conspiracy*, pp. 23, 24.
8. John G. Bennet, quoted by Barry McWaters, *Conscious Evolution*, pp. 84, 85.
9. LaVedi Lafferty and Bud Hollowell, *The Eternal Dance*, p. 468.
10. Statistics from the promotional flyer of the Spiritual Emergency Network, Menlo Park, California.
11. Donald Keys, *Earth at Omega*, p. 88.

CHAPTER 5: *The New Age Antichrist and His Will to Power*

1. Levi, *The Aquarian Gospel of Jesus the Christ* (Los Angeles: DeVorss & Co., 1970).
2. Lola Davis, *Toward a World Religion for the New Age*, p. i.
3. *Ibid.*, p. 186.
4. *Ibid.*
5. *Ibid.*, p. 228.
6. Alice Bailey, *The Externalization of the Hierarchy.* Also see *The Reappearance of the Christ.*
7. Benjamin Creme, full-page ad.
8. *Directory for a New World* (Los Angeles: Unity-in-Diversity, 1979), p. 30.
9. LaVedi Lafferty and Bud Hollowell, *The Eternal Dance*, p. 2 (Epilogue).
10. Elissa Lindsey McClain, *Rest from the Quest* (Lafayette, La.: Huntington House, 1984), pp. 66, 67.
11. Elissa Lindsey McClain, quoting Eklal Kueshana, *Rest from the Quest*, p. 25.
12. John Randolph Price, *The Planetary Commission*, pp. 163, 164.
13. LaVedi Lafferty and Bud Hollowell, *The Eternal Dance*, p. 153.
14. *Ibid.*

CHAPTER 6: How Will We Know the Antichrist?

1. Peter Lemesurier, *The Armageddon Script*, p. 228.
2. *Ibid.*, p. 231.
3. *Ibid.*, p. 239.
4. *Ibid.*, p. 233.
5. Benjamin Creme, full-page ad.
6. LaVedi Lafferty and Bud Hollowell, *The Eternal Dance*, p. 483.
7. George Bernard Shaw, quoted in Dave Hunt, *The Cult Explosion* (Eugene, Ore.: Harvest House, 1980).
8. F. Aster Barnwell, *The Meaning of Christ for Our Age* (St. Paul, Minn.: Llewellyn Publications, 1984), pp. xiii-xxxiv, 75-78.
9. *Ibid.*, pp. xx-xxviii, 70, 75-78.
10. Jean Michael Angebert, *The Occult and the Third Reich: The Mystical Origins of Nazism and the Search for the Holy Grail* (New York: McGraw Hill, 1975), Preface.
11. Aleister Crowley, quoted by Kathryn Paulsen, *The Complete Book of Magic and Witchcraft* (revised edition) (New York: New American Library/Signet Books: 1980).

CHAPTER 7: Come, Lucifer

1. This is a teaching of Freemasonry, given to holders of the 30th, 31st, and 32nd degree of Freemasonry. See J. Edward Decker, *The Question of Freemasonry* (Issaquah, Wis.: Free the Masons Ministries). Decker, coauthor of the best-selling *The God-Makers* and a former Mason, also quotes Masonic teachings that instruct members: "Yes, Lucifer is God. . . ," "Everything good in nature comes from Osiris" (Osiris is the ancient Egyptian god derived from the Babylonian Mystery Religion), and "When the Mason . . . has learned the mystery of his craft . . . the seething energies of Lucifer are in his hands. . . ." New Age spokespersons Lola Davis and Alice Bailey spoke highly of Freemasonry as a precursor to the New Age World Religion.
2. David Spangler, *Reflections of the Christ* (Scotland: Findhorn, 1977), pp. 36-39.
3. *Ibid.*, pp. 40-44.
4. *Ibid.*
5. Eklal Kueshana, *The Ultimate Frontier* (Chicago: The Stelle Group, 1970).
6. Elissa Lindsey McClain, *Rest from the Quest*, pp. 24-26.
7. Lola Davis, *Toward a One World Religion for the New Age*, p. 186.
8. Letter from the Lucis Trust, reprinted in Constance Cumbey, *A Planned Deception: The Staging of a New Age Messiah*, pp. 244, 245.
9. Shirley G. Clement and Virginia Fields, *Beginning the Search: A Young Person's Approach to a Search for God* (Virginia Beach, Va.: ARE Press, 1978), pp. 60-62.
10. *Ibid.*
11. Alexander Hislop, *The Two Babylons*, pp. 5-9, 13, 40, 74, 75.
12. See Barbara G. Walker, *The Woman's Encyclopedia of Myths and*

Secrets (San Francisco: Harper & Row, Publishers, 1983), pp. 450-452; and Alexander Hislop, *The Two Babylons*, pp. 103-110, 307-310.

13. Barbara Walker, *The Woman's Encyclopedia*, p. 553.

14. Matthew Fox, interview by William Rodarmar, "Original Blessing," *Yoga Journal*, November/December 1986, pp. 28-31, 64-67.

15. *Ibid.*, p. 31.

16. Constance Cumbey, *Hidden Dangers of the Rainbow* (Lafayette, La.: Huntington House, 1983), pp. 33, 34.

17. Hal Lindsey, *Satan Is Alive and Well on Planet Earth* (New York: Bantam, 1985). This book is an excellent rebuttal to those who discount the existence or the power of Satan and his horde of demon angels.

18. See *The Dictionary of Bible and Religion*, William H. Gentz, general editor (Nashville, Tenn.: Abingdon Press: 1986), p. 699; Kurt Koch, *Occult ABC* (Germany: Literature Mission Aglasterhausen, 1978; distributed in the U.S.A. by Grand Rapids International Publications, Grand Rapids, Michigan), pp. 172-174; and Alexander Hislop, *The Two Babylons*, pp. 260-264.

19. Kurt Koch, *ibid.*

20. From promotional brochure, Church Universal and Triumphant, Malibu, California.

21. Association of Sananda and Sanat Kumara, *The Sibors Portions* (Mount Shasta, Calif.).

22. Benjamin Creme, *The Reappearance of the Christ and the Masters of Wisdom* (London: The Tara Press, 1980), p. 135.

23. Alice Bailey, *The Externalization of the Hierarchy*, p. 86.

24. Benjamin Creme, *The Reappearance of the Christ and the Masters of Wisdom*, p. 165.

25. Jack Boland, "The Master Mind Principle," *Master Mind Goal Achievers Journal* (Warren, Mich.: Master Mind Publishing Company, 1985), p. 2.

26. *The Urantia Book* (Chicago: Urantia Brotherhood, 1955).

27. *Ibid.*, p. 1193.

28. *Ibid.*, p. 1192.

29. *Ibid.*, p. 1194.

30. "Kwan Yin" (channeled by Pam Davis), "The Power of One," *Life Times*, Winter 86/87, p. 84.

31. *Ibid.*

32. *Ibid.*

33. Szandor Anton LaVey, *Satanic Bible* (New York: Avon Books, 1969), p. 146.

34. Nigel Davis, *Human Sacrifice in History and Today* (New York: William Morrow), pp. 86-96.

35. Carl Olsen, editor, *The Book of the Goddess* (New York: Crossroad Publishing Company, 1986), pp. 110-123. Also see Barbara G. Walker, *The Woman's Encyclopedia of Myths and Secrets*, pp. 488-493.

36. Fritjof Capra, *The Tao of Physics*, 2nd edition (New York: Bantam Books, 1984; originally published by Shamballa Publications, Boulder, Colo.), p. xix.

37. *Ibid.*, p. xv.
38. Edward Rice, *Eastern Definitions* (New York: Doubleday/Anchor Books, 1980), pp. 398-400.
39. In this passage, many Biblical scholars believe that Isaiah was comparing the king of Babylon to Lucifer because the Babylonian ruler had required the nations to worship him as a god.
40. The term *Adonay* (or Adonai) is subject to some confusion. Some scholars contend that Adonay was the Greek and Semitic (Jewish) God equivalent to Shiva, the Hindu god. But most note that in early Hebrew translations of the Old Testament, this term, meaning "Lord," is simply used as another form of address for God Jehovah. (See Alexander Hislop, *The Two Babylons*, p. 70.) Obviously Satan has no objection whatsoever to either meaning as long as the worshiper is addressing *him* as Lord.
41. Kathryn Paulsen, *The Complete Book of Magic and Witchcraft*, p. 24.
42. Alice Bailey, *Problems of Humanity* (New York: Lucis Publishing Company), p. 166.
43. The use by the New Age of the words "Secret Place" should not be confused with the verse, "He that dwelleth in the secret place of the Most High shall abide under the shadow of the Almighty," found in Psalm 91:1. In the Psalms context, the phrase is taken from the Aramaic language and means "fortress" or "protection." Psalm 91:1 tells those who obey ("dwelleth in") God that they will receive divine protection because God is like a fortress. As George M. Lansa, editor of *Old Testament Light* (San Francisco: Harper & Row Publishers, p. 517) points out, "God has no secret place, nor does He need protection."
44. David Spangler, *Revelation: The Birth of a New Age*, p. 150.
45. *Ibid.*, pp. 152, 153.
46. Lola Davis, *Toward a World Religion for the New Age*, p. 180.
47. David Spangler, *Revelation*, p. 144.
48. *Ibid.*, pp. 222-224.
49. Helena P. Blavatsky, *The Secret Doctrine* (Calif.: Theosophical University Press, 1888), pp. 472, 473.

CHAPTER 8: Messages from Demons: Communicating Satan's Blueprint for Chaos

1. Stories about "Ramtha" and his human channeler, J. Z. Knight, have multiplied throughout the media. Knight and Ramtha were profiled on ABC television's "20/20" program (January 22, 1987) and Knight has been a guest on "Good Morning, America" and the "Phil Donahue Show." Also see "Channels, the Latest in Psychic Chic," *USA Today*, January 22, 1987, p. D-1.
2. Kurt Koch, *Occult ABC*, p. 215.
3. Vera Alder, *When Humanity Comes of Age* (New York: Samuel Weiser, 1974), pp. 19, 20.
4. *Ibid.*, p. vii.
5. LaVedi Lafferty and Bud Hollowell, *The Eternal Dance*, pp. 36, 37.
6. David Spangler, *Revelation: The Birth of a New Age*, p. 178.

7. John Randolph Price, *The Superbeings*, p. 3.
8. *Ibid.*
9. *Ibid.*
10. Lola Davis, *Toward a World Religion for the New Age*, p. 4.
11. *Ibid.*, p. 220.
12. *Ibid.*, p. 186.
13. John Randolph Price, *The Superbeings*, pp. 51, 52.
14. *Ibid.*
15. Willis W. Harman, "Rationale for Good Choosing," *Journal of Humanistic Psychology,* Winter 1981.
16. David Spangler, *Revelation: The Birth of a New Age*, p. 64.
17. Paul Twitchell, *Eckankar: The Key to Secret Worlds* (Menlo Park, Calif.: IWP Publishing, 1982), p. 72.
18. *Ibid.*, pp. 72, 73.
19. *Ibid.*

CHAPTER 9: *"It Said It Was Jesus"—the Leadership of the New Age Revealed*

1. William Plummer, "Turmoil in a California Camelot," *People Weekly,* July 1, 1985, pp. 75-77.
2. Jose Silva and Philip Miele, *The Silva Mind Control Method* (New York: Pocket Books, 1977).
3. Helen Schucman, *A Course in Miracles* (Foundation for Inner Peace, 1975).
4. John White, "A Course in Miracles: Spiritual Wisdom for the New Age," *Science of Mind*, March 1986, pp. 10-14, 80-88.
5. *Ibid.*
6. *Ibid.*, pp. 13, 14, 80, 81.
7. Melanie Chartoff, interviewed in *Magical Blend*, Issue 14, 1986, p. 51.
8. *Ibid.*
9. Reported in the *Christian Information Bureau Bulletin*, December 1986, p. 4.
10. Promotional flyer, "1987 International Seth Seminar," Austin Seth Center, Austin, Texas. Also see Jane Roberts, *The Seth Material* (Englewood Cliffs, N.J.: Prentice-Hall, 1970) and other "Seth" books.
11. *Ibid.*
12. Promotional flyer, "Lazaris," Concept: Synergy, Fairfax, Calif.
13. *Ibid.*
14. *Ibid.*
15. Roy Eugene Davis, quoted in *Yoga Journal*, July-August 1986, p. 22.
16. Barry McWaters, *Conscious Evolution*, p. 141.
17. John Randolph Price, in *The Quartus Report*, Report No. 11, Vol. V, 1986.
18. Kurt Koch, *Occult ABC*, p. 259.
19. *Ibid.*, pp. 209, 210.
20. Jose Silva, interviewed as a guest on *The John Ankerberg Show,* aired December 1986-January 1987. Also see Jose Silva, *The Silva Mind Control Method.*

21. Johanna Michaelson, *The Beautiful Side of Evil* (Eugene, Ore.: Harvest House, 1982).
22. *Magical Blend,* Issue 14, 1986, p. 71.
23. Mark and Elizabeth Prophet, *The Science of the Spoken Word* (Colorado Springs, Colo.: Summit University Press, 1974), pp. i, ii, 12, 13.
24. Reported in *Omni* magazine, January 1984, p. 129.
25. In the article "OM: The Sacred Syllable and Its Role in World Peace," the New Age publication *Life Times,* Winter 1986-87, p. 35, the author states, "He who meditates on OM attains to Brahman (God). Hindus and Tibetan Buddhists have consciously used the power of OM for centuries, especially chanting OM while sitting in the configuration of a circle. . . ." The article also remarked that OM is "sometimes also pronounced AUM."
26. J. Z. Knight, interview by Paul Zuromski, *Psychic Guide,* Vol. 5, No. 2, December 1986, p. 16.
27. *Ibid.,* pp. 16-18.

CHAPTER 10: *The New Master Race*

1. Meher Baba, quoted by Allan Y. Cohen, "Meher Baba and the Quest of Consciousness," *What Is Enlightenment?,* edited by John White (Los Angeles: Jeremy P. Tarcher, Inc., 1984), p. 87.
2. Julian Huxley, *Religion Without Revelation* (London: Max Parrish, 1959).
3. Arthur C. Clarke, *Profiles of the Future* (New York: Holt, Rinehart, Winston, 1984).
4. Ruth Montgomery, *Threshold to Tomorrow* (New York: Ballantine/ Fawcett Crest, 1982), p. 206.
5. John Randolph Price, *The Superbeings,* back cover.
6. John Randolph Price, *The Planetary Commission,* p. 29.
7. Bernadette Roberts, quoted by Stephen Bodian, "The Experience of No-Self," *Yoga Journal,* November/December 1986, p. 35.
8. John White, editor, *What Is Enlightenment?* (Los Angeles: Jeremy P. Tarcher, Inc., 1984), p. 219.
9. *Ibid.,* p. 126.
10. Ruth Montgomery, *Threshold to Tomorrow,* pp. 206, 207. Also see W. Scott-Elliott, *The Story of Atlantis and the Lost Lemuria* (Wheaton, Ill.: Theosophical Publishing House, 1968) and John Mitchell, *The View over Atlantis* (New York: Ballantine Books, 1969).
11. Edgar Cayce, *Edgar Cayce on Atlantis* (New York: Paperback Library, 1968).
12. Ruth Montgomery, *Threshold to Tomorrow.*
13. *Ibid.,* pp. 9, 10.
14. *Ibid.,* p. 1.
15. LaVedi Lafferty and Bud Hollowell, *The Eternal Dance,* p. 89.
16. *Ibid.,* pp. 89, 90.
17. See Alice Bailey, *The Externalization of the Hierarchy* and Benjamin Creme, *The Reappearance of the Christ and the Masters of Wisdom.*

18. Hayward Coleman, quoted by Susan Woldenberg, "Mime Yoga: Meditation in Motion," *Yoga Journal*, July/August 1986, pp. 23, 24.
19. Peter Roche de Coppens, Foreword to F. Aster Barnwell, *The Meaning of Christ for Our Age* (St. Paul, Minn.: Llewelyn Publications, 1984), pp. xix-xxxi.
20. *Ibid.*, p. xxiii.
21. See James Bolen, "Teilhard de Chardin, 1881-1981," *New Realities*, Vol. IV, No. 1 (1981).
22. Richard M. Bucke, *Cosmic Consciousness* (New York: E. P. Dutton, 1901).
23. *Ibid.*
24. See my discussion in *Rush to Armageddon* (Wheaton, Ill.: Tyndale House, 1987), pp. 47, 48, 242, 243.
25. *Ibid.*, p. 48.
26. For a brief but revealing discussion of the concept of "root races," see Corinne Heline, *New Age Bible Interpretation*, pp. 250-255.
27. LaVedi Lafferty and Bud Hollowell, *The Eternal Dance*, p. 503.
28. *Ibid.*, pp. 504, 505.
29. Vera Alder, *When Humanity Comes of Age*, p. 154.
30. John Randolph Price, *The Planetary Commission*, p. 48.
31. *Ibid.*
32. *Ibid.*, p. 153.
33. *Ibid.*, pp. 47, 48.
34. Barry McWaters, *Conscious Evolution: Personal and Planetary Transformation*, p. 55.
35. John Welwood, "On Love: Conditional and Unconditional," *Yoga Journal*, July/August 1986, pp. 7-10.
36. Rainer Maria Rilke, *Letters to a Young Poet*, translated by Stephen Mitchell (New York: Random House, 1984), p. 92.
37. International Society of Divine Love, full-page ad in *Yoga Journal*, May/June 1986, p. 25.
38. *Ibid.*
39. Vera Alder, *When Humanity Comes of Age*, p. 154.
40. Edward O. Wilson, quoted in "Biological Diversity: Going . . . going. . . ?," *Science News*, Vol. 130, No. 13, September 27, 1986, p. 202.
41. Jeremy Rifkin, *Algeny* (New York: Viking Press, 1983), p. 252.
42. Robert Mueller, *The New Genesis: Shaping a Global Spirituality*, p. 37.
43. The pompous doctrine of self-love is so important to the New Age religion that its promotion sometimes reaches incredulous heights. For example, consider the titles of two recent New Age books: *Dear Me, I Love You* and *What to Say When You Talk to Yourself*. Unfortunately, this is also a doctrine that is being spread by a few Christian ministers. See Dave Hunt and T. A. McMahon, *The Seduction of Christianity* (Eugene Ore.: Harvest House, 1985), pp. 11-22.
44. *UN Declaration*, quoted in Marilyn Ferguson, *The Aquarian Conspiracy*, p. 369. Also see *Houston Chronicle*, November 3, 1975, p. G-12.
45. Lola Davis, *Toward a World Religion for the New Age*, p. 9.
46. Edgar Cayce, quoted in Moira Timms, *Prophecies and Predictions: Everyone's Guide to the Coming Changes*, p. 156.

47. See Shirley G. Clement and Virginia Fields, *Beginning the Search: A Young Adult's Approach to a Search for God,* p. 61.
48. Douglas R. Groothuis, *Unmasking the New Age* (Downers Grove, Ill.: InterVarsity Press, 1986), p. 174.

CHAPTER 11: The Dark Secret: What Will Happen to the Christians?

1. Matthew Fox, *Whee, Wee, We, All the Way Home . . . A Guide to a Sensual, Prophetic Spirituality,* p. 242.
2. Marilyn Ferguson, *The Aquarian Conspiracy: Personal and Social Transformation in the 1980s,* pp. 19, 34.
3. Moira Timms, *Prophecies and Predictions: Everyone's Guide to the Coming Changes,* p. 289.
4. *Ibid.,* pp. 125, 126.
5. Association of Sananda and Sanat Kumara, *The Sibors Portion* (Mt. Shasta, Calif.).
6. David Spangler, quoted by Barry McWaters, *Conscious Evolution: Personal and Planetary Transformation,* pp. 120, 121.
7. Barry McWaters, *Conscious Evolution: Personal and Planetary Transformation,* p. 130.
8. G. I. Gurdjieff, quoted by Barry McWaters, *Ibid.,* p. 124.
9. *Ibid.,* p. 113.
10. *Ibid.*
11. Moira Timms. *Prophecies and Predictions: Everyone's Guide to the Coming Changes,* pp. 276, 277.
12. Maharishi Mahesh Yogi, *Inauguration of the Dawn of the Age of Enlightenment* (Fairfield, Iowa: Maharishi International University Press, 1975), p. 47. See Dave Hunt, *The Cult Explosion* (Euguene, Ore.: Harvest House, 1980), pp. 229-234 for an examination of the Maharishi's plan for a world government.
13. Ruth Montgomery, *Threshold to Tomorrow,* pp. 196-207.
14. *Ibid.,* p. 196.
15. *Ibid.,* pp. 206, 207.
16. *Ibid.,* p. 206.
17. Ruth Montgomery, interview in *Magical Blend,* Issue 13, 1986, p. 23.
18. David Spangler, *Revelation: The Birth of a New Age,* pp. 163, 164.
19. *Ibid.*
20. Moira Timms, *Prophecies and Predictions: Everyone's Guide to the Coming Changes,* pp. 57, 58.
21. *Ibid.*
22. John Randolph Price, *The Planetary Commission,* pp. 163, 164.
23. *Ibid.,* pp. 162, 163.
24. LaVedi Lafferty and Bud Hollowell, *The Eternal Dance,* p. 153.
25. *Ibid.*
26. *Ibid.*
27. "Djwhal Khul" (channeled by Alice Bailey), "Food for Thought," *Life Times,* Winter 1986/1987, p. 57.
28. Corinne Heline, *New Age Bible Interpretation.*
29. *Ibid.,* pp. 197, 198, 202, 228.

30. *Ibid.*, p. v.
31. *Ibid.*, p. 44.
32. *Ibid.*, p. 226.
33. *Ibid.*, p. 227.
34. *Ibid.*, p. 230, 231.
35. *Ibid.*, p. 232, 233.
36. *Ibid.*, p. 244.
37. *Ibid.*, p. 245.

CHAPTER 12: *New Age Zeal . . . New Age Aggression*

1. Jack Underhill, "My Goal in Life," *Life Times*, Winter 1986/1987, p. 90.
2. Lisa Moore, letter to the editor, *Yoga Journal*, July/August 1986, p. 4.
3. Miriam Starhawk, quoted in *Yoga Journal*, July/August 1986, p. 4.
4. Kurt Koch, *Occult ABC*, p. 201.
5. David Spangler, *Revelation: The Birth of a New Age*, p. 89.
6. Alice Bailey, "Externalizing the Mysteries," Part I, *The Beacon*, November/December 1975, p. 171.
7. Alexander Hislop, *The Two Babylons*, p. 291.
8. LaVedi Lafferty and Bud Hollowell, *The Eternal Dance*, p. 473.
9. *Ibid.*, p. 468.
10. Sue Sikking, *Seed of the New Age* (New York: Doubleday, 1970).
11. See Kenneth Boa, *Cults, World Religions and You* (Wheaton, Ill.: Victor Books, 1977), pp. 81-89.
12. James Sire, *The Universe Next Door* (Downers Grove, Ill., InterVarsity Press, 1976), p. 142.
13. Alexander Pope, *Essay on Man*. Also see discussion in James Sire, *The Universe Next Door*, p. 53.
14. LaVedi Lafferty and Bud Hollowell, *The Eternal Dance*, p. 367.
15. Stuart Litvak and A. Wayne Senzee, *Toward a New Brain* (Englewood Cliffs, N.J.: Prentice-Hall, 1986), pp. 199, 200.
16. Corinne Heline, *New Age Bible Interpretation*, pp. 248-255.
17. Moira Timms, *Prophecies and Predictions: Everyone's Guide to the Coming Changes*, p. 58.
18. *Ibid.*, p. 99.
19. David Spangler, *Revelation: The Birth of a New Age*, pp. 63-65.
20. *Ibid.*, p. 94.
21. *Ibid.*
22. *Ibid.*, p. 156.
23. *Ibid.*

CHAPTER 13: *A New Culture, a New Barbarism*

1. Vera Alder, *When Humanity Comes of Age*, p. xii.
2. *Ibid.*, pp. 5-7.
3. *Ibid.*, p. 8.
4. *Ibid.*, p. 10.
5. *Ibid.*, p. 11.

6. *Ibid.*, p. 13.
7. Robert Mueller, *The New Genesis: Shaping a Global Spirituality*, p. 164.
8. *Ibid.*, p. 183.
9. Vera Alder, *When Humanity Comes of Age*, p. 20.
10. *Ibid.*, p. 21.
11. *Ibid.*, pp. 20-24.
12. *Ibid.*, p. 22.
13. *Ibid.*, p. 29.
14. *Ibid.*, p. 23.
15. Robert Mueller, *The New Genesis: Shaping a Global Spirituality*, p. 155.
16. *Ibid.*, p. 8.
17. Peter Lemesurier, *The Armageddon Script*, p. 247. Also see Brad Steiger, *The Gods of Aquarius* (New York: Harcourt Brace Jovanovich, 1976).
18. Lemesurier, *ibid.*
19. Discussed in Brad Steiger, *Gods of Aquarius.*
20. Texe Marrs, *Rush to Armageddon*, pp. 27-52, 77-90; Texe W. Marrs and Wanda J. Marrs, *Robotica: The Whole Universe Catalogue of Robots* (Briarcliff Manor, N.Y.: Stein & Day, 1987); and Texe Marrs, *High Technology Careers* (Homewood, Ill.: Dow Jones-Irwin, 1986), pp. 110-113, 121-127.
21. Jonathan Glover, *What Sort of People Should There Be?* (New York: Penguin Books, 1984).
22. Vera Alder, *When Humanity Comes of Age*, pp. 32, 33, 36-40.
23. *Ibid.*, pp. 68-76.
24. *Ibid.*, p. 67.
25. *Ibid.*, pp. 48, 49.
26. Texe Marrs, *Rush to Armageddon*, pp. 77-90.
27. Vera Alder, *When Humanity Comes of Age*, p. 83.
28. *Ibid.*, p. 82.
29. *Ibid.*, pp. 83, 84.
30. *Ibid.*, p. 148.
31. Robert Mueller, *The New Genesis: Shaping a Global Spirituality*, p. 191.
32. Erwin Chargaff, quoted by Michael Saloman, *Future Life* (New York: Macmillan, 1983).

CHAPTER 14: The Unholy Bible of the New Age World Religion

1. Vera Alder, *When Humanity Comes of Age*, p. 31.
2. Miriam Starhawk, "Witchcraft and the Religion of the Great Goddess," *Yoga Journal*, May/June 1986, p. 56.
3. Vera Alder, *When Humanity Comes of Age*, p. 31.
4. *Ibid.*
5. *Ibid.*, p. 35.
6. *Ibid.*, pp. 33-35.
7. *Ibid.*, p. 37.

8. *Ibid.*
9. *Ibid.*, p. 39.
10. Lola Davis, *Toward a World Religion for the New Age,* pp. 187, 188.
11. Alice Bailey, *Problems of Humanity* (New York: Lucis Publishing Company, 1947), pp. 142, 143.
12. David Spangler, *Reflections on the Christ* (Scotland: Findhorn Publications, 1982), p. 73.
13. Robert Mueller, *The New Genesis: Shaping a Global Spirituality*
14. Lola Davis, *Toward a World Religion for the New Age,* p. 25.
15. LaVedi Lafferty and Bud Hollowell, *The Eternal Dance,* pp. 451-453.
16. Alexander Hislop, *The Two Babylons,* p. 7.
17. "The Way of the Heart," *Austin American-Statesman,* March 13, 1986, p. B-8.
18. *Ibid.*
19. John White, editor, *What Is Enlightenment?,* pp. 228, 229.
20. William Kingsland, *The Gnosis or Ancient Wisdom in the Christian Scriptures* (London: Allen and Unwin, Ltd., 1937), p. 93.
21. Randall King, quoted by William Plummer, "Turmoil in a California Camelot," *People Weekly,* July 1, 1985.
22. William Plummer, *ibid.,* pp. 75-77.
23. "Scientology Scripture Held Sacred," *Austin American-Statesman,* January 6, 1986, p. A-9.

CHAPTER 15: *Doctrines of Devils*

1. Joan Halifax, *Shaman: The Wounded Healer* (New York: Crossroad, 1982).
2. Miriam Starhawk, "Witchcraft and the Religion of the Great Goddess," *Yoga Journal,* May/June 1986, pp. 38-41.
3. Lola Davis, *Toward a World Religion for the New Age,* pp. 178, 180-182, 193-195, 222.
4. Elizabeth Clare Prophet, "In Search of the Power of Moses: Reclaiming our Spiritual Heritage," *The Coming Revolution,* Summer 1986, pp. 12, 13.
5. Alice Bailey, *The Rays and the Initiations* (New York: Lucis Publishing Company, 1960).
6. *Newsweek,* February 7, 1983.
7. Ruth Montgomery, *A World Beyond* (New York: Ballantine/Fawcett Crest Books, 1972) p. 12.
8. Paul Twitchell, *Eckankar: The Key to Secret Worlds,* pp. 41, 42.
9. Vera Alder, *When Humanity Comes of Age,* p. 55; also see pp. 85, 93, 101, 114.
10. *Planetary Commission Update,* July 1986, Austin, Texas.
11. Swami Muktananda, quoted in Dave Hunt, *The Cult Explosion* (Eugene, Ore.: Harvest House, 1982).
12. Benjamin Creme, *Reappearance of the Christ and the Masters of Wisdom.*
13. Allan Y. Cohen, "Meher Baba and the Quest of Consciousness," in John White, editor, *What Is Enlightenment?,* p. 83.

14. Charles Bullock, sermon at Christ Memorial Church, Austin, Texas, January 18, 1987.

CHAPTER 16: Apostasy: The New Age Plan to Take Over the Christian Church

1. Marilyn Ferguson, *The Aquarian Conspiracy: Personal and Social Transformation in the 1980's*, p. 222.
2. William Thompson, Introduction, in David Spangler, *Revelation: The Birth of a New Age*.
3. Kevin Ryerson, quoted in Shirley Maclaine, *Out on a Limb* (New York: Bantam Books, 1983), p. 181.
4. Elizabeth Clare Prophet, *The Lost Years of Jesus* (Malibu, Calif.: Summit University Press, 1984).
5. J. Finley Cooper, quoted in *The Coming Revolution*, Summer 1986, p. 102.
6. Anne Read, *Edgar Cayce on Jesus and His Church* (New York: Paperback Library, 1970).
7. LaVedi Lafferty and Bud Hollowell, *The Eternal Dance*, p. 172.
8. Mark and Elizabeth Clare Prophet, *The Science of the Spoken Word*, p. 73.
9. Peter Lemesurier, *The Armageddon Script*, pp. 139-173.
10. Benjamin Creme, *The Reappearance of the Christ and the Masters of Wisdom*, p. 95.
11. *Ibid.*
12. Emmett Fox, *Diagrams for Living: The Bible Unveiled* (New York: Harper & Row, 1968), pp. 158, 159.
13. LaVedi Lafferty and Bud Hollowell, *The Eternal Dance*, pp. 471, 472.
14. F. Aster Barnwell, *The Meaning of Christ for Our Age* (St. Paul, Minn.: Llewelyn Publications, 1984).
15. *Ibid.*, pp. 10-13.
16. *Ibid.*, pp. 165, 166.
17. *Ibid.*, p. 46.
18. *Ibid.*
19. John G. Bennett, *The Masters of Wisdom* (England: Turnstone Press, Ltd., 1980), p. 74.
20. Helen Schucman, *A Course in Miracles*.
21. Susan Jacobs, "Psychic Healing," *Yoga Journal*, July/August 1986, p. 30.
22. Michael Doan, "A Unisex Bible? Reformers Run Into a Storm," *U.S. News & World Report*, December 17, 1984, p. 70.
23. *Ibid.*
24. Peter Roche de Coppens, Foreword, in F. Aster Barnwell, *The Meaning of Christ for Our Age*.
25. *Ibid.*, pp. xix-xxii.
26. *Ibid.*, p. xxiii.
27. *Ibid.*
28. *Ibid.*, xxii.
29. Levi, *The Aquarian Gospel of Jesus the Christ*, p. 76.

30. Benjamin Creme, *The Reappearance of the Christ and The Masters of Wisdom,* pp. 159, 160.
31. John Randolph Price, *The Planetary Commission,* p. 54.
32. *Ibid.,* p. 144.
33. Marilyn Ferguson, *The Aquarian Conspiracy: Personal and Social Transformation in the 1980s,* p. 368.
34. Norman Boucher, "A Faith of Our Own," *New Age Journal,* April 1986, p. 27.
35. Ruth Montgomery, interviewed in *Magical Blend,* Issue 13, 1986.
36. Miriam Starhawk, *Circle Network News,* April 1983.
37. *Christian Information Bureau Bulletin,* December 1986, p. 4.
38. "Britain's Doubting Bishop," *Newsweek,* June 17, 1985, p. 91.
39. Col. Minter L. Wilson, Jr., "Peacemaking: Are We Now Called to Resistance?," *The Retired Officer,* October 1986, p. 5.
40. *Christian Information Bureau Bulletin,* April 1986, p. 1.
41. *United Methodist Report,* December 6, 1985.
42. Thomas H. Trapp, "Ecumenical," *The Northwestern Lutheran,* October 15, 1985, p. 32.
43. Joseph A. Harriss, "Karl Marx or Jesus Christ?," *Readers Digest,* August 1982, pp. 130-134.
44. Edmund W. Robb and Julia Robb, *Betrayal of the Church* (Westchester, Ill.: Crossway Books, 1986), p. 64.
45. *Ibid.,* p. 45.
6. Lola Davis, *Toward a World Religion for the New Age,* p. 212.
7. Rael Jean Issac, "Do You Know Where Your Church Offerings Go?," *Readers Digest,* January 1983, pp. 120-125.
   Christian Information Bureau Bulletin, December 1986, p. 4. Also see Norman Boucher, "A Faith of Our Own."
   ger Spence, "Father Bede Griffiths: Unity at the Source of All ngs," *Magical Blend,* Issue 13, 1986, pp. 7-11.
   ʊ A. Jackson, "Keeping the Faith: Western Religion's Future," *The st,* October 1985, p. 261.
   ʊvis, *Toward a World Religion for the New Age.*
   ante, quoted by Carlos Vidal Greth, "High Priest of Prosperity Plenty," *Austin American-Statesman,* March 1, 1986, p. F-1.

   ph Price, *The Superbeings,* pp. 101-103.
   der, *The Millionaire from Nazareth: His Prosperity Se-Marina del Rey, Calif.: DeVorss & Co., 1979).
   uoted in *USA Today,* July 22, 1986, p. 2-D.

for Our Children

bruary 17, 1986.
quoted by Marilyn Ferguson, *The Aquarian nd Social Transformation in the 1980s,* pp. 231,

oster Bailey, *Things to Come* (London: Lucis ɔ. 252-257.

4. Marilyn Ferguson, *The Aquarian Conspiracy: Personal and Social Transformation in the 1980s,* p. 293.
5. Phil Phillips, *Turmoil in the Toy Box* (Lancaster, Pa.: Starburst, Inc., 1986), p. 25.
6. John Dunphy, "A Religion for the New Age," *The Humanist,* January-February 1983.
7. Beverly Galyean, quoted in Marilyn Ferguson, *The Aquarian Conspiracy,* pp. 313, 314.
8. Beverly Galyean, quoted by Francis Adenay, "Educators Look East," *Spiritual Counterfeits Journal,* Winter 1981, p. 29.
9. David Hunt, *Peace, Prosperity, and the Coming Holocaust,* p. 78.
10. Marilyn Ferguson, *The Aquarian Conspiracy,* p. 312.
11. Charlotte Iserbyt, quoted in *Child Abuse in the Classroom,* edited by Phyllis Schlafly (Westchester, Ill.: Crossway Books, 1985), p. 391.
12. Marilyn Ferguson, *The Aquarian Conspiracy,* p. 203.
13. *Spin,* September 1986, p. 32.
14. *Chicago Tribune,* April 19, 1986.
15. *Associated Press,* "Satanism Tied to Death of Michigan Teen," February 20, 1986.
16. *Associated Press,* "Satanic Teen Fad Feared in El Paso," February 17, 1986.
17. *Ibid.*
18. Irene Park, interviewed by host Doug Clark, "Praise the Lord," Trinity Broadcasting Network, December 8, 1986. (Irene Park is author of the book *The Witch That Switched.*)

CHAPTER 18: Dress Rehearsals for the Main Event

1. Ruth Montgomery, *A Gift of Prophecy: The Phenomenal Jeanne Dixon* (New York: Bantam Books, 1966), p. 172. Note: Subsequent to this prophecy, Jeanne Dixon changed her mind regarding the source of her vision because so many Christians came to her and mentioned the parallels with the teachings of Eastern mysticism. Reportedly Dixon now believes her vision came from an "evil source."
2. On January 12, 1987, a full-page ad by the Tara Center appeared in *USA Today* announcing once again the imminent worldwide appearance of the New Age "Christ." This time a specific date for his appearance was not given.
3. Dave Hunt, *Peace, Prosperity, and the Coming Holocaust,* pp. 124-127.
4. Foster Bailey, *Things to Come* (London: Lucis Press, 1974). Also see Constance Cumbey, *A Planned Deception,* p. 88.
5. Joseph J. Carr, *The Twisted Cross* (LaFayette, La.: Huntington House, 1985).
6. *Ibid.,* p. 87.
7. *Ibid.,* p. 276.
8. *Ibid.*
9. David Spangler, *Revelation: The Birth of a New Age,* pp. 148, 149.
10. *Ibid.*
11. *Ibid.*

Randolph Price, *Planetary Commission Update*, August 1986, p.

l Healing Meditation," The Planetary Commission, Austin, Tex-
6.
Randolph Price, *The Planetary Commission*, pp. 29, 30.
16. *Ibid.*, p. 30.
17. *Ibid.*
18. Ruth Montgomery, *Strangers Among Us* (New York: Ballantine/Faw-
cett Crest Books, 1979).
19. Kurt Koch, *Occult ABC*, p. 59.
20. *Ibid.*, p. 58.

CHAPTER 19: *What Must Christians Do?*

1. Biblical scholars say that Peter addressed this remark to the early
   Christian Church, which was then suffering intense persecution by the
   Roman authorities. Certainly Peter's comment is also applicable to
   Christians in the last days.
2. Billy Graham, *Approaching Hoofbeats: The Four Horsemen of the
   Apocalypse* (Waco, Tex.: Word, 1983).
3. *Ibid.*
4. Charles Bullock, sermon.

About the Author

Texe Marrs, author-evangelist, and president of Living Truth Ministries in Austin, Texas, has thoroughly researched Bible prophecy, the New Age Movement, and the occult challenge to Christianity. Author of the recently released *Rush to Armageddon* (Tyndale House, 1987), Texe is a firm believer in the inerrancy of the Bible and salvation through Jesus Christ.

Prior to answering a call to the ministry, Texe was a high-tech consultant and successful author of thirteen books on robotics, computers, and related topics for such major publishers as Simon & Schuster, Dow Jones-Irwin, John Wiley, and Stein and Day. Previous to to that, he was a career officer in the U. S. Air Force. For five years he was assistant professor of aerospace studies at the University of Texas at Austin, and he has taught international affairs, political science, and American government for two other universities. Texe graduated summa cum laude from Park College in Kansas City, and earned his Master's degree at North Carolina State University.

Currently active as a seminar speaker and workshop leader, Texe frequently addresses church congregations and groups. He is now working on a sequel to *Dark Secrets of the New Age* and has recently filmed a documentary further exposing the New Age Movement.

For More Information

Texe Marrs and Living Truth Ministries offer a free newsletter about Bible prophecy, the New Age Movement, cults, the occult challenge to Christianity, and other important topics.

If you would like to receive this newsletter, please write to:

Texe Marrs
Living Truth Ministries
8103 Shiloh Court
Austin, TX 78745